MARIANNE NEIFERT, M.D., is a pediatrician and Associate Clinical Professor of Pediatrics at the University of Colorado Health Sciences Center, as well as the mother of five children. The author of *Dr. Mom* (Signet), she is a frequent lecturer and writes a column for *Parenting* and *Baby Talk* magazines. She lives in Denver.

⇒DR. MOM'S⇐

PARENTING GUIDE

Commonsense Guidance for the Life of Your Child

Marianne Neifert, M.D.

To Becky,
With appreciation and
warm wishes!
  Marianne Neifert MD
        2-7-98

A PLUME BOOK

PLUME
Published by the Penguin Group
Penguin Books USA Inc., 375 Hudson Street,
New York, New York 10014, U.S.A.
Penguin Books Ltd, 27 Wrights Lane,
London W8 5TZ, England
Penguin Books Australia Ltd, Ringwood,
Victoria, Australia
Penguin Books Canada Ltd, 10 Alcorn Avenue,
Toronto, Ontario, Canada M4V 3B2
Penguin Books (N.Z.) Ltd, 182–190 Wairau Road,
Auckland 10, New Zealand

Penguin Books Ltd, Registered Offices:
Harmondsworth, Middlesex, England

Published by Plume, an imprint of Dutton Signet,
a division of Penguin Books USA Inc.
Previously published in a Dutton edition
and in a Signet edition.

First Plume Printing, June, 1996
10 9 8 7 6 5 4 3 2 1

   REGISTERED TRADEMARK—MARCA REGISTRADA

The Library of Congress has catalogued the Dutton edition as follows:
Neifert, Marianne R.
    Dr. Mom's parenting guide : commonsense guidance for the life of your
child / Marianne Egeland Neifert.
    p.   cm.
    Includes index.
    ISBN 0-525-93373-5 (hc.)
    ISBN 0-452-26864-8 (pbk.)
    1. Parenting—United States.   2. Child psychology—United States.
3. Parent and child—United States.   I.Title.
HQ755.8.N45   1991
649'.1—dc20   91-10035
                                                                    CIP

Printed in the United States of America

PUBLISHER'S NOTE
The ideas, procedures, and suggestions contained in this book are not intended
as a substitute for consulting with your physician. All matters regarding your
child's health require medical supervision.

This book is dedicated to families . . .

To my cherished birth family,

my parents, Andrew and Annabelle Egeland,
and my brothers and sisters, Andy Egeland,
Marcy Poncelow, Aleta Egeland,
and Tommy Egeland

To my precious life partner, Larry

To the extraordinary family Lar and I created,
Peter, Paige, Tricie, Heather, and Mark

To the remarkable and vulnerable families
who have touched my life

And to each unique family who is
reached by this book.

CONTENTS

ACKNOWLEDGMENTS

Many authors agree that writing a book is analogous to having a baby. The metaphor certainly held true for me. This book was not simply published; it was born. The project began with a thesis, which, once conceived, was compelled to find its expression in written word. The lengthy process of gestation involved the intellectual development of ideas, the adherence to specific self-disciplines, and an ever deepening emotional commitment. The entire developmental period required elaborate support and encouragement from many significant people. The intense final stages of labor necessitated expert professional guidance, sensitive coaching, and focused energy. Upon delivery, I find myself viewing the finished work with a mixture of relief, pride, and wonder, while expectantly awaiting the reception from its readership.

I would like to gratefully acknowledge the following individuals whose input and support have been invaluable to me during the birth of this work:

The many parents, grandparents, and daycare workers who have attended my parenting talks, for it was their genuine interest and obvious enthusiasm that prompted me to write a parenting book incorporating the content of those popular presentations;

My literary agent for this work, Sherry Robb, who successfully marketed the book proposal;

Senior editor at Dutton Signet, Alexia Dorszynski, who initially embraced the project and diligently nudged it along, and who provided expert editing, valuable feedback, and lavish support;

My capable editor at Dutton Signet, Deborah Brody, who gave the book another life in paperback.

My husband, Larry, who tirelessly showered me with enormous support, and who enthusiastically contributed a chapter of his own on stress management; Larry, my confidant and friend, with whose affirmation this book was completed;

My five terrific children, Peter, Paige, Tricie, Heather, and Mark, who graciously allowed me to use examples from their lives and who kept me ever buoyed by a continuous infusion of encouragement and praise;

My parents and siblings, whose lifelong unconditional acceptance and approval have given me the courage to risk;

The countless families with whom I have interacted over the years, particularly those extraordinary people who have shown me how to turn adversity into creativity and those whose personal stories I have told;

The many children and youths who so generously have articulated their intimate feelings about sensitive topics;

Betsy Sturges-Murray, who helped launch the project and offered early creative input;

Charles Poncelow, my brother-in-law, whose thoughtful discussions generated valuable insights for the chapter on instilling values;

Velois Whiteside, who provided an exceptional model of peak parenting, who periodically reinstilled the confidence I needed to complete the work, and who thoughtfully reviewed the manuscript;

My entire office staff, whose cooperative support and frequent encouragement miraculously enabled me to fit this endeavor into my life (Phyllis Fantin; Nancy Spohnholtz; Karla Yegge; Suzie Henderson; Pamela Leite, P.A.-C., M.S.; Sandra DeMarzo, P.A., M.S., who thoroughly reviewed the manuscript; Cathy Darden, P.A.-C., M.S., who also reviewed the work; and my staunch partner and advocate, Joy Seacat, P.A., M.S.).

My heartfelt thanks is extended to all those others who helped breathe life into this project.

—*Marianne Egeland Neifert, M.D.*

1

PARENTING TODAY

A number of years ago, I pre-boarded a flight from Denver to Washington, D.C., making my way along the ramp with several others who were "traveling with small children or needed extra time." I settled into my bulkhead seat, cradling my two-month-old son, who nuzzled contentedly at my breast. I was twenty-seven years old, traveling alone with my infant to visit my parents and introduce them to their new grandchild. I looked forward to the trip, anticipating the doting attention of my folks, their demonstrative pride in my progeny, and their usual concern about my physical well-being. This long-awaited journey promised a brief respite from the daily demands that crowded my busy life. As a sleep-deprived new mother, I craved the emotional refueling that a visit with my parents always offered and that I had come to require periodically.

A smiling flight attendant paused at my seat and beamed her approval at my precious baby. "How old is he?" she politely inquired. "Nine weeks," I responded, automatically figuring the interval since Mark had permanently changed our lives.

"Is he your first?" she followed expectantly. "No, my fifth," I replied without hesitation. But the sound of my answer startled even me, as I suddenly recalled the two-, three-, five-, and seven-year-old munchkins who had clamored to kiss me good-bye before their daddy drove me to the airport.

"Gee," the flight attendant gasped in amazement. Then, attempting to be facetious, she quipped, "What do you do in your spare time?"

"I'm a pediatrician," I admitted wearily, and the weight of my answer momentarily oppressed me. I had finished my residency the day Mark was born.

Now speechless, the flight attendant continued down the aisle, greeting other passengers and leaving me alone with the self-doubts her questions had brought to the surface.

"How will I ever raise five little children so close in age, preserve my marriage under such strain, and still make a significant contribution after pursuing so much professional training?" I wondered in silence. "How will I balance the needs of other people's children with those of my own? How will I care for myself sufficiently to be able to nurture so many others? Will my husband and I ever again find the time or energy to focus on one another? How will the different facets of my life fit together in a meaningful way?"

Seventeen years have elapsed since I wrestled with those thoughts. It has been an exhausting, exhilarating adventure, albeit through uncharted territory at times. Much of that experience is summarized in this book, which is a collection of my personal and professional childrearing knowledge and philosophies. It was written for those of you who have ever felt underprepared for parenthood and disillusioned with the on-the-job training approach to raising children. The material I have selected to present was partly gleaned from my pediatric training and practice. My profession has offered me the awesome privilege and responsibility of hearing the private fears, conflicts, disappointments, and frustrations shared in confidence by many hurting families. Another important dimension to my parenting perspective, however, comes from firsthand experience gained in the raising of my own five children, while juggling a full-time career.

Today I am convinced that having a successful, older role model with whom I could identify would have made my own struggles to balance medicine and motherhood considerably easier. Thus it is very gratifying to me now to hear some young, busy parents confide that I represent a role model for them. To serve as an example for others generates an uncomfortable mixture of pride, humility, and accountability. This book, which represents an outpouring of affection and empathy for other parents, was written with the hope and expectation that it would impart some useful insights, practical suggestions, and supportive encouragement, intermingled with a touch of humor. In it I have summarized my professional knowledge of several of the most challenging contemporary parenting issues and openly shared some of the parenting successes I have enjoyed—and some of the mistakes that have taught me the most. In the end, I trust its contents will help minimize your parenting anxieties and multiply your family joys!

Parenting Through the "Ages"

Somehow Larry and I fulfilled the physical demands of our early childrearing years that once seemed so overwhelming. With the help of babysitters, daycare centers, neighbors, and extended family members, we tenuously juggled the needs of our small children, the demands of our careers, and the essentials of our household and marriage. For an uninterrupted decade, we toted diaper bags full of baby supplies everywhere we went. Carseats, cribs, high chairs, playpens, strollers, swings, toy boxes, and diaper pails seemed permanent furnishings in our home. While our childless friends made down payments on tasteful living room sets upholstered in the finest fabrics, we kept the same vinyl couch and chair, impervious to wet bottoms, drooling mouths, sticky fingers, and spilled drinks.

We solely frequented family restaurants that offered children's options like "Three Little Pigs" and "Chicken Little" dinners. We scanned marquees for telltale phrases like KIDS WELCOME, CHILDREN ADMITTED FREE, and FAMILY NIGHT. We knew all the cartoons and kiddie shows, watched for G ratings at the movies, and became familiar with every new doll, Barbie accessory, and Star Wars figure. We shopped at discount stores, bought in bulk, and waited for "blue light specials."

Ultimately, I became quite comfortable parenting little ones, and I readily identified with new mothers in my practice. By the time our youngest was potty trained and could make a mustard sandwich on his own, I had almost forgotten the intense physical demands of young, dependent children. Occasionally, I even wondered why I hadn't had a few more babies!

Then, all too soon, I was out of my comfort zone again, as I realized that the parenting skills I had finally mastered were being outpaced by our rapidly growing children. One day I was surprised to learn that the kids no longer accepted the clothes I had selected and bought for them in their absence. In the past, if I brought home a dress or a pair of jeans, I would be met with adoring appreciation. "It's so-o-o pretty. It has a zipper on the pocket!" Now my convenient selections were either the wrong color, wrong brand, or wrong style. The kids not only insisted on picking their own clothes, but they started to expand their world in a myriad of ways. They began to choose friends outside our immediate neighborhood, and they arranged to spend the night at their homes. They wanted to take gymnastics, play soccer, and join scouts, and they expected me to drive them everywhere. They boldly asked me to take off work to hear their debates, chaperone their outings, or teach their sex education classes at school. They needed braces, sports uniforms, music lessons, and a private chauffeur. They wanted jeans jackets, pierced ears, and perms.

Larry and I rallied to the new set of expectations. We built a home that looked like a dormitory, with a bedroom for each child, a recreation room, a bathroom for the girls and one for the boys. We held birthday parties, holiday parties, ice cream parties, pizza parties, and slumber parties. We let the kids decorate their own rooms, choose their own clothes, play their own music, style their own hair, and acquire their own pets. We chauffeured, carpooled, begged and borrowed rides to get them to their extracurricular activities, and we cheered their participation from the sidelines whenever we could. Eventually, I was proud to admit that we were parenting our preteen and early teen children pretty comfortably. After all, several had even survived puberty, and I had actually considered becoming a foster parent someday.

Before long, however, we started to feel out of our element again. The same children who as preschoolers felt secure only in our presence gradually preferred the company of their peers to that of their own family members. Repeatedly I would be admonished, whether in the registration line at high school or when encountering other teens at the mall, "Just promise you won't say anything, okay?"

No longer satisfied to be driven everywhere, our kids soon required a new kind of labor-intensive parenting endeavor—teaching them all to drive a car as they turned sixteen in rapid succession. I expected to relish the much-deserved freedom a new driver in the family would bring. Instead, I found myself passing long, worry-filled hours every week, anxiously waiting for a novice driver to pull safely up our driveway. More than once I allowed myself to imagine how reassuring it would be momentarily to transform an independent teen into a helpless baby once again, and to confine her even briefly in the safety of her playpen. I would recall with fond nostalgia those peaceful scenes with five little heads sleeping undisturbed under a single roof. Instead, on a growing number of nights, Larry and I would find ourselves at home alone, with Peter on his own, Paige and Tricie at college, Heather out on a date, and Mark spending the night at a friend's. Simply trying to orchestrate everyone's presence for our traditional holiday family photo had become a scheduling nightmare.

Then a most amazing thing started happening. The same youths who only recently were inseparable from their peers and embarrassed to be seen with Larry and me now began to seek our opinions about their colleges, careers, personal lives, and world affairs. They undertook to coordinate summer jobs and outside activities in order to be present for our traditional family camping trip.

Peter, my oldest, lived at home the summer after he graduated from college and chose to carpool to work with me. This son—the first child I had carried, delivered, nursed, bathed, clothed, sheltered, guided, humored, and worried about—had emerged as a delightful, mature, thoughtful, sensitive adult whose company I thoroughly enjoyed. That summer, while Peter drove us to and from work, we offered one another valuable insight and perspective on a variety of personal and professional issues. We would reach his destination first, and I would exit from the passenger side in order to take the driver's seat. For a brief moment each morning, a forty-two-year-old mother and her twenty-two-year-old son tenderly embraced one another in a 7-Eleven parking lot. Invariably, a few people would glance in our direction, trying to interpret this outward display of affection between such an odd couple. "Hasn't it been great?" I would reflect with deep satisfaction before starting each workday. "Hasn't it been great!"

The Yardstick of
Successful Parenting

Recently, Larry and I survived a new rite of parenthood, or perhaps it would be more accurate to state that we experienced a familiar passage in a new way. We enrolled our middle daughter in an out-of-state college located two days' drive from our home. Since Tricie is our third child to attend college, I thought myself a veteran when it came to "letting go" appropriately. In actuality, our eldest two children had attended in-state institutions, making it possible for them to come home on some weekends. It was relatively easy for me to touch base with them emotionally. We could discuss sensitive issues in person, and they could join a family gathering if they so desired. Amid saying good-bye to Peter or Paige, I was always comforted by the knowledge that I would likely see them again within a matter of weeks and would still have opportunities to fill in any gaps in my parenting that became evident once they started living on their own. The fact of the matter is that I had grown comfortable with in-state schools, which offered a way to complete the separation process gradually—and not end it with the separation itself.

But Tricie, our indomitable middle child, sought her own identity. She wanted to go out-of-state, in part because no one else had done it. As a result, I had to face the reality of not seeing one of my children for several months at a time. During the drive to her college, I was confronted with multiple fears, doubts, and anxieties about whether we had adequately prepared Tricie to handle the diverse challenges that would accompany her youthful independence. In the car, I thought of countless things I should remind her about and conjured up all sorts of traumas from which I desperately wanted to shield her. Intellectually, I knew that she would need to make some bad choices and experience a few failures of her own in order to learn many valuable lessons. She would have to weather some rejections in order to fully accept herself. And she would need to feel insecure and vulnerable at times in order eventually to assume full responsibility for her life circumstances. As a parent, however, I still felt compelled to protect her from the very experiences that would ultimately strengthen her character.

As the campus loomed in sight, Larry broke the silence, spontaneously offering a wonderfully insightful commentary. "Tricie," he began, "I'm going to give you only three words of formal advice. I have every confidence in your ability to apply this simple three-word formula to every new situation you will face at college."

"Three words," I reflected to myself. "Call me anytime," I almost blurted out, but didn't. As Tricie listened expectantly, Larry offered his carefully chosen words with measured evenness, "Figure it out. . . . Figure it out intellectually, figure it out socially, figure it out ethically, figure it out practically. Whatever the challenge, Tricie, know that you have within you the ability to 'figure it out' successfully."

At that moment, my fears began to dissipate. I intuitively knew that Larry's advice was appropriate for both Tricie and for us. His challenge to her had also summarized our ultimate responsibility as parents: to imbue our children with the appropriate personal tools and skills to enable them to solve life's problems in our absence someday. No parent can ever hope to leave a child at college having specifically prepared her for every eventuality she may face. Nevertheless, we can realistically impart to our youngsters during their childhood some fundamental ingredients for personal success. So long as Tricie could maintain a positive self-image and hold on to her unique identity, so long as she had internalized our past discipline into self-control and self-discipline, so long as she consistently displayed respect for others, acknowledged the natural consequences of her actions, identified her own values, and chose a positive attitude in life, I was confident she could deal successfully with any situation she might face. But I still hoped she would call me anytime—to tell me something new that she had figured out!

Challenges of Contemporary Parenting

If Grandma Neifert were alive today, she might assume at first glance that parenting had gotten easier than she remembered it nearly seventy years ago. She lost one of her eight babies delivered at home to respiratory distress syndrome of prematurity, which is readily treatable now. She was widowed with five young children and left penniless, after her beloved first husband died in a fiery trucking accident. Grandma initially breastfed each baby, then mixed a crude formula without benefit of refrigeration. After scraping excrement off the diapers, she washed them by hand in water she had to heat on the stove. She used a brick heated in the oven to warm the bed at night before putting a bundled infant to sleep beside her. Changing a diaper on a frigid winter night was unthinkable. Grandma never owned an infant

19

seat, a stroller, a playpen, or a changing table. She sold eggs, took in ironing, and cleaned other people's houses just to feed and clothe her children.

Caring for the physical needs of infants and children today is certainly easier than it was in the 1920s. All manner of baby equipment, baby supplies, and household appliances now expedite the daily routines of feeding, diapering, bathing, clothing, transporting, and safely confining our babies. Yet I would never suggest that parenting today is easier than in the past. In many ways, while the physical requirements have been modified, contemporary parenting is potentially more anxiety-provoking and mentally demanding than ever before. Let's examine some of the distinctions between parenting roles in the past and present.

Knowledge

Parents today have more informational resources available to them than any preceding generation. Countless childrearing books, babycare manuals, instructional audiotapes and videotapes, educational TV programs, and parenting classes are designed to prepare expectant, new, and experienced parents to handle everything from infant feeding to childhood safety to adolescent acting-out. Despite this plethora of information, it is my observation that many contemporary parents with the best of intentions make fundamental childrearing errors. Low self-esteem and underachievement are epidemic among today's children. Inappropriate discipline techniques and outright child abuse remain widespread. Most children are permitted to spend more time in front of a TV than in a classroom, while nearly a quarter of all American children do not graduate from high school.

Childbearing Options

Couples today are able to choose if and when to have children. More couples are electing to postpone child-bearing until their thirties, when they may be more mature as individuals, more stable as couples, more financially secure, and more established in their careers. The large family is rapidly becoming an anachronism; two children is the norm. Unfortunately, the trend toward smaller families hasn't necessarily translated into more time spent with each child. In fact, most parents spend less than fifteen minutes a day in focused, positive interaction with each of their children.

Contemporary childbearing options also encompass possibilities that Grandma could not have mentally or physiologically conceived. With routine use of ultrasound, many parents can learn their baby's sex before delivery and prepare specifically for the birth of a boy or girl. Egg and sperm now can be united outside the fallopian tubes and injected into the uterus, where implantation occurs. A surrogate mother can carry a fetus conceived from her own egg, or she can loan her uterus to carry a child conceived from another couple's egg and sperm. Recently, I encountered a young woman with two small children who has agreed to become a surrogate mother for another couple. Sheila's four-year-old, Ryan, showed great interest in her previous pregnancy and clearly adores his new brother. I inquired what explanation Sheila planned to offer to Ryan when the next baby does not join their family after her anticipated surrogate pregnancy. My question made Sheila realize she had not yet considered young Ryan's reaction to the unusual reproductive option she was weighing.

At-risk mothers can undergo amniocentesis or chorionic villi sampling to screen for chromosomal anomalies and other genetic defects. As a result, many parents will gain peace of mind, while a few necessarily will be forced to make heart-wrenching decisions about elective termination of their pregnancy. And how can one begin to comment about the individual and collective impact of more than a million fetal deaths each year as a result of legalized therapeutic abortions?

Health Care Decisions

Parents are increasingly becoming joint partners in their children's health care by providing thoughtful and informed consent for procedures previously viewed as routine, such as neonatal circumcision or repeat C-section or the timing of repair for a baby's cleft lip. This joint decision-making is certainly a refreshing change from the days when a physician unilaterally made the decisions about patient management. Few would dispute the value of having parents weigh options about infant feeding or immunizations. On the other hand, the need to participate in difficult health care decisions can impose a heavy burden of responsibility on some parents. I know a couple who had to make the agonizing decision about whether to have their baby undergo a single amputation procedure or lengthy conservative management of a congenital limb deformity. I am confident they made the best possible decision and will feel good about their involvement in the process, but I am equally sure that selecting the right option was extremely stressful for them.

Disrupted Families and Absent Fathers

Only 50 percent of American children presently live in traditional families with both biological parents. Divorces in America have doubled in the past thirty years, while out-of-wedlock births have increased four-fold. Today, nearly 40 percent of children do not live with their natural fathers, and more than half of children will spend at least part of their childhood without a father. The resulting "father hunger" is jeopardizing children's welfare economically, morally, emotionally, and intellectually. The trend toward fatherlessness also is robbing men of one of their most fundamental and rewarding roles. The absence of a father in the home is more than just an alternative lifestyle; it is a national crisis. Social scientists now insist there is a definite two-parent advantage. Father absence is linked with poverty, suicide, drug abuse, school dropout, teenage pregnancy, and criminal activity.

Employed Mothers

One of the most dramatic recent changes in the American family is the increased number of women in the paid workforce. Since 1950, the percentage of wives who work outside the home has doubled, while the percentage of working mothers has quadrupled. For most younger families, it is now assumed and expected that the wife and mother will contribute economically to the family. Purchasing power has dropped over the last twenty years, making it necessary for more mothers to work in order to keep family income from declining. Despite the growing number of employed mothers, women still assume most of the responsibility for child-rearing and do the majority of household chores, while men enjoy significantly more leisure time than women. In addition, employed mothers often are in conflict about putting the needs of others above those of their own children. For instance, a nurse in a neonatal intensive care unit may find she is unable to continue breastfeeding her three-month-old infant once she returns to work to care for other women's babies.

Dual working couples and single heads of households necessarily reduce the parental time and energy that can be devoted to childrearing. Our society has not yet assessed the full impact of this radical change on family life or children's outcome. No doubt the type of substitute childcare is of paramount importance to the proper nurturing and care of children whose mothers work for pay. Yet too many children are placed in either inadequate or inappropriate daycare settings, while others are left completely unattended.

Poverty

Despite admirable rhetoric about children being our most valuable resource, Americans have allowed children to become the poorest segment of our society. Nearly a quarter of all American children under the age of six now live in households with incomes below the official poverty line. Most of these families are headed by a single mother, often living in inadequate, unaffordable housing. A disproportionate percentage of children are without health insurance, and many fail to receive adequate preventive care and immunizations. To a large degree, the basic needs, including health care, education, daycare, and emotional support, of the present generation of children remain unmet. Even the people who work with children receive lower pay and less status than other professionals. Rising rates of childhood poverty are strongly correlated with changes in family structure—specifically absent fathers. Among children under the age of six who live with only their mother, 66 percent live in poverty, whereas only 12 percent of children under six residing with married parents live in poverty.

Media Influence

Never before has a generation of parents faced such awesome competition with the mass media for their children's attention. While parents tout the virtues of premarital virginity, drug-free living, nonviolent resolution of social conflict, or character over physical appearance, their values are daily challenged by television soaps, rock music lyrics, tabloid headlines, and movie scenes extolling the importance of physical appearance, conformity, and violent solutions to conflict. A child's admired Hollywood or sports heroes and heroines may be overtly involved in marital infidelity, drug use, domestic violence, or fraud. Personal appearance now claims such cultural importance that cosmetic surgery and adolescent anorexia and bulimia are widespread. TVs and VCRs are found with increased regularity in college dorm rooms, and fewer children than ever read for enjoyment, preferring instead to be passively entertained by a television screen.

Violence

While the family was meant to be a physical and emotional sanctuary for children and their parents, a growing number of families are tyrannized by violence. Two million cases of child abuse and a million violent domestic crimes are reported each year. Indeed, violence in America has become a public health emergency. The availability of handguns among urban high school students is pervasive, and gunshot wounds are now the leading cause of death in both black and white teenage boys in America. The extensive viewing of television violence is directly related to increased levels of physical aggressiveness among today's youth and is a major contributing factor in the present epidemic of violence in our society.

Drug Abuse

The national drug abuse crisis has reached horrifying proportions, and represents a major threat to our children and youth. Presently, one in ten newborns has been exposed to an illicit drug during pregnancy. The majority of children will have tried illicit drugs before leaving high school, with a disturbing trend toward polydrug use and earlier initiation of drug use. Three million children between fourteen and seventeen are problem drinkers.

Societal Fears

While every age has had its crises, contemporary families live with multiple overhanging clouds of oppressive fears. AIDS, a uniformly fatal disease, still eludes modern science's attempts to conquer it. Even if we succeed in averting a deadly nuclear war, we have so over-populated our world and ravaged our environment that the future of our planet remains in jeopardy. No wonder many parents battle emotional fatigue and a pervading sense of dread. Some even ask whether they should bring children into such a world as ours.

Few would contest that parenting is much different today than in the past. Indeed, most would contend that it is more challenging than ever before. Yet with sufficient support and practical advice, it is still possible to rear children with confidence instead of fear, while considering the pressing needs of our era.

The Future of the Family

My ultimate purpose in writing this book is to nurture and uplift families, specifically by offering emotional support and parenting skills for those adults who have primary responsibility for children. The family is both the fundamental unit of society as well as the root of culture. It represents a child's initial source of unconditional love and acceptance and provides lifelong connectedness with others. The family is the first setting in which socialization takes place and where children learn to live with mutual respect for one another. A family is where a child learns to display affection, control his temper, and pick up his toys. Finally, a family is a perpetual source of encouragement, advocacy, assurance, and emotional refueling that empowers a child to venture with confidence into the greater world and to become all that he can be.

It should come as no surprise that when the family unit is strong, this strength ripples throughout society. Strong families make strong neighborhoods, which create strong communities and businesses, which in turn produce strong local and national governments. The converse is also true: the erosion of the family unit heralds the decline of all society. I wrote this book because I believe one of the fundamental ways to strengthen the family is to teach parenting skills and nurturing techniques to caretaking adults.

Despite widely promoted stereotypes, family forms vary from one society to another and undergo radical changes over time within the same society. While many people still cling to the image of a working father, homemaker mother, and one or more children as the "traditional American family," this characterization was true for only a brief period in our history and presently describes only 16 percent of U.S. households. The beauty of the contemporary American family lies in its enormous diversity and its individual strengths. In order to affirm all families effectively, we must first discard our former idealized notions about the "perfect" family in favor of a broader definition that acknowledges and celebrates the differences in people.

For most of us, the word *family* carries very personal and emotional connotations, but it is essential that we learn to view all of humanity as part of the earth's family. While we have no trouble cherishing our own children, we must also appreciate our broader responsibility to the world's children. Only when we learn to value other people's children as our own will all children have the opportunity to reach their full potential. And only then can we be assured of our collective future and the future of our planet.

ADDITIONAL READING:

Blankenhorn, David. *Fatherless America*. New York: Basic Books, 1995.
Medved, Michael. *Hollywood vs. America*. New York: HarperCollins, 1992.
Pearsall, Paul. *The Power of the Family*. New York: Doubleday, 1990.

2

THE MYTH OF THE SUPERPARENT

The Changing Roles of Modern Parents

The myth of the superparent—who can pursue a career or hold a job, keep a spotless house, be a flawless host or hostess, as well as a loving spouse *and* raise disciplined children who are delightful to be around—has evolved during the recent decline of traditional parenting sex-role stereotypes. In less than two decades, the working mother has been transformed from novelty to norm. While the reality of maternal employment has indelibly impacted modern motherhood, the accompanying redefinition of today's father also has placed unique stresses on contemporary men. It seems that removing former arbitrary limits on parenting roles has not merely broadened the opportunities for some parents, but has also increased the expectations for all parents.

Contemporary Fathers

Traditionally, fathers have been expected to be gainfully employed, and the importance of assuring their family's financial security was accepted as ample justification for the prolonged daily separation from spouse and children that was a necessary prerequisite to "success" in a career. Until recently, this breadwinner role outweighed the value of a father's input in day-to-day childrearing. Fathers were expected to be final arbiters of disciplinary decisions and to play with older children, but they were given few childrearing responsibilities and shared few of the basic joys—or burdens—of a primary caretaker.

But once fathers demanded, and were given access to delivery rooms in the 1970s, they got "hooked" on their children and genuinely wanted to spend more time with them. The involvement of fathers in all aspects of parenting rapidly accelerated. How refreshing that so many contemporary fathers are committed to playing a dynamic role in parenting their children! Despite having only their own fathers' outdated parenting model, many men today struggle to balance traditional career aspirations and shifting family priorities.

New terminology has evolved to describe some of the circumstances unique to modern fatherhood—*paternity leave, house spouse, shared custody*, and *parity parenting*, among them. Many personal examples have made news, and movies like *Kramer vs. Kramer* have championed the cause of the newly involved father. An ex-governor gained much publicity when he took a six-month leave after departing office in order to travel with his wife and four children and re-establish their family unity. A movie star with grown children turned house spouse in his new marriage and became the primary caretaker for the young son he has decided to parent differently than he did a generation ago with his "first family." No one is shocked today when a father turns down a once-coveted promotion because it would require him to travel too often or give up too much time with his family.

Employed Mothers

While the societal changes facing fathers are indeed significant, those facing women are colossal in comparison. Out of economic necessity, personal choice, or societal pressure, more mothers than ever are presently employed outside the home, even while the vast majority of them continue to assume the primary parenting role. A growing number of employed mothers are single heads of households, with sole responsibility for their children's financial, physical, and emotional welfare. A disproportionate number are in low-paying, monotonous, or dead-end jobs that provide minimal fulfillment and promise little chance of advancement. Others are professional women holding high-pressure positions that leave them physically and emotionally depleted at day's end and demand that additional time be spent on work outside office hours. Too few succeed in obtaining positions well-matched to their skills and offering a network of supportive colleagues, a combination that can actually enhance one's self-esteem.

Parents at Home

Parents who work in the home certainly experience their own unique pressures and stressors. In fact, at-home parents may be even more vulnerable to the expectations of the superparent myth, compelled to achieve perfection as a homemaker, spouse, and parent since they are not perceived as being "gainfully employed." Such parents are over-represented in neighborhood volunteer activities, serving as homeroom parents, field trip chaperones, scout troop leaders, emergency contact people for children of working parents, and providers of before- and after-school supervision for latch-key children.

I am very much aware that my own children never would have been able to participate in scouting, soccer, cheerleading, softball, or other activities were it not for the often thankless efforts of at-home parents who quietly chauffeured my kids along with their own. Furthermore, I am ashamed to admit that I was so preoccupied at the time with my work demands that I often failed to express my gratitude appropriately or to acknowledge the magnitude of the contribution these gracious individuals made to our family. In lieu of the personal recognition my conscientious at-home neighbors deserved a decade ago, I am now publicly sharing just how much their efforts meant to my kids and to me. (Thank you Wilma, Ruth, Sue, Nora, Kevin, Cherie, Carol, and all of you others!) I find it regrettable that employed and at-home parents have not been more supportive of one another. Perhaps both groups are so insecure and guilt-ridden about our personal employment choices that we idealize the alternative lifestyle and become defensive about our own. If every family were to respect the differences in their neighbors, we would be far more effective in collectively meeting the needs of our children.

Regardless of individual circumstances, contemporary parents share a number of stresses in common, ranging from unrealistic expectations for ourselves and our children; having too much to do in too little time; battling chronic guilt and fatigue; preserving our own health and sense of well-being; taking time for ourselves; communicating with our partners; and for employed parents, trying to obtain and maintain affordable, competent childcare. I will not attempt to discuss the merits of the changes in family life that have resulted from a new norm of working mothers and the expanded parenting role among fathers. Instead, my purpose is to try to offer some practical suggestions for all parents who feel overcommitted, with the goal of helping them maximize their parenting enjoyment with minimal stress to themselves and their children.

I don't claim to have any magic formulas, but I do have nearly twenty-five years of experience precariously juggling a demanding career, a large family, and a unique marriage. Larry and I started this journey long before it was socially permissible for a "good" mother to pursue a career and well before it was considered admirable for a father to be intimately involved in child-care. While I had no female role models in my particular field, my own parents had already challenged the television stereotype of June and Ward Cleaver. My mother taught high school while raising five children, and my Dad would don an apron after work each evening and pitch in to fix dinner, solely because it made good sense in a big, busy family.

Of course there have been highs and lows, pros and cons, rewards and disappointments. In reflecting on the personal course I chose, I feel the positives have out-numbered the drawbacks, and on balance, I have been pleased with my own decisions about working. This is easier to admit from my present advantage, since my children are now old enough to appear to have turned out well, and my marriage is sturdy enough for me to predict cautiously that it is permanent. I have also had the opportunity and privilege to observe firsthand how countless other couples have struggled to prioritize the demands of parenting with other facets of their lives. My hope is that I can provide some insights that will help you make the parenting decisions that are right for you and your family. Whatever commitments you find yourself juggling, I wish you all the joys of successful parenting, along with the personal fulfillment that can come from satisfying work.

The Superparent Myth

What exactly is a superparent and how do we fall victim to its myth? The myth, an outgrowth of the newly expanded roles for both mothers and fathers, is the compelling, yet highly unrealistic, expectation that we can be all things to all people. Because the superparent myth affects women more dramatically than men, many of my comments will be directed specifically toward women. However, I trust that most of the following material is applicable to fathers as well.

The myth is not just believing we can "do it all," but includes the notion that we can do everything both superbly and effortlessly. To do less is equated with being a complete failure. Thus, in her attempt to be "everything to everyone," the superparent may try to be all at once:

- the perfect mother who bakes fresh cookies for her child's class, makes a Halloween costume from scratch, leads a Girl Scout troop, gives her child piano lessons, and checks her homework every night;

- the competent business executive who strives to be as competitive, assertive, and professional as her male counterpart;

- the seductive partner who dresses impeccably, has her nails done weekly, and sips wine with her husband over candlelit gourmet dinners;

- the fulfilled individual who is a long-distance runner, takes flying lessons on weekends, is earning her Ph.D. at night, and reads at least one best-selling novel each week on her lunch hour.

Intellectually, we acknowledge that no one, regardless of how talented or energized or motivated, can really fulfill these multiple roles well, certainly not without incurring tremendous personal expense and compromise. Intellectually, we know all marriages have some conflicts, all partners can be bitchy sometimes, and many marriages end in divorce. All kids act rude and cranky sometimes, and all children have some problems and bring some disappointments, if not outright misery at times. Every working woman gets tired and discouraged and will surely have some down days. All mothers act grouchy at times, make mistakes, and inflict some emotional trauma on their kids. All people experience some failures in their lives, which provide wonderful opportunities to learn and grow.

For some perverse reason, however, we insist on perpetuating the superparent myth, despite knowing that it is harmful to our own mental health. I blame television for a lot of our apparent addiction to such surrealism. Actually, I think television first introduced the myth with the popular Aviance perfume commercials years ago. I can still visualize this gorgeous professional woman bustling through the doorway after work, swinging her briefcase onto the couch, confident in her ability to both bring home the bacon and fry it for her man. Before the commercial ends, she slips into seductive evening wear to greet her husband, who is rapidly overcome by her Aviance essence.

I have yet to meet the woman who actually looks or feels like the Aviance woman at the end of the day, but many of us still cling to that image of the idealized, multidimensional woman. While our own family's flaws are self-evident, we insist on believing that the picture-perfect families on television really exist. Even when our own mirror reflects the realities of the aging process, we want to believe that some people really are as naturally and eternally beautiful as those captured by the

TV cameras. We know too well the extent of our own personal shortcomings and daily disappointments, but we wish it were true that some people are perpetually smiling, their teeth whiter, their breath fresher than the laws of nature allow.

Don't get me wrong. I'm all for heroes and ideals when the individual or standard effectively motivates us to achieve something difficult yet within our reach. When the ideal is superhuman and unattainable, however, then holding it up can be as destructive as promising a youngster he can soar above the clouds if he will only emulate an eagle long enough!

Sadly enough, many women still believe that someone truly can "have it all" with relative ease. But, the superparent myth is just that, a myth. Pretending that superheroes really do exist just makes life harder for the rest of us ordinary humans by making us feel inadequate and guilty for not living up to the inflated standard. Let me share an illustrative story that first opened my eyes to the dangers of mythical behavior. This true account reminds me that you may dream the impossible dream, but you can't do the impossible.

During much of my own early training, I shared the conviction that I was prepared to do whatever it took physically, mentally, and emotionally in order to enter the then male-dominated profession of medicine. "Perseverance" and "willpower" were my middle names, and thus far in life they had carried me to my goals.

During the first year of medical school, we conducted various experiments in physiology lab. Often the experiments were performed on laboratory animals, but at other times we monitored body functions on ourselves. One day the instructor explained that we would be studying variables in our twenty-four-hour urine output and announced that everyone was to bring to the next class a twenty-four-hour urine sample. I don't recall any other instructions being offered and my immediate assumption was: "Oh, my word, we have to hold it for twenty-four hours!"

I looked around at my thirty classmates, but no one appeared distressed at this seemingly phenomenal assignment. Thus, I determined to carry out the requirement without complaint. I certainly wasn't going to suggest that women have some minor difficulty with bladder capacity that prevents them from becoming doctors. Still awed by my classmates' ability to accept the task so readily, I began to plan how I would contain twenty-four hours' worth of urine in my poor bladder, which had already endured one pregnancy.

I decided to begin the countdown in the evening, so I would be well on my way to the deadline by morning. I awoke the next morning and headed for the bathroom, anticipating the usual relief, before I remembered that I was not permitted to urinate. Suddenly the weight of my full bladder started to preoccupy me. Running water to brush my teeth created an almost overwhelming power of suggestion. I went to make myself a cup of coffee but immediately rejected that thought. Peter's weight pressed on my bladder as I carried him down our front stairs to the car. Fastening my seat belt further aggravated the uncomfortable pressure.

I arrived at school and made it through biochemistry, but found it difficult to concentrate. By midmorning, my eyeballs were floating. I doubted I could "hold it" any longer. My classmates were drinking coffee as usual and appeared quite comfortable. No one mentioned "the assignment."

Finally, I could stand it no longer. "Clark," I asked my closest friend at school, "how are you doing it?"

"Doing what?" Clark sincerely inquired.

"Don't act like you don't know." I was irritated enough already. "How can you not pee for twenty-four hours? My bladder is going to burst!"

"Marianne, you're not trying to *hold it* are you?

You're supposed to collect a twenty-four-hour urine sample. You know—like in a jar—not in your bladder!"

I nearly died of embarrassment at that moment and considered muttering something unconvincing like "I knew that," but the sentiment was overridden by the compulsion to empty my bladder.

"Here," said Clark. "Take this beaker to the bathroom and go right now." As I headed off in the direction of the bathroom, I doubted that anyone had ever anticipated urinating with such relief.

This story is more than just a funny and embarrassing account. It is a lesson in life. You see, there are some things that are simply not possible, regardless of how determined or motivated you are. The only reason I tried to do the physically impossible in this case was that I mistakenly thought everyone else was doing it without difficulty. You might desperately want to stay married and be willing to work hard at your relationship, but if your spouse decides to run off with his secretary, there may be nothing humanly possible that you can do to preserve your marriage. Accepting the inevitable does not mean you lack perseverance or motivation—it simply means you are being appropriately realistic.

The problem with the superparent myth is that it sets up extremely unrealistic expectations that leave many parents feeling inadequate and guilty. The mistaken conviction that countless others are coolly and capably juggling their careers, marriages, and children with minimal stress and maximal fulfillment leaves the rest of us feeling woefully inadequate about our own unglamorous daily struggle to meet everyone's needs.

The reality is that for most of us the myth is more like the *Cathy* cartoon poster in which she is shown sitting at her desk, looking forlorn. All her job-related projects are piled several feet high on one side while her laundry and home demands are stacked equally high on the other. Below reads the telltale caption: "Having it all—the worst of both worlds!"

Being honest about the compromises we have to make paints a more realistic picture for all parents and protects them from extreme disillusionment when their own lives fail to match the touted norm. I am often asked, "How do you do it?" by women who automatically assume that I do all things well and easily. That is simply not true, but it's still tempting at times to maintain a façade and perpetuate the superparent myth by letting stay-at-home mothers believe that I magically do everything they spend all day on *and* have a glamorous career. Fortunately for everyone, my kids (who have threatened to write *Dr. Mommie Dearest*) usually tell all and keep me humble. The truth is, most of our alleged superheroes make meals, make beds, make ends meet, make mistakes, make up, make amends, make love, and mostly make do.

Once when Peter was in the second grade and I was still a pediatric resident, he completed a class assignment called "About My Family." My husband and I were reviewing his work at a parent-teacher conference when we came across the questionnaire. In the section "About My Mother," he had filled in answers as follows:

"The favorite thing my mother likes to cook for me is tomato soup.

"The favorite thing my mother likes to do is sleep."

Well, Peter was simply telling it like he saw it. I was a walking zombie much of that time; I was on call every third night and chronically sleep-deprived. We ate a lot of tomato soup, and I tried to catch up on sleep every chance I got. I was ashamed to face the teacher after reading my son's perception of me, the supposedly great doctor-mother.

Shortly after the *Dr. Mom* book came out, a reporter from the *Los Angeles Times* came to Denver to interview my family and me. She was to visit me at the office and then drive to my home after work. My secretary, who knew I seldom baked, was worried that I wouldn't have anything to offer the reporter to eat. So, the day before the reporter was to arrive, my secretary brought a freshly baked bundt cake to work and told me to take it home and pretend I had baked it myself. At first I thought this was a great idea, but after considering it further, I had to admit that it was highly unfair to all women to suggest that I bake cakes from scratch in my spare time! Besides, such a story would never fly. The reporter might ask me to name the ingredients, or my kids might collapse with laughter when I tried to explain that I had baked it myself. In the end, I offered the reporter a piece of cake, but I also admitted that my secretary had baked it.

I once served as a member of the planning committee for a seminar sponsored by our local medical society. The program was planned for female physicians and was designed to address the various stresses that resulted from their multiple life roles—as physicians, mothers, wives, and women. During a brainstorming session to select an appropriate title for the conference brochure, someone wrote on the board, "The Disparate Roles of the Female Physician." After initial enthusiasm for the title, we ultimately had to reject this selection because everyone in the room admitted they had at first mistakenly read it as "The Desperate Roles of the Female Physician." Surely, every parent who has periodically experienced stress, guilt, fatigue, and inadequacy might claim to be "desperate" at times.

Practical Strategies for Busy Parents

Much of what follows will focus on enhancing your parenting enjoyment by learning to identify priorities, make compromises, lower your standards, accept imperfection, and be willing to do a "good enough" job instead of a superb job. There's a fine line, but a critical distinction nevertheless, between "doing your best" and "doing the best you can with the circumstances you have."

Define Your Values and Establish Priorities

Defining your values is easier said than done. It requires honest introspection and unrestricted time. I urge you to set aside a couple of hours and actually write down your personal values in order of priority. What are the things in your life that are truly important to you? What will matter most to you ten years or twenty years from now? What people or principles would you put your life on the line for?

A couple of years ago, I took a seminar on time management because I felt overwhelmed with too much to do in too little time. I thought I could get more done if I just managed my time better. The first assignment was to spend two to five hours clarifying your values and priorities. Being a busy person, I tried to skip this first exercise, arguing that I didn't have enough time to spend that long on the assignment, and besides, I already knew what was important to me in life. But, I learned you can't really begin to establish a daily list of things to do unless you know precisely what activities will be a priority for you.

When the techniques presented at the seminar didn't seem to be working for me, I realized that unless I thoughtfully established my values and priorities, I would continue to let *other people* determine the way I spend each day. "Dr. Neifert, will you give a lecture at the medical school on Thursday?" "Marianne, will you write a letter of recommendation for me?" "Dr. Mom, would you fly to Los Angeles and appear on television?" "Dr. Neifert, can we schedule a patient for you at one o'clock this afternoon?" and on, and on, and on. Unless you identify what is most important *to you* to get done, you will find yourself filling your days with *everyone else's* priorities. I was busy *all the time*, but lots of the things I was doing were not very important to me. They just got onto my list because someone else asked me to do them. I couldn't rank each request in relation to my personal priorities because I had failed to establish clear priorities in the first place. I simply said yes to everything until I was overwhelmed and miserable. Since I was unwilling to live my own life, I discovered that everyone else was more than happy to live it for me!

So don't schedule another thing until you first identify your own governing values. Write them down, carry what you have written with you, and read your espoused values daily. Then ask yourself whether your daily actions really support those stated values. If not, then something is out of synch between the values you express and the value system you act out. For example, let's say you rated your family above everything else. You would readily lay down your life for your children or your spouse, and you realize that everything else you are spending time on right now will be dwarfed in comparison to the importance of your family ten years from now. But meanwhile, you are so preoccupied with work demands that you seem to have only leftovers for your family, in terms of energy and enthusiasm. You snap at them after work, and you have missed several activities important to your children because of "just this one special crisis at work." The best years of your life are slipping by and you are giving your "first fruits," as it were, to your work instead of to your family. You profess to others that your family rates first in your life, but your actions regularly put them at a lower priority than your work.

It's time to take stock. Are you doing all this for the money? Would you rate money higher than your relationship with the ones you love best? Are you doing it to enhance your own self-esteem? Do you need so much approval from others because you disapprove of yourself? Years from now, will you wish you had spent more time with your family? These are some of the tough questions that haunt working parents.

Every time you schedule something to do, examine it to see if it fits any of your stated priorities. When I am asked to travel somewhere, give a lecture, write something, or otherwise spend time on an activity, I have to ask myself whether it helps me meet one of my personal goals or whether I would be giving up something more valued, like time with my husband and kids or time for myself, in order to do it.

I "had my colors done" several years ago, at which time I also received a palette of the specific autumn colors that were supposed to make me look my best. While I wasn't limited to wearing only these colors, I was advised that they were particularly becoming on me. Indeed, I began to observe that when I wore my teal suit I always received compliments about my appearance. One morning, when I had had only two hours of sleep and certainly wasn't feeling very attractive, I wore my teal suit to the hospital, and, sure enough, someone commented on how nice I looked. Maybe there really is something valid about having your colors analyzed and wearing the colors that bring out the best in your appearance!

Recently, I thought, "Wouldn't it be nice if we could 'have our *values* done' as simply as having our colors analyzed?" If only we could make choices according to our values as easily as we choose clothes according to our colors. Then, when asked to compromise our family priorities by coming in to work this weekend on that "special project" or traveling out of town on business, we could just spread out our values palette and announce, "Sorry, that option doesn't become me. It doesn't match my values."

This concept came to me after meeting a photographer who had traveled to Denver from New York to photograph my family for a magazine interview. This man was a highly reputable professional who was in great demand and thus traveled often. He also had a wife and young son who were important priorities in his life. To maintain some balance between his demanding career and a family he loved deeply, the man had identified and tenaciously adhered to a particular value—he refused to work on weekends. Whether commissioned to photograph a rock star, the president, or the queen of England, if the job involved a weekend, he simply said no. He had vowed that weekends would be devoted to his family, and he refused to make exceptions.

This man didn't need to conduct any lengthy, energy-depleting, soul-searching debates about the particular merits of one weekend offer over another. If the job involved a weekend, he simply declined it, without waffling or speculating, and without looking back later. I admired and envied this man very much, for he had identified a governing value for his life, which in turn had ordered his priorities. Then he had stuck to his convictions and daily acted out his value system. Although he had many lucrative offers and career-advancing weekend opportunities, he made *simple* decisions by first examining his imaginary value palette. At times these must have been *difficult* decisions, I'm sure, but they were always simple, based on his acknowledged values and priorities. Like committing to wearing your best colors, you can learn to say, "That decision doesn't become me; it doesn't bring out the best in me."

Lower Your Standards

Once you have honestly identified your values, your priorities can be easily ordered, based on your value system. Then you can choose to lower your standards in low-priority areas so that you won't have to compromise your standards for your highest priorities.

My first lesson in lowering my standards after becoming a parent was a real shocker that challenged my whole identity, but it was a tremendous learning and growth experience. When my first baby was born, I was terribly naive and had no concept of how drastically motherhood would change my life. Peter arrived in the middle of my third and final year of college, shortly after I had been accepted to medical school. But I still had to finish the semester and attend summer school in order to graduate from college and enter medical school in the fall.

I managed to return to my college classes a week after Peter was born, but I was totally unprepared for the constant care and attention required by a newborn. I was so overwhelmed with being a new mother that I essentially did no homework for six weeks! Until this point in my life, being an A student had been an important part of my identity. Determined to be a good mother and a good wife, I soon discovered that there was simply no way I could devote as much time to my studies as I had when Larry was overseas and I carried Peter inside me.

Now, here I was, a little more than a month before the end of the semester, and I wasn't even sure I could complete the necessary coursework for graduation. For several weeks, I considered dropping out of school. I engaged in "all-or-nothing" thinking and felt that not getting an A would be the equivalent of failing. Then, as if to dramatize my dilemma, I received two contrasting pieces of mail one day. The first was an announcement that, based on my academic record to date, I had been selected to receive an award for "Outstanding Achievement in Chemistry." The second was a failure notice in one of my current chemistry courses that was not yet represented on my transcript!

This was the last straw. I had to make a decision about my future. Would I give up and drop out of school or try to graduate and enter medical school? When I went to class the next day, I noticed something that changed my life. I noticed that Jim Thompson didn't even show up at class. At least I'd been attending regularly and I had taken good notes. If some kids could pass despite skipping classes, I reasoned, maybe I could get through too, even though I was hopelessly behind in homework. It occurred to me that all I really needed to do was to pass since I already had been accepted to medical school. I *wanted to get A's*, but I *didn't have to get A's*. I simply had to get by, and I resolved to lower my standards at school, to do only a "good enough" job for the first time in my life. I couldn't willfully neglect my baby, but I could perform less than perfectly in my coursework. I wouldn't like it, but it was a viable compromise.

I went to see each professor, explained my situation, and requested permission to catch up on my assignments and turn them in late. Then I made a list of every overdue English essay, chemistry lab report, physics problem, and computer assignment that faced me and resolved to tackle them one by one. It took me until the end of the semester, but I completed everything that was essential. My performance was "good enough." I earned low B's that semester instead of A's, but I had passed everything, and I was going to graduate after all. I've never regretted that I lowered my performance standards, finished college, and entered medical school. And no one has ever asked me what grades I earned during my final semester of college!

Later, as a young wife and mother in medical school, I often had to reorder my priorities when I simply had too much to do in too little time. The first compromise I chose to make was to lower my housekeeping standards, which clearly ranked lower than nurturing my children, preserving my marriage, and caring for patients. I adopted and popularized the motto, "Housework is a cinch, provided your standards are low enough." When things got too hectic, we used paper plates and "threw the dishes away" instead of washing them. (Now I am more environmentally conscious.) For support, I recalled my own mother's observation years after her children were grown and she had retired: "You know," she reflected, "I can't even remember today the addresses of all the places I struggled to keep clean when you kids were growing up."

Paige, our oldest daughter, is in medical school studying to become a physician and expects to marry and have a family. Thus, she will face the same juggling act among multiple roles that I struggled with throughout her childhood. Several years ago, Paige's novel approach to a dilemma involving her youngest sister convinced me that she is well on her way to setting priorities and making practical compromises.

Our youngest daughter, Heather, was a Girl Scout at this point in time. Many of the mothers of other girls in her troop did not work outside the home and were far more successful homemakers than I. These mothers could bake, sew, make a costume, French-braid hair, and decorate a living room. One night near Christmas, when I was attending physician in the pediatric clinic at University Hospital, Heather called me and announced that each Girl Scout was to bring a batch of home-baked cookies, along with the cookie recipe, to tomorrow's scout meeting. They would sing carols at a neighborhood nursing home, serve the homemade cookies to the residents, and then exchange cookie recipes. What kind of cookies was I planning to bake?

Now Heather always amazed me by her "magical thinking" at times like this. Perhaps she is a perpetual optimist or maybe she was still young enough to retain a flicker of hope that I would rally to the occasion, arrive home after midnight, and mix the ingredients for the Neifert family's "traditional holiday cookies." Paige, on the other hand, was old enough to realize that we don't keep on hand the ingredients to mix anything to be baked from scratch, nor do we have any traditional family recipes, with the single exception of chestnut stuffing that I ceremoniously make each Thanksgiving.

I was "discussing" the matter with Heather, who was starting to become emotional, and my feelings of guilt and inadequacy were mounting. I tried to be humorous. "Look, I'll stop at the grocery after I get off and buy a package of Double Stuff Oreos. The 'recipe' could be a description of how to eat them by pulling them apart, licking off the white center, and throwing away the black circles." I was actually pleased with my originality and sense of humor and thought Heather just might buy this creative approach, but instead she wailed in disgust, "You never do anything the way the other mothers do." Just then, Paige came on the line, "Don't worry, Mom, I'll handle it. She'll have her cookies."

Several hours later, I called to tell the girls I was on my way home. "Do you want me to stop by the grocery?"

"No, Mom, everything's under control," Paige explained calmly. "Heather's got her cookies and her recipe."

"What did you possibly come up with?" I asked.

"Well, I found a box of generic oatmeal cookies in the cupboard. I arranged them on a plate and covered them with foil so they'd look fresh-baked. Then I copied an oatmeal cookie recipe from *Joy of Cooking*. Heather thinks it's great."

It was a perfectly *adequate* solution to Heather's minor crisis. While her cookies certainly weren't going to be the best ones brought to tomorrow's meeting, they would do. Paige had learned to make a "good enough" compromise under the circumstances. I think of this story often whenever I start to worry about the future struggles Paige will undoubtedly face someday as a physician mother juggling too much at times. Somehow, I know she's going to handle it all pretty well.

Just Say No

Many contemporary parents, both those employed and at home, are greatly overextended with family, work, and community commitments. We have said yes to every demand made upon us, and despite "running as fast as we can," we can't seem to find quality time for our families, personal time for ourselves, or any time for adult relationships. Many employed mothers I know start their day at 4:30 A.M., getting up to run the washer and dryer before preparing breakfast, packing diaper bags, putting ingredients in the crockpot, and loading the car. An at-home mother of three described becoming so involved in her children's numerous athletic and extracurricular activities that she found herself chauffeuring them to multiple daily practices and weekly sports events, as well as heading up the booster club, volunteering in an organization, and taking a college class three evenings each week. One day, as the family ate dinner in their van on the way to a football game, this woman conceded that her life was out of control. Both her daughters and her son were participating in four different activities, orchestrated and cheered on by their mother. In the course of a week, she chauffeured to and applauded for their swimming, gymnastics, dance, piano, choir, trombone, cheerleading, football, and scouting.

"That night when we all got home, I sat everybody down and told them I wasn't happy with the way our family life was going. Actually, we all had to agree that the pace and the pressure had become unbearable. 'You each presently have four extracurricular activities,' I said. 'Pick two.' "

While the decision was painful, each child quickly identified their two most important activities. "The quality of our lives dramatically improved," she commented. "We discovered that sometimes more is not necessarily better; less is better."

If you are uncomfortably overextended in your personal or professional life, start saying no today, cut back on anything that isn't absolutely essential, underschedule yourself instead of overscheduling yourself. Practice telling others, "I prefer not to. My family comes first right now." Put your current commitments in perspective by asking yourself how you will want to have spent your time forty years from now. For example, I have never heard a white-haired retiree insist, "My only regret is that I didn't come into the office on weekends more often." Instead, what older mentors invariably lament is that they didn't spend more time with their families.

Manage Your Time

In today's fast-paced world, time is our most valuable resource. My own working mother taught me early that "time is money," and I have repeated that phrase often. Everywhere we turn today, advertising attracts our attention with promises to save us time. We have fast foods, express mail, instant potatoes, Minute Rice, quick oatmeal, one-hour photo developing, and even rapid dialing! As a busy parent, your time is most precious. We can't even begin to talk about quality time when we have so little total time available with our child.

Work expands to fill the time available. One of the most fundamental principles of time management is the caveat that work expands to fill the time available. This principle is so true that I find I do best when I assign an appropriate time limit to a specific task, instead of permitting the task to take as long as it seems to need.

After I was married and became a mother, I always budgeted my studies in this way. I would retire with some of my work undone (not everyone can fall asleep with their work undone, however!) and then I would arise in the wee hours of the morning, allowing a limited amount of time to complete my assignments before getting my kids up and leaving for class. I found I worked more efficiently in this way than if I tried to stay up at night indefinitely, taking as long as necessary to complete my work. I'm not giving a blanket endorsement to this method, but it has worked for me. After a brief, rejuvenating sleep, and without other distractions in the middle of the night, I found I got more accomplished between three and six in the morning than if I had stayed up late at night to complete my work.

Perfectionists, especially, will benefit from allotting only a certain length of time to a particular task. Perfectionists usually take *all* the available time to complete something, because their expectations of their work are so high that it never quite seems good enough. They are only able to finish something when there is simply no more time left. Often perfectionists are so immobilized by their fear of not doing a perfect job that they become classic procrastinators. They put things off until the last possible minute, finally rationalizing, "Well, it may not be a perfect term paper, but it's not bad for one written in just two nights!"

I know a well-intentioned perfectionist who has scores of half-written letters to people she really cares about, but she seldom finishes or mails a letter because it never seems good enough to send. Her family and friends would love to receive even a sloppy note, a scribble on a greeting card, or a plain postcard, but she is still waiting to write the perfect message—and never gets it done. When her friends and family don't hear from her, they assume she doesn't really care, when, in fact, she cares too much.

Someone like her would function better if she said to herself, "I've got ten minutes to wait until my daughter is out of dance class. I think I'll jot a note to Lu Ann in that time and mail it on the way home." Then she could use the perfectionist's argument: "It may not be a great letter, but it's not bad for having spent only ten minutes."

Like the perfectionist I just described, I have trouble getting my Christmas cards mailed on time. Although I buy and address them well before the holidays, I stew at length about composing the perfect message that will make up for a whole year of not corresponding with someone. In actuality, people are more interested in our enclosed annual family picture than in anything I might write. If I just mailed the cards with our names printed at the bottom, I could use the remaining time and energy to enjoy the holidays more.

As I should do with my Christmas cards, try focusing

on doing a "good enough" job of most things. You'd be surprised how few things in life really need to be done exceptionally well—like performing surgery, packing a parachute, sitting on a jury, writing a letter of recommendation, driving a school bus, watching a baby near a swimming pool. For most things, an adequate or "good enough" job is all that is called for— for preparing a meal, cleaning the house, selecting a gift, writing a letter, holding a birthday party, choosing something to wear, washing the car, or leading a scout meeting. Don't let the "perfect" become the enemy of the "good" in your life.

The tyranny of the urgent. Another issue that dictates the way we manage our time is the concept of "the tyranny of the urgent." Most of us spend a great deal of time doing things that are urgent, but few of those things are really important. The important things in life are often long-range goals that do not have daily deadlines associated with them: "Someday I'd like to get my degree." . . . "I really must let my parents know how much they mean to me." . . . "I sure would like to adopt a healthier lifestyle and get in shape."

Thus, a ringing telephone is always urgent, even though only a tiny fraction of the calls we receive are actually important. We will get up from our dinner, come out of a shower dripping wet, or even interrupt lovemaking to answer the shrill ringing of a phone, which could end up being a wrong number or a computerized telemarketing call. But we seldom think twice about indefinitely postponing things like a vacation with our spouse, spending time alone with our child, writing a letter to someone we love, taking a self-improvement class, finally learning to play the piano, starting an exercise program, or visiting a relative in a nursing home. Since none of these is technically urgent, they may never achieve sufficient priority importance actually to get done.

For example, writing this book was important to me, but until the deadline closed in, it wasn't urgent. Something else was always urgent; something else was always overdue and needed to be Federal Expressed. In retrospect, most of those commitments were not very important in the total scheme of things, but they almost kept me from writing this book. Personally, I believe that distinguishing between *urgent* and *important* priorities is one of the hardest things to do well in life.

Television. I can't talk about time management without addressing what I consider to be the greatest time-waster in our century—television. The typical family watches three or more hours of television each day. I realize that watching television can offer an outlet for stress. It can provide a temporary escape from the pressures of life. And it can provide unprecedented educational opportunities, including the nightly news, special documentaries, presidential debates, Senate hearings, space shuttle launchings, symphonies, operas, African safaris, underwater adventures, and other programming that broadens our intellectual horizons.

In reality, however, the majority of time an individual sits in front of the TV each day is spent viewing sitcoms, adventure dramas, soap operas, music videos, made-for-television movies, and reruns. Watching television is an entirely passive activity that typically precludes interactions with other family members. In many families, the television even prevents the family from dining together. Perhaps worst of all, television paints an entirely unrealistic view of life with an overemphasis on personal appearance, the perpetuation of sex-role stereotypes, and the idealization of family life where problems are always resolved in a thirty-minute segment.

Several years ago, in a proposed study of family television viewing patterns, five hundred dollars was offered to selected families if they would unplug their television for one month. Surprisingly few families agreed to participate because they didn't feel they could forgo television viewing for that long. In a recent national telephone poll of more than one thousand adults, nearly half of the respondents said they wouldn't give up television for less than a million dollars. Put simply, television viewing is addictive; advertisers and programmers have designed it to be that way.

The first question I like to ask an overly busy parent is: "How much TV do you watch?" Many people could add four or more hours to their day if they simply turned off the television! Would you consider turning off even one TV program an evening and devoting that time to your child, giving him one-to-one focused attention by playing a game or talking to him? I urge you to try it.

Enlist Support

Parents don't magically get an extra eight or ten hours in their day, and they don't suddenly need less sleep. No matter how much more responsibility we assume, we still are allotted only twenty-four hours in each day, and we still have to sleep away some of those hours. So how do busy parents cover all the bases? We've talked about setting priorities, managing our time, lowering our standards, and relinquishing perfectionism. But it's also necessary to ask for and enlist as much extra help as possible. All conscientious parents have too much to do. So start by examining each task and asking yourself, "Can I get some help with it, delegate it entirely to someone else, pay to have it done, do it less well, or skip it altogether?"

Sadly, despite working mothers becoming a new societal norm, women still do 80 percent of all housework. And, for the most part, it is mothers who take over when a child announces those five words that strike terror into every working parent's heart: "Mommy, I don't feel well."

Your spouse. The most likely source of help is your own spouse and your older children. Negotiate some of these issues early in your relationship, and begin to delegate age-appropriate responsibilities to children by the time they are three. Don't chronically whine or be unpleasant, but using a matter-of-fact tone in a noncrisis situation, outline everything that needs to be done to run the family. Then discuss among all members how to divide the responsibilities fairly. Include the options of hiring help or dropping a duty completely. For example, you might decide to just quit making the bed if no one has time to do it, to find a new home for a pet if no one is willing to care for it, or to hire someone to clean the house or do yardwork. One thing is certain. If you begin to work outside the home and try to maintain all your stay-at-home standards, you'll probably develop a stress-related illness and make yourself and everyone around you miserable. Remember, you can't make a car fly!

With all due respect, I must say that some men have never given a thought to all that goes on behind the scenes to make a household run smoothly. Many fathers consider their contribution to the family to be largely over once they arrive home after a hard day's work. These men view home as the sanctuary where they can unwind for the evening, relax in front of the TV, and emotionally refuel for another day at the office. They aren't so much thoughtless as they are just plain oblivious to the fact that their wives may feel like they're starting a second shift of duty when they walk through the door after work.

For a mother, coming home after work is a far cry from unwinding. There is still dinner to prepare and clean up, kids to help with homework, baths to be given, stories to read, lunches to pack, and washing to do.

Couples must negotiate how this workload will be distributed so no one feels abused. I've seen marriages break up because one partner perpetually feels like they are giving too much and consequently becomes resentful. Martyrs make lousy parents and marriage partners! But it's not enough for one member to acquiesce to "help" the other with "their work." Rather, when both parents are employed outside the home, there must be a joint commitment to get done equitably whatever it takes to run the family.

Delegate. If you are going to delegate a task, you have to be willing to relinquish control of it. Acknowledge at the outset that the other party will probably do the task less well, and certainly differently, from the way you've always done it. But at least it will get done. A woman I know complained about folding the laundry, so her husband stepped in to help. Instead of totally abdicating the chore, however, she was very critical of the way he folded clothes. As a result, her husband was reluctant to offer his help again. Kids, too, are vulnerable to such negative feedback when they're trying to pitch in. You can't have your cake and eat it too. The best way to get more help is to delegate tasks effectively and then accept how they get done—and even compliment the ones who perform them.

I recall a particularly adaptive new mother who brought her baby for a two-week checkup. While I was undressing the infant, I noticed that her disposable diaper was taped on backward. I was a little curious about the diaper, since the mother happened to be an experienced pediatric nurse.

"Peggy, why is Troi's diaper on backward?" I inquired.

"It's not backward," Peggy deliberately responded. "It's on perfectly. Reggie did it, and it's perfect."

I immediately broke into a grin. After all, how much could it really matter which way a diaper caught a baby's excrement? With some four thousand diapers yet to come, how wise of Peggy to graciously accept her husband's help with changes. Eventually, he would probably catch on to the correct way to position a diaper under his baby daughter, but Peggy certainly wasn't about to criticize adequate help when it was offered!

Hire help. If you don't have time to do a job yourself and you can't delegate it, ask yourself if you can hire someone to do it for you. When honestly considering whether you can afford to hire help, weigh the money you would spend against the enhanced quality of your life that a few extra hours each week could bring. Many women have been so acculturated to doing their own housecleaning that they can't bring themselves to pay someone else to do it, no matter how overextended they may be with other responsibilities. I, too, felt that way for a lengthy period of my life until I broke down and hired the Merry Maids some years ago. Today, when I come home to a clean house on Merry Maid day, I feel like an oppressive weight has been lifted off my shoulders.

Women need to move beyond the ingrained perception that housework is always "our" responsibility and come to view it instead as one of many aspects involved in running a family. Most of us don't give a second thought to paying a teen to mow the lawn or shovel the snow, to paying someone to deliver our paper, to paying a service station to change our oil, to paying someone to paint our house, or to paying a hairdresser to cut our kids' hair. In fact, we now even have the option of paying a minimal charge to order our groceries over the phone and then have them delivered store to door. Remember, our time is more finite than our money and is thus more precious. I decided long ago that if spending a little extra money will buy me and my family some quality time, then I'm all for it.

Your extended family. Another invaluable source of

support for parents is the extended family network. Throughout history, extended family members traditionally have been a mainstay for young couples, helping smooth out the rough spots in married life and parenthood. A couple's own parents lived either nearby or in the same house, serving as a source of practical knowledge, as relief caretakers, confidants, counselors, and helpers. Unfortunately, however, most Americans are now so mobile that contemporary nuclear families are often far removed from extended family members. Furthermore, the changing profile of women in the workforce means that even if Aunt Dorothy does live nearby, she may be relatively unavailable because of her own work schedule. Nevertheless, I still believe that extended family members represent an underutilized source of support, and I encourage you to solicit more help from them.

When we moved to Colorado in 1970 for my third year of medical school, Peter was two and Paige was eleven months old. Essentially we had agreed to sacrifice every security we had known as a family in pursuit of my medical degree. We had left our home in Hawaii, Larry's job, my school, and our friends. Upon arriving in Colorado, Larry had no employment leads, and we had scarcely any money left and no idea where we would live. We had less than one hundred dollars to spend on a car and also needed to find adequate childcare and acquire winter clothes. I knew I would be on call at an unfamiliar hospital essentially every third night for the coming year. It was a discouraging, frightening time of transition . . . until we met Aunt Betty and Uncle John, that is. Larry's father was divorced from his mother when Larry was just a preschooler. Although he had a number of paternal aunts and uncles, Larry had had only minimal childhood contact with them, and we hadn't viewed these distant relatives as a potential source of family support. While we were still in Hawaii,

Larry's Uncle Don, a naval officer stationed at Pearl Harbor, "discovered" us. When we first considered that I would finish medical school in Colorado (Hawaii had only a two-year school at the time), Uncle Don championed the idea, noting that several of Larry's aunts and uncles lived there. Looking back, I'm not sure we ever would have made it through the next five long years of medical training without the support and constancy provided by this network of extended family, especially Aunt Betty and Uncle John Rau. We just walked into their lives one day, empty and needy, and for some unknown reason, they responded and filled us up. To this day, we still don't know for sure whatever possessed Aunt Betty and Uncle John to acknowledge their relationship to us, take us under their wing, and nurture us so effectively—except that they are simply wonderful people with an abiding devotion to "the family," of which they were convinced we were a part. At any rate, we will always be indebted to Aunt Betty and Uncle John and to the great Neifert tradition of extended family support.

I spent most of the next several years in a state of physical and emotional exhaustion. Larry carried heavy childrearing responsibilities and the burden of childcare arrangements while maintaining a job during the day and attending college at night. With an every third night on-call schedule, I was either on call, had just gotten off call, or was anticipating being on call again. You might say we weren't at our best very often. Neither of us had much left over to give to the other.

It was actually on weekends at Aunt Betty and Uncle John's that everyone was most nurtured. We usually managed to spend one day at their house and that served to revitalize us. As soon as we arrived, their preteen daughters would scoop up our toddlers and happily play with them all day. If I had just gotten off call, Aunt Betty would get out one of her nightgowns and let me crawl into her bed and crash. I could easily have brought my own nightgown, but I deliberately would borrow one of hers, symbolically wrapping myself in her warmth and love. The other adults would huddle in the family room, watching a Bronco game and cheering wildly. As evening approached, we'd all gather for a big dinner, after which Larry and I would return home replenished.

Every family needs an Aunt Betty and Uncle John. Young families weren't meant to be islands unto themselves. They were meant to be strengthened and sustained by a network of supportive relatives. We receive help when we need it, and then we extend help to someone else when we are able. While I may never repay Aunt Betty and Uncle John directly for their support, I do try to return their *measure* of support to other friends and relatives, so that my extended family ledger ultimately will be balanced.

Other sources of support. If you have no extended family available, you can still enlist help from friends and neighbors—if you will only risk sharing your need and asking others. While most of us derive great enjoyment from opportunities to serve others, we still hesitate to ask for help when we need it because we have an irrational fear that others will be reluctant to help us. In fact, we all have a fundamental need to be needed. And serving others raises our self-esteem and brings us personal fulfillment.

A young working mother I know is married and has two small children. Her friend and co-worker is a divorced mother whose own children live in another city with their father. One day, the married woman commented that her relationship with her husband was strained because they had so little time together. Upon hearing this remark, her single colleague promptly offered to babysit the children one weekend so the young couple could spend some time together. It was a win-

win arrangement for everybody, as the usual weekend solitude of the single woman was broken by children's laughter and play; the children thoroughly enjoyed their special time with "Aunt Nancy"; and the young couple was able to renew their relationship by devoting two whole days to one another.

The older I get, the more comfortable I am requesting support from others. When I need help from someone, I first ask myself if I would be willing to do for them what I am about to ask. If the answer is yes, then I plunge forward with my request. Although we seldom repay the specific individuals who have helped us, all families ultimately benefit if we each ask for support when we need it and offer support when we can.

Take Time for Yourself

Parenting involves almost constant giving and guiding and caring. Unless you make it a priority to replenish yourself periodically, it's easy to become so emotionally and physically depleted that you have little energy left for your family. Remember, we all nurture others from our own emotional overflow. That is to say, "You can only parent a little better than you feel." Years ago, my kids and I discovered the following truism: "When I'm feeling resentful, it means I'm giving too much." This is why martyrs make such poor parents. No child wants a tired, irritable, emotionally drained parent to oversacrifice for him. In the first place, such a parent is likely to be unpleasant to be around. Furthermore, the parent who constantly gives too much will eventually expect the child to fulfill all her own unmet needs. Thus, the child of a martyr is burdened with the untenable responsibility of needing to "be enough" for the self-denying parent who has no personal life of her own.

Ironically, many parents are reluctant to take time for themselves because they mistakenly believe that to do so is somehow selfish or unfair to their child. Rather, taking adequate care of yourself not only makes you a more effective parent, it allows you to derive more joy from the role. Remember, there's a good reason behind a flight attendant's advice to put your own oxygen mask on before assisting your child with hers!

Nurture your relationship with your spouse. The common practice of always putting children first in a family often contributes to undermining the parents' marriage relationship. Instead of regularly sidestepping their own needs, parents would do their children a great favor by spending adequate time strengthening their own relationship as a couple. Children are reassured if you have a solid relationship with your partner, and they experience uncomfortable anxiety when they witness frequent parental conflict. It has been said that the nicest thing a father can do for his children is to love their mother—and the reverse is also true.

Your relationship with your partner provides your children with a model of adult intimacy, but perhaps most significantly, it provides a potential source of emotional support for both parents. The best way to nurture your relationship is mutually to commit yourselves to spending time alone with one another. You might reserve some private time each evening after the children are asleep or make it a practice to go on a "date" together each week. Perhaps you could meet for lunch in the middle of the workday or spend a weekend alone at a nearby hotel every couple of months while a friend or relative watches your children. Cultivate joint hobbies, such as bowling on a team, playing golf or tennis together, joining a bridge club, or taking dance lessons. The chief requirement for maintaining a fulfilling relationship is to give one another focused attention periodically, and to communicate, laugh, and just have fun together.

Although Larry and I have seldom been able to take a formal vacation together, we often have celebrated our birthdays or anniversary by spending the night at a local hotel. Long ago, we agreed we would rather spend precious time alone together than receive a tangible gift. And over the years, we have asked our relatives, former students, neighbors, and even my brother-in-law's parents to babysit our children so we could get away overnight.

Cultivate your friendships. Another effective way to replenish yourself is to regularly spend time with other adults. Perhaps you can get together on Saturday evenings with another couple, go to breakfast with some friends once a week, participate in a neighborhood Bible study, or play a weekly game of bridge or golf. I know a group of ladies who regularly gather in each other's homes for coffee and dessert. They each bring some type of needlework and enjoy lively conversation while working on their craft. These devoted friends affectionately call their support group "Stitch and Bitch."

A group of low-income single mothers I know found a way to get together without the luxury of childcare arrangements for their small children. Each Friday afternoon the women would gather at one of their homes. All the kids would agree to play together in one area of the house, while another area was designated for their mothers. The women talked, played tapes, danced, and sang together, while the children played happily in the next room. The children looked forward to these weekly get-togethers with their friends as much as the parents did.

One of my favorite examples of supportive adult relationships is a particular group of twelve women who meet each month to play a game called Bunko. They rotate their gatherings among one another's homes, and the host of the meeting does not have to provide the food that evening. The women are deeply committed to their group, as all twelve must be present in order to play Bunko. Their meeting is really more like a support group than a game. They play in groups of four, rotating the groups all evening so that each woman spends time with everyone else present. I'm told that Bunko requires minimal concentration, thus allowing the emphasis to be on relating to one another, rather than on the intricacies of the game. Each woman eagerly anticipates Bunko night and returns home emotionally uplifted and re-energized. In the end, her family also reaps the rewards of her brief, replenishing interlude.

Exposing the myth of the superparent forces us to relinquish the alluring fantasy that, with supreme effort and gifted ability, we just might achieve perfection in ourselves and our children. Like admitting we no longer believe in Santa Claus, puncturing the legendary superparent ideal can represent a loss of mystique and magical thinking. Once we shed the illusion, however, we discover we are suddenly free to feel good about ourselves, our children, and our choices. Released from the constricting bonds of perfectionism, we can focus our energies on being good enough parents. We can be challenged to respect our unique priorities, to make inevitable mistakes and learn from them, and to give and accept vital support from others. Perhaps most important, in rejecting the myth that doesn't work for us, we are inspired to accept ourselves honestly and to enjoy our families fully. It's definitely a worthwhile trade-off!

ADDITIONAL READING:

Bateson, Mary Catherine. *Composing a Life*. New York: Plume, 1990.

Covey, Stephen. *The 7 Habits of Highly Effective People*. New York: Simon and Schuster, 1989.

Garfield, Charles. *Peak Performers*. New York: Avon Books, 1986.

McGrath, Ellen. *When Feeling Bad Is Good*. New York: Henry Holt and Company, 1992.

Shaevitz, Marjorie Hansen. *The Superwoman Syndrome*. New York: Warner Books, 1984.

Stern, Ellen S. *The Indispensable Woman: Beating the Perfection Addiction*. New York: Bantam Books, 1988.

Taffel, Ron. *Why Parents Disagree*. New York: William Morrow and Company, Inc., 1994.

3

YOU AND YOUR CHILD'S SELF-ESTEEM

When we consider the awesome responsibilities of parenthood, we tend to focus on the concrete duties involved in the physical care and safety of children. It's obvious that we need to provide our baby's daily nutritional requirements and eventually teach our child sound eating habits. Parents know that infants require regular medical supervision, routine immunizations, and acute care for the inevitable illnesses of childhood. We realize we're obligated to learn and adhere to numerous safety guidelines that will enhance our children's chances of reaching adulthood physically intact. On top of all this, many of us are deeply committed to exposing our children to music, art, literature, athletics, and higher academics in an effort to cultivate their innate talents and to expand their opportunities.

With these goals and responsibilities in mind, most of us will expend tremendous time, energy, and financial resources giving our offspring the "best" childhood possible, hoping to shower them with all the joys we recall from our childhood and to shield them from the pains we experienced.

With no formal training, we throw ourselves into the parenting role with tireless effort and daily self-denial in hopes of producing progeny who will exceed our own accomplishments. To this end, we see that our children have fashionable haircuts, new shoes, designer jeans, Barbie dolls, bikes, Walkman radios, Nintendos, and pets. We pay for encyclopedias, insurance policies, speech therapy, braces, contact lenses, music lessons, and private schools. We chauffeur kids to preschool classes, religious training, dance lessons, birthday parties, medical appointments, soccer games, gymnastic meets, scouting activities, and band concerts. We adhere to holiday rituals, plan family vacations, make trips to the zoo, hold picnics in the park, check homework, monitor television viewing, and teach the skills involved in riding a bike, swimming, and driving.

In the end, we take genuine pride in having given and sacrificed so much, proudly proclaiming that we were "good parents." But the best yardstick of good parenting is actually an intangible measure that may or may not be related to the things you did *for* your child, like straightening her teeth or sending her to camp.

The ultimate measure of successful parenting is whether you raised a child with a positive self-concept— that is, a youngster who likes himself, who feels good about the unique individual that he is, who has an honest assessment of his strengths and abilities, and who accepts himself and others.

A child with positive self-esteem is confident that you love her unconditionally, no matter what her accomplishments, appearance, or behavior. A child with a good self-image is so sure of your love for her that she readily loves herself and doesn't hesitate to love and respect others. A child with a good self-concept strives to achieve her best in life—not just to capture your love and attention, but to satisfy her own goals of becoming all she is capable of being. Such a child can handle great success without feeling either undeserving or falsely proud. She can withstand great failures without fearing the loss of your approval and without losing her own self-respect or confidence. For those with positive self-esteem, failures are just "major learning experiences"; such people not only rise above failures and disappointments, but become stronger persons for them.

Children with a positive self-concept do not rely on external criteria to judge themselves or others. They are so comfortable with themselves that they are able to celebrate the achievements of their peers without being threatened. Children with self-respect resist peer pressure, honoring their own values instead of compromising them to gain the approval of others. Children with positive self-esteem want to look their personal best, but not necessarily better than anyone else. They can accept their inevitable weaknesses and separate these traits from their overall self-worth. They don't link their individual value to their grades, athletic ability, or popularity. And in the future, when misfortune strikes, they won't allow divorce, loss of a job, failure to get a promotion, physical injury, or the aging process to threaten their self-worth.

Children with positive self-esteem are less likely to get pregnant out of wedlock, use drugs, drop out of school, display delinquent behavior, develop an eating disorder, get divorced, or commit suicide. Rather, they are likely to be happy, well-adjusted, self-directed, confident individuals who make and keep friends, stay married, and find fulfillment. In a nutshell, positive self-esteem is the most basic foundation for long-term personal health and happiness. It is the most precious gift you can offer your child.

Examining Your Own Self-Esteem

In my opinion, every other parenting duty is dwarfed in comparison to the critical importance of instilling a positive self-concept in your child. Unfortunately, however, so many of us have problems with our own self-esteem that we unknowingly inflict poor self-image on our children, as if it were a genetic disease. In actuality, the more we enhance our own self-esteem, the better we can nurture our children's self-concept.

If your own childhood wasn't the best and left you with weakened self-esteem, you needn't pass these wounds onto your children. In a sense, our past is "perfect" in the dictionary sense of the word—that is, "it cannot be improved upon." But this doesn't mean we must remain victims of our past, whether it was clouded by physical or sexual abuse, alcoholic or neglectful parents, poverty, chronic illness, handicaps, discrimination, personal tragedy, or excessive parental pressure. We can help break negative family patterns and work on healing ourselves from our past and giving ourselves and our children a brighter future by obtaining professional counseling, joining a support group, reading self-help books, attending parenting classes, and seeking spiritual guidance.

If you feel inadequate, are often depressed or feel guilty, have unresolved childhood conflicts, often seek the approval of others, feel unlovable or unworthy, have trouble handling anger, or just plain don't like yourself, I urge you to seek professional help. Begin by telling your physician and asking to be referred to a mental health resource for counseling. You deserve to be happier and more hopeful—and your child will function immensely better when you get the help you need. Remember, you can't give what you don't have; you can only nurture others when your own emotional tank is full, not empty.

The Key Ingredient for Positive Self-Esteem

So how do we give our children healthy self-esteem? The most fundamental ingredient for positive self-esteem is unconditional parental love. By unconditional, I mean love with no strings attached: loving your children no matter what they look like, no matter what their abilities turn out to be, no matter how they act. Unconditional love is total acceptance of your children, even if you don't accept everything they do. Children who feel they are loved unconditionally by you believe they are lovable by others. Feeling lovable makes children feel capable and ultimately makes them capable of loving others. To a child, her parents are all-knowing and all-powerful; she looks to her parents for messages about her own self-concept. A tape is playing in the child's head all her life, on which she records her parents' reactions to her and draws conclusions about her self-worth.

Think about people you know who have trouble demonstrating their love to others. My guess is you'll find that these people weren't themselves made to feel lovable in childhood. Now think about the most loving people you know. I'll bet these individuals feel very loved and lovable themselves and because of this assurance, they are able to radiate love to others.

In his elegant books *How to Really Love Your Child* and *How to Really Love Your Teenager*, Ross Campbell makes the important distinction between *being loved* and *feeling loved*. Surprisingly, although most parents love their children dearly, most children do not *feel* unconditional parental love. Parents may be shocked to learn that their child is unsure of their love for him or her. They recite the litany of things they did and the sacrifices they made as proof of their love, yet somehow their child doesn't *feel* loved.

How to Convey Your Love to Your Child

Children's self-worth is largely formulated by our everyday interactions with them, by those spontaneous and mundane things we do and say, often without fully considering their impact on our child. Children's self-esteem is shaped positively or negatively based on whether they receive our regular, undivided attention or frequent neglect, whether we listen to or ignore them, whether we accept or reject their feelings, how we set limits, handle their misbehavior, respond to their needs, answer their questions, compliment or criticize them, and by how much we expect of them. With renewed awareness and a little daily effort, you can enhance your child's self-image.

For at least twenty minutes daily, give each of your children your focused attention—in other words, your undivided attention. This doesn't mean giving an empty "uh-huh" every so often while reading the paper during your child's description of her day. Instead, it means putting the paper down, taking your child seriously, looking her in the eye, and listening intently to her account. It means giving verbal feedback when appropriate, nodding or using other body language to show you have heard what she is saying, and giving an empathetic response when she has shared her feelings. It means listening to your child the way you would listen to your boss. This says to her that she is important and worthy of your attention. It tells her she matters to you and has sufficient worth to command your full attention, if even for a short period.

If you have several children, I can't emphasize how critical it is to spend even a few minutes of one-to-one time daily with each child. As one of five children, I regret not having had more individualized time with my parents when I was growing up in a busy household. Now, as my own five children are nearly grown, I wish I had spent more time with each one individually. While doing things as a family certainly has its rewards, each of my kids fondly recalls those extra-special times Larry or I did something together with them, alone—like letting one child accompany me to a distant speaking engagement, taking a child out to dinner on his birthday, playing a game one-on-one, going to breakfast with a child after an orthodontic appointment, talking out a problem together, taking a child clothes shopping alone, letting one spend the day with me at the office, staying home with and pampering a child when she's sick, preparing a meal or doing a chore together.

Don't try to cheat once you've made a commitment to give your child focused attention. I've been caught at it! I vividly remember the time I brought the newspaper to Heather's soccer game. While Heather was playing her heart out to impress me, she looked up after a particularly sterling play to find my face buried in the newspaper. She was utterly disappointed that I had promised to come but was not giving her my full attention—and she trapped me at halftime. "Did you see me head the ball?" she asked. "Uh, yeah, great play!" I attempted. "You lied!" she challenged. "You weren't even watching me; you were reading the paper most of the time. I never headed the ball, but I almost made a goal, and you missed it! I don't know why you bother to come if you don't want to see me play."

Painful as this experience was, I consider myself lucky that my kids are so willing to tell me outright when I let them down. Their blunt and prompt feedback encourages me to improve my parenting. Countless other kids don't have the nerve to confront their parents when they've been let down. They silently nurse their emotional hurts, and many are left with permanently damaged self-esteem.

I can't tell you what precise, magical amount of focused attention your child requires from you each day. You will be shocked to learn that most American parents don't spend even ten minutes a day talking with their children one-to-one without raising their voices, scolding, criticizing, or correcting. Ideally, we would all give our children liberal doses of focused attention beginning at birth, but even if that hasn't occurred, it is never too late to start parenting a little better. You can begin talking to your teenager or grade-schooler right now and still make a difference in their self-esteem.

I know one father who decided to start spending at least ten minutes talking and listening to each of his children each day. When he announced, "Come here, son, I'd like to spend some time talking with you," his teenager immediately became defensive. "Gee, Dad, I haven't done anything wrong. What are you going to yell at me about?" There had been so few times that the boy and his father had actually discussed something together, the adolescent just assumed "talking" meant some kind of reprimanding. But the father persevered and this personal interaction was so meaningful to the boy that soon their conversations expanded to twenty or thirty minutes of special time together for father and son. Now, even when this man is out of town, he makes a point to talk by phone individually with each child.

Be an empathetic listener and accept your child's feelings. Acceptance is very important to the development of self-esteem, yet often we transmit rejection to our children by rejecting their legitimate feelings. For example, suppose dinner isn't ready yet and five-year-old Jeff complains, "I'm hungry." You answer, "You can't be hungry; you had a big lunch." This is both confusing and frustrating to Jeff because he genuinely feels hunger. How can you presume to know what Jeff really feels or expect him to stop feeling hungry on command? When a child shares his or her feelings, we need to accept them as legitimate and express empathy. "It's hard to wait for dinner when you're feeling so hungry. Maybe you could snack on some raw vegetables while you wait."

Even if Jeff is hungry now because he refused to eat his lunch, you can still empathize with his feelings while teaching a lesson about natural consequences: "It must feel miserable to be so hungry. Maybe if you had eaten your lunch, you wouldn't feel so starved right now. Fortunately, dinner's almost ready."

Suppose three-year-old Megan is having trouble adjusting to her new sister and is feeling jealous and displaced. When you sit down to nurse the infant, Megan blurts out, "I hate that baby! I wish you never brought her home!" "No, you don't," you try to insist. "You love your baby sister." Megan has just risked baring her innermost feelings of displacement, and you have neatly negated them, thereby discounting how she really feels. In Megan's mind, rejecting her feelings is akin to rejecting her. A better response would acknowledge her painful feelings as legitimate and accept them. "Babies take a lot of time, don't they? It must be hard for you not having as much time with Mommy as you used to. But babies can't swing at the park like we're going to do later, can they? Come on, let's look at your baby album and see what a cute little baby you were. You were Mommy's first special baby."

Children are often deeply upset about things that seem inconsequential in our adult world. If five-year-old Cheryl's pet goldfish died, or nine-year-old Sean was picked last when the class chose teams today, it may not seem very important—especially when compared to your own worries about the overdue mortgage payment, your mother's positive mammogram results, or the big report due at the office tomorrow. But the magnitude of Cheryl's sadness or Sean's disappointment is very real by their youthful standards, and your child needs your empathy when he or she expresses such pain. Empty comments or attempts at rationalization like "It was only a fish!" or "So what, lots of kids have been picked last" give a child the impression their feelings don't matter. This is easily translated into "I don't matter, either." Expressing true empathy, saying, "It really hurts to lose a pet" or "It must have felt awful to be the last one standing there," conveys acceptance, understanding, and support. Such empathy often enables the child to take action to resolve her disappointment, to say, "Let's go bury Goldie, and then maybe I can get another fish this weekend" or "I played really hard anyway. I bet someone will want me on their team next time."

Adolescents are especially vulnerable when they risk sharing their innermost feelings. Your rejection of these feelings easily feels like total rejection of them. So when your teen reveals that he didn't make the varsity team, don't jump in too quickly with your rationalization: "After all, you're only a junior. I'm sure you'll make it next year. Besides, it's probably better this way. You'll get to play in every game on the JV team." While all that may very well be true, your first reaction should be to empathize with your child's feelings about not making varsity and to show your acceptance of those feelings: "You must be really disappointed. I know how much a varsity letter means to you, and I've seen how hard you've practiced to make the team. You must really hurt right now."

Such acceptance and validation of his feelings are likely to provide the impetus your son or daughter needs to begin to resolve his or her immediate disappointment and refocus on having a good JV year and making varsity next time.

Make a point of giving daily nonverbal messages of love and acceptance, through eye contact, touching, and hugging. All children need physical expressions of your love, no matter how old they get. Most infants are lavished with intimate contact during feedings, bathing, rocking, dressing, and diaper changes. As children grow older, we tend to diminish physical contact, sometimes deliberately avoiding it. But even older children who feign disgust at Aunt Elsie's hugs and kisses actually crave physical displays of affection. Why do you think rubbing lotion on a sunburn or massaging a sore muscle helps make it feel better? Even my college kids still love to get a hug when we greet or depart. The popular bumper sticker slogan HAVE YOU HUGGED YOUR KIDS TODAY? should serve as a guiding rule of conduct for parents. It reminds us there is simply no substitute for the daily nonverbal communication of our love.

Some children are naturally less demonstrative than others about receiving and displaying affection, so don't give up if your child doesn't seem to respond after you've made a few attempts to display nonverbal affection. Instead of withdrawing your physical contact, be prepared to keep giving those hugs and kisses even when you don't always get one in return.

Another effective way to demonstrate affection is to make eye contact with your children when speaking or listening to them. Eye contact gives a powerful message to the speaker that the listener is really interested in hearing them. Have you ever been in the process of pouring your heart out to someone and then noticed they were looking away, glancing at their watch, or trying to read something while you were talking? It sure makes you doubt that you have their full attention. A really good listener maintains eye contact with the speaker to communicate their sincere interest.

A man I know conducts training seminars for a living. In describing his work, he happened to mention how uncomfortable it made him when a class participant brought her knitting to one of his lectures. While I'm sure the attendee means no disrespect (it was probably a busy woman who felt obliged to be doing at least two things at once!) and is quite capable of grasping the speaker's message despite looking down periodically, the seminar leader explained that the regular loss of eye contact with this listener was very disruptive. Every time the knitter glanced at her work, the speaker automatically felt he had briefly lost her attention. After a day-long workshop with one or more knitters, he always felt particularly drained.

After thinking about this, I realized that whenever I speak professionally, I scan the audience to identify several listeners who appear particularly interested and empathetic. Their periodic nonverbal feedback makes me feel connected with my audience and enables me to give a much better talk. I automatically direct my remarks to those captive listeners who are smiling, nodding in agreement, and making constant eye contact. In fact, I find it very difficult to speak effectively without at least a few listeners providing such regular supportive feedback. Vacant expressions, drooping eyelids, side conversations, frowns, and negative headshakes are powerful nonverbal messages of disagreement or disinterest, signaling that I've spoken too long or lost my connection with my listeners.

Use positive words with your child. Compliment and praise her at every opportunity. It has been wisely observed that compliments are biodegradable and need to be replenished every couple of hours. Everyone can always use another compliment or an extra word of praise. Child discipline experts agree that children would misbehave far less if we regularly praised their good behavior before they act up. This principle has been summarized by the popular phrase "Catch them being good." In spite of the well-established effectiveness of positive reinforcement, however, most of us make the mistake of regularly ignoring our youngsters' predominantly good behavior and instead, blast them for occasional misbehavior, screaming the distorted accusation "Can't you ever be good?!"

To use positive words regularly, you need to learn to focus on the positive side of things in general. Most of us can use some help in learning to recognize and emphasize the positives in our lives instead of dwelling on the negative side of things.

When my son Peter was a senior in high school, he had an irritating habit of leaning back on his chair at the kitchen table. "You're leaning back on your chair again," I would admonish almost daily. "You're going to tear the tiles off the floor. Can't you see it's dangerous to lean back like that? Your chair might tip over. I'll bet I've told you this a thousand times. What's wrong with you?"

One day Peter brought his chair forward, looked directly at me, and said evenly, "You're right, I lean back on the kitchen chair. I can't seem to stop it. But I also make straight A's; I'm student body treasurer; I'm on the varsity soccer team; and I'm graduating second in my class. I don't smoke, drink, do drugs, have sex, or stay out late. And I've just won a full-tuition college scholarship. But you're right, I do lean back on the kitchen chair. Is that so bad after all?"

I felt two inches high. Here I was the lucky parent of one of the most outstanding teenagers in Colorado and I was harping on one insignificant, if irritating, behavior. When was the last time I had complimented Peter on one of his exceptional traits or told him what a special young man he was or what a joy he had been to me? He would be leaving for college in a few short months, and I was using our precious final time together to nag about something inconsequential. I never mentioned the habit again!

Let me share one particularly effective method of using positive words with yourself and your child. First, consider how often you talk to yourself in a way that reinforces your negative behaviors. Suppose you waited to the last minute to prepare for a holiday and are now flustered with too much to do. Disgusted with your tendency to procrastinate, you tell yourself, "That's just like me—I always wait till the last minute. Why can't I get my act together?" Or you're playing tennis and you make a great play that quite amazes you. "How'd I do that?" you exclaim to yourself. "That's just not like me!" Then you flub the next serve as if to prove to yourself that you really weren't capable of the great play you just made.

Now consider how often we use this same style of talking to unconsciously reinforce undesirable behavior in our children. For example, your child misbehaves during a lengthy shopping trip and you find yourself shouting, "Why can't you ever be good? It's just like you to ruin my whole day." As predicted, your child then continues to misbehave, as if to fulfill your negative expectations of her. If you really think about it, you'll notice that we tend to talk to ourselves and our children in this way all day long, reaffirming our negative qualities and proclaiming surprise at our positive ones. With such daily reinforcement, a lifelong conviction about our unalterable negative traits will emerge, and the conviction alone will trap us in the negative behavior.

If we make a concerted effort, we can learn to talk to ourselves and our children in a different way. When you arrive late to the big meeting at work, try looking around at everyone and announcing, "Gee, sorry I'm late this time. That's just not like me." Your colleagues might silently think, "What do you mean that's not like you? Everyone knows you're always late." But if you diligently use positive self-talk, I promise you can change your behavior.

This technique is guaranteed to work wonders with children too. When four-year-old Brandon breaks his sister's doll, we're tempted to shout, "Shame on you for breaking Heidi's dolly. You're always naughty. Why can't you behave?" Instead try saying, "Brandon, I can't believe you broke Heidi's doll. That's just not like you to damage other people's property. You're usually so considerate of others." When Brandon pats his new brother tenderly after trying to smack him earlier, you can announce, "Now that's just like you, Brandon, to be nice to your new baby. You're such a kind big brother." Try this verbal method of altering your own and your children's self-concept and see how soon behavior patterns can change!

Make it a point to put your positive comments in writing too. While verbal compliments certainly can be recalled, your written expressions of love and praise will be treasured by your child and re-read in their entirety over and over. There's nothing like the indelible written word to give permanence to a compliment. You can use birthdays and holidays to write personal messages to your children, telling them how much they mean to you.

A special out-of-town friend we seldom see sends separate gifts to each member of our family at Christmas. Attached to each present one year was a note to the individual telling him or her how much Lucy loved and missed them. Each message also included a personal memory about the individual, recalled from one of our visits together. Those handwritten individualized notes actually meant more to each of us than the accompanying gifts.

But you don't need a formal occasion to write a message of love. You can drop a short note in your child's lunch bag, leave a message on her pillow, or stick a

"Post-it" to her computer screen. Don't agonize about what to say. A one- or two-line compliment will do, such as "I liked the way you helped your brother with his homework today. That's just like you to be so thoughtful. I'm proud that you're my daughter."

One evening recently, Heather reminded me to write a note to her school, excusing her absence that day due to illness. Early the next morning, remembering the excuse, I quickly jotted a note and left it where Heather was sure to see it. As an afterthought, I stuck a small yellow "Post-it" note to the excuse and scribbled, "Hope you're feeling better and that you have a good day, Heather. I love you, Mom." That evening, Heather thanked me several times for the "note" I had left for her. Initially assuming she was referring to the excuse I had written, I kept insisting it had been no big deal. Only later, when Heather mentioned it a third time and described the "little yellow note" that had meant so much to her, did I realize that she had been deeply touched by my simple gesture that morning. I had taken only a few extra seconds to express my love for her, yet Heather had remembered it all day! I immediately resolved to display my love more often.

As you become more comfortable expressing yourself in writing, you can compose whole letters to your child. You might even venture writing a letter of recommendation if your child needs to apply for a job, school, or camp. Sometimes the indirect compliments contained in such a letter are the most meaningful of all.

Set realistic, firm limits. Children, whether those struggling for independence at two or at fourteen, feel more confident and secure when they know that you are in charge and that their behavior is limited appropriately. Consistently enforced limits tell a child that she is safe and loved and that her environment is ordered and predictable. (See "Understanding Misbehavior," Chapter 5.) However, consistent discipline can require tremendous parental willpower and commitment, especially at the end of the day, when our defenses are down. It is easier to give in to whining, tantrums, pleading, cajoling, and manipulative behavior than to consistently and lovingly enforce the limits that have been established for your child's own well-being.

With older children, and especially adolescents, it's important to let them participate in the negotiation of limits. Children will adhere to limits better if parental rules don't seem arbitrary. The standard fallback—"Because I said so"—is an inappropriate response that provokes power struggles with your children and undermines their self-esteem. Even if they don't agree with the limits, older children will feel more respected if you share your reasoning behind the rules. Eventually, adolescents and their parents can mutually agree on reasonable curfew times, the kinds of parties they can attend, and where they are allowed to drive. Regular family meetings provide an ideal forum for members to air their feelings and viewpoints and mutually agree on ground rules.

In addition to open communication, successful limit setting also involves providing appropriate supervision to help a child resist temptation. Don't set your child up for failure, then come down hard when she inevitably breaks the rules. Don't, for example, tell your two-year-old not to eat any cookies before dinner and then walk away, leaving the plate of cookies within her reach. Similarly, don't tell your teenage son not to have sex, then let him go camping alone with his girlfriend. Don't tell your teenage daughter not to drink, then permit her to attend unchaperoned parties.

I know a single mother who went out of town and left her teenage son unsupervised for several days. Although sixteen-year-old Jordan had his license, he was strictly forbidden to drive while his mother was gone.

But the prolonged absence of adult supervision proved too tempting for an adolescent testing his independence. So when his peers pressured him to drive to a football game, rationalizing "How would your mother ever know?" Jordan finally gave in and broke the parental rule.

Upon his mother's return, Jordan was praised for being so responsible in her absence. Shortly thereafter, however, a neighbor casually mentioned having seen Jordan in the car on the highway the previous weekend. His mother was furious that Jordan had breeched her trust in him. Her demeaning lecture ("I should have known I couldn't trust you"), accompanying reprimands, and harsh punishment lowered Jordan's self-esteem and made him feel like a "bad," unworthy person, doomed to misbehave. In actuality, Jordan did what many other teens would have done under the same circumstances. The real error in judgment was made by his mother, who gave him too much freedom at an inappropriate age.

Perhaps if another adult had been asked to stay with the teen during his mother's absence, Jordan would have been able to resist peer pressure and succeed in adhering to the rules. Then, when he was praised for his responsible behavior (accomplished with appropriate supervision), he would have experienced elevated self-esteem and an internal conviction that he was worthy of love and respect—as well as capable of resisting future misbehavior with even less supervision.

Give your child responsibilities so he will feel valued, capable, and needed. Doing everything for your child doesn't make you a model parent. It only makes your child feel incapable, overly dependent, and insecure. And it makes you a resentful martyr, for no good cause.

Traditionally, children have always played an invaluable role in a family's mission by helping with gardening, farming, cooking, cleaning, and caring for

animals or younger siblings. Part of a child's emerging
sense of self-worth is defined by his role within his own
family. When you delegate responsibilities, make them
age-appropriate and provide enough supervision to in-
sure that your child succeeds in her assignment. Let
your three-year-old carry the plastic cups from the table, but not your best crystal glasses. You might do a
chore together until you are confident your child can
accomplish the task alone. If you decide to let your
teenager do the grocery shopping, either jointly make
a list or resolve to eat whatever she buys. But don't
delegate the shopping, only to criticize her selections.
That will simply serve to undermine a child's self-esteem
and make her reluctant to assume responsibility again.

When our oldest, Peter, was in kindergarten, we attended a parent-teacher conference and were shown
some of his paperwork. A large sheet of drawing paper
had been labeled at the top WHY I AM IMPORTANT.
Larry and I studied Peter's drawing and discerned a
little boy in a backyard with a large dog. The boy was
holding a shovel twice his size. On the spade were arranged numerous large black lumps. Suddenly, it hit
us! Peter's chore was that of chief pooper-scooper for
our German shepherd. You bet he was important—and
at age five he knew it!

Because I worked outside the home even when my
children were small, they had a lot of responsibility at
a young age. They packed their own lunches as early
as the second grade and learned to run the washer before they were ten. One of their neighborhood friends
was an only child whose well-meaning, doting mother
packed his lunch even after he was in high school,
cleaned his room, washed his laundry, fed his pet, and
handled all meal preparation and cleanup. Patrick had
virtually no chores of his own. For a while, my kids
tried to make me feel guilty by frequently reciting all
the things that Patrick's mother did for him, contrasted

with all the chores they were stuck with in our home. Later, however, they admitted that they were proud to have had household responsibilities and realized that Patrick wasn't so lucky after all for being pampered. They concluded that having chores had made them "more mature" than Patrick.

As important as giving your child responsibility is helping your child feel powerful, not powerless. For example, if eight-year-old Jimmy wets the bed from time to time, teach him how to wash and change his own sheets so he will own both the problem and the solution. The whole world doesn't have to know whether Jimmy "had an accident" last night, because he can handle the consequences of his enuresis himself. It's demoralizing enough for a child not to have control of his bladder at night when he really wants to. Having his mother check his sheets each morning and then complain about the extra load of washing he just created for her can erode his self-esteem still further. But teaching a child to take responsibility for managing the bed linen himself is one way to empower a youngster who may be feeling powerless about his bladder control.

Similarly, when your child brings home her report card, make it clear that the grades she earned are hers, not yours. Instead of launching into an angry diatribe about the fact that Emily is "certainly capable of better marks than these," begin by asking Emily how *she* feels about the grades she earned. One indignant teen, whose parents were devastated by his D in Algebra, surprised them by insisting: "I worked hard for that D! Some kids didn't even pass."

If Emily admits she is not pleased with her report card, respond by empathizing with her: "It must be disappointing to have grades that don't reflect your true ability. You must feel bad right now." This keeps the ownership of the problem with Emily. You can additionally explore what she thinks might be the consequences of her grades, like needing to retake a subject or being required to attend summer school. Her acknowledgment of such natural consequences will have more impact than exaggerated comments such as "At this rate you'll never get into college." Finally, inquire what Emily would like to do about her poor grades. Remain empathetic and offer your support in helping her achieve her goal of improving her grades. "I'd be willing to check your homework each night and to drive you to the library on Saturdays."

Do things with your child, not just for your child. Many parents worry about having enough money to allow them to *do* things for their child—to buy brand-name clothes or popular toys, travel to Disneyland, or pay for lessons. We worry about making meals, making costumes, making cookies, and making beds *for* our children. Many working parents go overboard with material things for their children as an exchange for not being able to spend more time with them. But children, almost without exception, prefer your *presence* to your *presents.* Doing things with your child is one of the most effective ways to give her focused attention.

I know a single working mother who typically came home hassled every night. She would proceed to fix a meat-vegetable-and-potatoes type of dinner for her daughter because she was determined to be a "good mother" during her limited time at home. Throughout the harried meal preparation and cleanup, however, the woman was short-tempered and irritable. You might describe the evening hours she spent with her only child as less than "quality" time. One night, she was simply too tired to cook. Feeling guilty, she took only a few minutes to make peanut butter sandwiches and slice some apples. The cleanup was minimal, and much to her surprise, she had a thoroughly enjoyable evening talking and playing with her daughter. This experience caused the woman to examine her evening routine. Fast foods, instant dinners, or frozen meals prepared on the weekends were preferable to a cooked-from-scratch dinner that left her too depleted to interact with her daughter.

Even a few minutes spent performing the most routine activities can provide opportunities for meaningful interaction. One mother told me she is so grateful that she has a double sink in her bathroom because each morning she and her teenage daughter stand together in front of the mirror curling their hair. Those few minutes together at the start of each day, doing something quite mundane, have sparked many short discussions, exchanges, and spontaneous reassurances that might have been missed if mother and daughter had done their hair separately in silence.

When I visit my young nieces in another state, I am shamelessly pleased by how excited they are to see me. At first I attributed this to the fact that I always have a little gift for them. But more than the material gift that holds their fancy for a moment, I believe Dana and Jenna look forward to my visits so much because I try to be with them totally during my brief stays. "Aunt Mari, will you play Barbies?" "Aunt Mari, look what I drew for you." "Aunt Mari, read us a story now." In my absence, these little girls recall the things we have done together, like buying a bunny, giving a birthday party, going to dance class, carving a pumpkin, making Valentines, and playing Barbies. I trust that I have contributed in some small measure to positively shaping their self-esteem during my brief, but attentive visits.

By the time my children were teenagers, they did not require much physical care. The older ones could drive and get the others to and from their activities. They could prepare a meal, wash their clothes, and buy groceries if I left them money. They spent a great deal of time with their peers, but they still loved to do things with me or Larry. They usually insisted on bringing one or more friends along, but they wanted us to be present, too.

At a busy point in my career, I often heard myself saying things like, "Not this weekend; I'm just too busy right now. I have too much to accomplish before Monday. Maybe next weekend." All my self-imposed deadlines and professional commitments seemed like once-in-a-lifetime crises to me, but before long, a never-ending string of external crises became an entrenched lifestyle. No matter what I said, my actions shouted to my children that they were less important than other people's demands on me.

Fortunately, something brought me to my senses and helped me prioritize better. Perhaps it was the fatal auto accident involving a teen in our community. Or it could have been the unexplained suicide of another youth. Maybe I just heard Harry Chapin's "Cat's in the Cradle" on the radio and started thinking about how quickly kids grow up and leave home. Anyway, something jogged me, and I began trying hard not to turn down my kids when they wanted to do something with me. "Let's go to the Chinese restaurant Thursday to celebrate midterms being over," they would say. Or "Let's go get a Christmas tree together today." Or "Let's go to the pet store and look at the new puppies." Or "Let's go miniature golfing this weekend."

Saying yes to these kinds of suggestions is what creates those everyday one-to-one interactions that enhance your child's self-esteem. Your child's self-worth skyrockets when your actions convince her she is worthy of your time and attention. Conversely, repeatedly saying no to such requests, regardless of the merit of your excuse, gives your child a clear message that she is less important than your other commitments. If children believe they are unworthy of their own parents' attention, they begin to doubt they are deserving of anyone else's attention.

A physician colleague of mine was extremely over-extended professionally, working seventy or more hours a week and handling a heavy on-call schedule. She was highly respected among her peers, admired by her residents in training, and adored by her patients. But she had little time or energy left for her only child. Although she increasingly recognized her life to be out of balance, it wasn't until her six-year-old son said something profoundly insightful one day that she took immediate action to change her lifestyle. As she was called to the hospital during a scheduled activity together, the youngster simply commented, "You're many different things, Mommy, but being a doctor is the most important thing to you." She had tears in her eyes when she recounted this incident. No matter how much she insisted to her son that he was important to her, her actions daily reinforced that being a doctor to other people's ills always came before his own needs.

Fortunately, it's never too late to rearrange one's priorities. We can take measures to improve our parenting whenever we gain new insights. The woman I just described took heed and cut her practice to part-time in order to tell her son both in word and deed that "being a mommy had become the most important thing." She gained immense satisfaction from her expanded parenting role and was grateful that her son had verbalized his true feelings, giving her an opportunity to reorder her life. Countless children never express their feelings of unworthiness and unimportance. They just assume that everything else in their parents' lives is more important than they are.

Admit when you are wrong and apologize to your child when your own behavior has been inappropriate. The act of apologizing can convey many valuable lessons in living. For example, seeing adults acknowledge their mistakes helps children appreciate that no one is perfect. Young children especially tend to idolize their parents and view them as invincible. Some children later become immobilized by their conviction that they can never match their parents' abilities or success. Learning to view their parents as humans who can err at times may help children better accept their own shortcomings.

Apologizing when we have lost our temper or failed to keep a promise or let our child down tells her that we value her feelings enough to ask her forgiveness. Showing such respect for a child does wonders for her self-esteem.

All children, and especially adolescents, despise hypocrisy in adults. I've often heard teens exclaim how upset it makes them to have their parents accuse them wrongly of something and then refuse to acknowledge their mistake or to apologize. Saying "I'm sorry" is one of the most humbling and honest things a person can do. If a child learns she can forgive her parents, it makes it easier to forgive herself and others.

Common Parental Mistakes
That Undermine
a Child's Self-Esteem

In addition to the preceding guidelines for enhancing self-esteem, most parents need to make a concerted effort to *avoid* the following common mistakes, which are guaranteed to erode a child's self-esteem. When we scrutinize the list, we will probably recognize several things our own parents did unintentionally that served to undermine our own self-concept. And if we're honest, I'll bet each of us can identify a couple of behaviors that we are presently using in a destructive fashion with our children. But feeling guilty about these mistakes won't help. What's important is to understand why they are so harmful to children and to become more aware of our use of them so we can begin to eliminate them from our daily interactions.

Repeatedly associating a child's character with his or her misbehavior. Your dislike of your child's behavior always must be separated from your feelings for your child. We must constantly reassure our children that we continue to love them unconditionally, despite their behavior. Associating a child's very character with his performance can be very damaging to self-esteem. Calling your five-year-old a "baby" because he wet the bed last night makes him feel terribly inadequate.

If your seven-year-old spills his milk again, you might be tempted to blurt out, "You clumsy slob! Can't you get through even one meal without spilling something? That's just like you!" Many parents have talked like this all their lives and they must work hard to start reacting in a different manner when their child's behavior is unpleasant. Describe how the behavior makes you feel and why you don't like it, but don't link the behavior to your child's worth. "Roger, I don't like to clean up spilled milk at the dinner table. Here's a sponge. Help me take care of this mess while I pour you another glass."

Tying a child's personal worth to his or her performance. This is a close cousin to the error just described. Overemphasizing a child's strengths eventually makes him feel he is loved for the strength only, instead of being loved unconditionally. Overemphasizing a child's abilities tends to promote "all-or-nothing thinking," in which a child sees his performance in black or white categories, and feels his self-worth is subject to cancellation any time his performance falls short of perfection. Thus, the straight-A student who gets a B may feel completely inadequate and unworthy. The Olympic athlete who wins the silver medal instead of the gold may feel like a complete failure. And the former beauty queen who succumbs to the natural aging process may

feel totally unattractive and unlovable. You can probably think of several people who are exceedingly talented or attractive, but who lack self-confidence and
base their entire self-worth on their performance or
appearance. This can result from our parents having
placed too much emphasis on the valued trait. Always,
the message must be that we love and are loved
unconditionally.

*Belittling, humiliating, criticizing, or putting down
your child*. Too many parents use degrading terms when
talking to or describing their children. Focus on using
positive words and praise instead, and eliminate criti-
cism from your conversation. There is no place for belittling labels like "crybaby," "clumsy," "fatso,"
"slowpoke," or "stupid."

Countless children will play the tapes of their parents'
criticisms in their heads for the rest of their lives. Every
time they fail or fall short, they'll reinforce that behavior
by mentally insisting, "I did it again!" Remember, our
children believe we are all-knowing, so they are particularly vulnerable to accept the labels we give them
in a fit of temper. Instead, try using affirming words
and frequent praise as described earlier. Use the technique of "That's like you, that's not like you," to foster
desirable behavior or to extinguish undesirable behavior. If you find yourself using derogatory labels, try
substituting new names like "pal," "sweetheart,"
"honey," or "buddy."

Revealing something confidential about your child in
front of others is another form of devaluing them and
eroding his or her self-esteem. If Haley overhears you
discussing her hair-pulling habit or her bed-wetting
problem with Theresa's mother, she's apt to feel be-
trayed. Try treating your child with the same respect
you would afford a good friend.

*Comparing siblings or other children with one an-
other*. Making comparisons is very destructive to a

child's self-esteem. Even if you usually compare your child favorably with another ("Boy, you sure played much better than Jason did today! He missed three goals"), comparisons make a child feel he is valued only when his performance is better than someone else's. A better way to convey your pride in how your son played would be, "Boy, you sure played a great game today. I enjoyed watching you try your hardest." Constant comparisons among siblings is particularly damaging. (See "Raising Siblings," Chapter 4.) Try to view each of your children as unique individuals with special strengths and qualities.

Comparisons convey to your children that your love for them is not unconditional; rather, it is linked to their performance. Because comparisons always carry the risk of coming out unfavorably, they jeopardize self-esteem. Imagine how easily threatened you might be if your children regularly compared your parenting performance to that of other mothers and fathers. Around Mother's Day, I often see cards that say "To the best mother in the world." Most of us are the "best mother we can be," (I certainly try to be the "best mother in my immediate family"), but none of us expects to rate "best mother in the world." I don't enjoy getting cards like that because they make me wonder whether I'd still be loved if my kids ever figure out that I really wasn't the best mother in the world after all.

Expecting too much from a child. One of the biggest mistakes parents make is having unrealistic or rigid expectations for their child. Your inevitable repeated disappointments then become the child's disappointment in herself. Perfectionist parents usually have miserable children. It's been said that "perfectionists take great pains and give them to other people." Everyone around a perfectionist feels like he or she is failing and thus has low self-esteem. Have the courage to be imperfect yourself and lower your expectations for your children.

Unfortunately, many parents have children in the first place in order to enhance their own self-esteem through their children's accomplishments. Other parents hope to overcome life's disappointments by vicariously reliving their own life through their child's experiences. Both of these parenting motives are highly inappropriate and will result in children who are not free to develop into unique individuals, but who are expected to fulfill their parents' preconceived expectations.

I know a father who places a high premium on athletic ability, who loves to hunt and fish, and who has a competitive personality. While he showed promise of real athletic talent himself, a mild disability kept him from achieving the degree of success he had coveted. When his wife gave birth to a boy, he placed a baseball in the baby's bassinet at the hospital and constantly visualized his son becoming a gifted athlete, in fulfillment of his own boyhood dreams. He anticipated baseball and soccer games, father-son hunting and fishing trips, awards ceremonies, and summer training camps.

As a result of the intense pressure from his father, however, the youth's interest in sports gradually diminished. Since he could never live up to his father's expectations, he played soccer and baseball without enthusiasm and lacked a competitive spirit. What the boy really enjoyed best and excelled at was playing the piano and writing short stories. But his remarkable talents in these areas were never fully acknowledged or appreciated by his father, who could not relinquish his preconceived and unrealistic expectations of his child. Thus, a sensitive and gifted youngster experienced perpetual feelings of inadequacy resulting from the daily knowledge that he was a disappointment to his father. How unfair that an innocent baby comes into the world facing a list of parental expectations he can never fulfill.

We should view our children as mystery seeds that we plant and nurture. Only when the seed sprouts can we start to guess what kind of plant it is destined to be. If we plant a cherry seed, we can't will it to grow into a tomato plant. So it is with our children. We should expect them to be exactly who they are and nothing else. When a baby arrives in the world, the greatest gift we can give her is the freedom to blossom into a unique individual, free of the burden of our expectations.

Putting yourself down. Many parents who make a concerted effort to foster their children's self-esteem make disparaging comments about their own self-worth in front of their youngsters without realizing the damaging effects this can have. For example, it does little good to try to convince your overweight adolescent that you love her unconditionally when she overhears you make a self-deprecating remark while trying on a bathing suit: "I just hate all this fat!" What your daughter may interpret from your remark is "I hate fat people." On the other hand, if you can accept and love yourself, flaws and all, it is much more convincing to your child that you really do love and accept her, despite her imperfections.

I can't emphasize how much children's self-esteem is linked to their parents' own feelings of self-worth. Children model both our attitudes and our behaviors, so work hard on acquiring a more positive image of yourself. Both you and your child will reap the rewards!

Fostering stereotypes. Stereotypes place arbitrary limitations on others based on our predetermined expectations of their ability, behavior, performance, or appearance. For example, despite our increased awareness of sex-role stereotypes in our society, many parents still maintain differing expectations for their sons and their daughters. They are apt to ask their daughter to help with dinner and their son to mow the lawn. While today women are entering medical school in almost the same numbers as men, sex-role stereotypes continue to keep women out of other professions. Many parents would still encourage their son to be a pilot and their daughter to be a flight attendant.

When we impose limits on our children as a result of such stereotypical expectations, we erode their self-esteem. Whether we discourage our short son from trying out for basketball or neglect to teach our teenage daughter how to change the oil in her car, we are implying that the opportunities open to our children are arbitrarily restricted by an unalterable physical trait. In fact, a boy can learn to sew, a girl can drive a truck, and a child who stutters can become a public speaker—if they have the desire and we give our support.

Fostering Self-Esteem in Vulnerable Children

This chapter has emphasized the critical role positive self-esteem plays in permitting a child to reach her full potential. While a healthy self-concept is essential for all youngsters, it is of paramount importance for those vulnerable children whose self-image is likely to be threatened by society or their peers. For example, children of an ethnic minority may be made to feel they aren't the norm in certain communities. Children who differ from their peers and classmates by virtue of a physical or mental handicap may be at increased risk for damaged self-esteem. Childhood obesity, precocious or delayed development, or a chronic medical condition can also chip away at a child's self-image.

If something about your child makes her more vulnerable to low self-esteem, you will need to double your efforts to convey your unconditional love and acceptance. When a child is absolutely convinced that his own parents find him lovable and capable, he is then equipped to venture out into the world and risk the acceptance of others.

When your child experiences hurt feelings, make yourself available to listen, empathize, reaffirm her worth, and explain that others sometimes act unkind only because they aren't comfortable with the differences in people. Reassure your child that once others get to know her better, chances are they, too, will readily like and accept her. Remind her that people's comments and actions cannot change her personal worth and that no one can *make* her feel badly if she chooses not to let them. Teach her to recite "Sticks and stones may break my bones, but names can never hurt me," just like many of us did during tough times in our childhood.

If your child is a member of an ethnic minority, be sure you provide plenty of successful role models for her. If he has a medical condition, participating in a support group will reinforce the fact that others share the same problem and still feel good about themselves. Remember, the unconditional love and acceptance you offer your child will be the most important factor determining how she handles the reactions of others, so resolve to build up your child as much as you possibly can at home. In the end, I am confident she will not only receive the acceptance of others, but she will have taught them a great deal in the process.

I often find it reassuring to recall that I am not solely responsible for my children's self-image. Fortunately, we can tap into the expertise, love, concern, and example of many others, including compassionate teachers, neighbors, daycare workers, relatives, and health professionals who also will contribute significantly to our child's development and help them feel good about themselves.

ADDITIONAL READING:

Berne, Patricia H., and Savary, Louis M. *Building Self-Esteem in Children.* New York: The Continuum Publishing Company, 1990.

Branden, Nathaniel. *Six Pillars of Self-Esteem.* New York: Bantam Books, 1994.

Briggs, Dorothy Corkille. *Your Child's Self-Esteem.* New York: Dolphin Books, Doubleday, 1970.

Campbell, Ross. *How to Really Love Your Child.* New York: New American Library, 1982.

Campbell, Ross. *How to Really Love Your Teenager.* Wheaton, Illinois: Victor Books, 1981.

Hart, Louise. *The Winning Family: Increasing Self-Esteem in Your Children and Yourself.* Oakland, California: LifeSkills Press, 1987.

Meeks, Carolyn Ann. *Prescriptions for Parenting.* New York: Warner Books, 1990.

Palmer, Pat, and Froehner, Melissa Alberti. *Teen Esteem.* San Luis Obispo, California: Impact Publishers, 1989.

Youngs, Bettie B. *How to Develop Self-Esteem in Your Child: Six Vital Ingredients.* New York: Fawcett Columbine, 1991.

4

RAISING SIBLINGS

When the second child enters a family, you can be
certain that sibling rivalry also has been born. So potentially destructive is this fundamental human dynamic
that its ravages are described in the first book of the
Bible, preceded only by the Creation story and the
account of the Fall of Man. When Cain and Abel present offerings to God, Abel's gift is received with favor,
while Cain's offering is scorned. Jealous of God's acceptance of his brother, Cain then murders Abel. While
this story certainly has theological implications, it is also
a frank account of sibling rivalry at its worst.

Anyone with two children will tell you that having
two is *more* than twice as hard as one. And three is
more than three times as hard. It's not just the predictable increase in physical care related to having to
feed, dress, bathe, protect, play with, and educate two,
three or four children that makes raising multiple children harder than raising an only child. It's the unpredictable thousand ways your kids will find to squabble,
fight, whine, complain, tattle, threaten, and irritate one
another. Parents tell me that intense sibling rivalry is
one of the main problems that daily threaten to take
the fun out of parenting.

It is simply not practical to attempt to eliminate sibling rivalry altogether. All children in the same family

naturally feel some jealousy, competition, and rivalry among one another. And it's obvious to bystanders that children actually enjoy sibling fights to some degree. The primary goal of this chapter is to learn effective techniques for minimizing sibling conflicts by conveying unconditional love to each child. In addition, methods will be offered for appropriately managing a child's anger when conflicts inevitably arise. It is my conviction that the effects of poorly handled sibling rivalry can last a lifetime and prevent children from reaching their full potential. On the other hand, well-managed sibling conflicts can actually enrich the relationship between sibs and encourage their individual development.

The Cause of Sibling Rivalry

Underlying all sibling rivalry is competition for the parents' love. When one child begins to feel at a disadvantage in the struggle for parental approval, then rivalry erupts, often in an active aggressive outburst of name-calling, flaunting something, hitting, grabbing a toy, or tattling. At the other extreme, a jealous child may react to the competition by passive aggressive behavior, such as soiling his pants, giving up and failing at school, or using drugs to escape the conflict. Whether mild or marked, sibling rivalry takes its toll on parents who soon grow weary of hearing, "He looked at me!" "She touched me!" or "Give it back; it's mine!" What is the source of all this conflict?

Most of us have heard the popular story that is commonly used to familiarize parents with the emotional trauma a child experiences when a new sibling is brought home from the hospital. When the dilemma is examined from an adult perspective, we gain instant insight into a young child's feelings of inadequacy and loss of parental love that accompany the arrival of a new baby.

When the story begins, you are asked to imagine that you are a happily married woman, confident of your husband's love. One day your husband announces with great delight that he is bringing home a second wife. At this point, every adult who hears the story accurately identifies the immediate reactions of the first wife—feelings of anger, hurt, jealousy, and self-doubt. Each privately thinks, "Why wasn't I enough for him?"

The account only gets more painful when your husband defends his actions by insisting that he's only bringing the second woman home so she can be a friend, helpmate, and companion for you, his beloved first wife. Usually, the illustration ends here, with adults agreeing that an older sibling would rightfully feel jealous of a new baby brother or sister. A discussion typically follows about ways to better prepare a youngster for the arrival of a sibling.

But Adele Faber and Elaine Mazlish, in their popular, practical and highly insightful book, *Siblings Without Rivalry*, carry the analogy several steps further. Before they have finished making their point, the adults participating in the exercise acknowledge actual outrage toward the intruder and voice extreme feelings of vulnerability and insecurity. In Faber and Mazlish's expanded version of the story, the new wife turns out to be rather adorable and everyone stops to compliment her, while they generally ignore you. Gushing over the new wife, someone may turn to you and ask how you like the new wife, as if they expect you also to bubble over with joy at her arrival.

Next, Faber and Mazlish suggest that the new wife needs clothes, so your husband takes several of your favorite outfits from your closet and gives them to her. When you object, he reminds you that you've put on some weight and the clothes don't fit you as well as they do the new wife. He's sure you won't mind sharing with her.

As the new wife adjusts to her new environment, she proves to be extremely bright and capable. While you're still struggling with the instructions to the computer your husband just bought you, the new wife starts using it with obvious ease. When you protest that the computer belongs to you, your husband acts disappointed, asking why you won't share with the new wife. Finally, just when you think you can bear this intruder no longer, your husband gets called away on urgent business and asks you to take good care of his new wife in his absence.

When adults are presented with this hypothetical scenario, many readily admit that they would harbor intense hostility toward the new wife. The sudden presence of this interloper also would shake their self-confidence and raise numerous self-doubts. All things considered, most parents would have to agree that our kids handle such displacement far better than we would.

Whom Do You Love the Most?

Those of us with more than one child are acutely aware of their constant jockeying for our attention and affection, as they fiercely attempt to secure a favored position in our imaginary hierarchy of love. The tensions generated by this undercurrent of sibling competition can periodically seduce us into secretly hinting that we love someone the best. Of course, we are careful to make such innuendos only when we are alone with one child, trusting that they will have the decency not to confide the indiscretion to their siblings. We tell ourselves that allowing each child to believe we love him or her best will help boost their self-confidence and allay any insecurities caused by sibling competition for parental love. "What harm can it do?" we rationalize. A mother depicted in Erma Bombeck's *Motherhood: The Second Oldest Profession* carried off this ruse more successfully than anyone could hope. Terminally ill with cancer, she wrote separate letters to her three nearly grown sons, professing to each boy that she had always loved him best. Each thought he had been the only one to receive a letter and each remained convinced he had been his mother's favorite child.

Like the dying mother Erma Bombeck wrote about, we are often tempted simply to tell each of our children that we've always loved him best, hope he buys our line, and then pray he never discusses it with his brothers and sisters. After a brief moment of reassurance, however, most kids will start to doubt the sincerity of our private confession and suspect that we have made the same promise to each child. Besides, being loved "the best" is not really very comforting to a child, because it inherently implies that he can eventually be displaced from the coveted first position, like being bumped from first chair, should circumstances change. The tenuousness of being loved best at a given moment makes parental love feel conditional, instead of unqualified. Besides, who really wants to lie to their children?

Loving Equally

If trying to convince each child that we love her "the best" is inappropriate, then what about insisting that we love our children *equally*? Most of us who have more than one child initially believed we could minimize sibling rivalry by emphasizing that we had enough love to share equally among them all. If we bought a needed item for one child, say a sweatsuit, we also selected a sweatsuit for the other child, regardless of whether that sibling already had a drawer full of sweatsuits.

When my kids were young, I remember taking elaborate pains to spend the same amount of money on each child at Christmas as proof of my equality. However, the children didn't know the monetary value of different gifts and were more interested in getting what they wanted than in knowing how much the presents had cost.

Trying to love *equally* can quickly become a drag, as kids maintain, "He got more than I did." "You gave him two red ones and I only got one." "Tricie got to have seven girls at her birthday slumber party last year." "You went to Mark's soccer game last week and you're going to miss mine today." My own kids have worked to dig up every inequality they can recall, ranging from who got their ears pierced at what age to who got to drive how far from home how soon after getting their license.

A few years ago, Heather was miserably sick with mono, the third daughter to succumb to the illness in her mid-teens. While I was home pampering Heather, bringing her juice and soup and dispensing medication, I overheard the older girls commiserating about their perception that I hadn't been as attentive to their needs when they were sick with mono. Meanwhile, it was my distinct recollection that I had been every bit as sympathetic and nurturing throughout their respective illnesses. As far as they were concerned, however, I was lavishing far too much attention on Heather and was guilty of having treated them unequally.

Trying to love your children *equally* is a losing battle. First of all, your children's scorecards will never match your own. No matter how meticulously you measure and mete out your love, attention, and material gifts, it will never feel truly equal to your children. Besides, life's various circumstances will never permit you to be as consistent as you had hoped. Your children will need different things at different times, and true equality won't really serve their differing needs very well, anyway. One child may require physical therapy while another needs braces. Or, one may be gifted musically and bég for private violin lessons, while his brother is satisfied taking trumpet lessons during band class at school.

Furthermore, it is extremely unrealistic for children to focus on dividing things equally with their siblings. Your children don't have equal talents now and they won't have equal opportunities later in life. You may be able to divide resources equally in childhood, but your best efforts won't succeed in shielding them from personal or physical crises. Both in childhood and throughout adult life, your children will vary in their specific talents, personality, physical attractiveness, and academic and athletic abilities. You can buy them the same clothes, give the same number of birthday parties, and take them to the circus the same number of times, but one child may develop leukemia, another may become paralyzed in an automobile accident, while another is selected homecoming queen. Your heart will be broken a thousand times if you really expect to equalize your children's happiness by striving to love them equally.

Loving Uniquely

How then do you love each of your multiple children, if not *the best* or even *equally*? The answer is, you love them *uniquely*. The depth of this precept touched me personally one day while I was reading a greeting card from my oldest daughter, Paige. The message read

". . . because there's a special place in my heart and in my life that's yours, and yours alone." On good days and bad, whether perfect or flawed, during success or amid failure, my daughter had promised me that there will always be a special place in her heart reserved only for me. Despite the intensity of the other relationships she develops with her sorority sisters, her future husband, or her own children, these will never supplant the unique love she holds for me. How gratifying and how comforting!

Do you suppose Paige subconsciously selected that particular card because that's all she really wants of me too? Just to know there's a unique place in my life and in my heart that will always be hers alone, whether or not she earns an A, gets a scholarship, sings a solo, or wins an election? Ultimately, I think that's all any child is really asking from us—the assurance that no one else, no brother or sister, will ever replace their unique significance in our lives.

Thus, no matter how much Seth protests, we can't promise to take his little brother back to the hospital. And, we won't lie to him and insist we'll always love him best. Neither can we cut our love in half and divide it equally between the two boys. But we can honestly promise Seth that we will always love him unconditionally for being the special and unique individual that he is. We can convey to him that no matter how many other children join our family, no one will ever be able to take his place in our lives.

Specific Strategies for Minimizing Sibling Rivalry

Honor the Individual in Every Child

One day while I was serving as attending physician in the newborn nursery at University Hospital, a woman gave birth to an infant who had a cleft lip and palate. The birth defect had been completely unexpected, and the young mother and her husband were initially shocked and dismayed. After meeting with them briefly, I called a plastic surgeon to examine their little boy and explain the options for repair. I remained with the family during and after the surgeon's discussion and witnessed their beginning attachment to their son.

While holding the baby and stroking his head, the mother suddenly looked up and announced with a smile, "I think he has Joey's eyes." Joey was their healthy toddler at home, and I believe her comment was one of the nicest compliments she could have given her new son. After her initial shock upon seeing his cleft, she had quickly identified in her new baby boy an admired facial feature of her firstborn, first-loved child. I think her comment was really saying, "I can handle this; I can love this child just like Joey." Somehow, at that moment, I knew that this young family would do fine with their new infant.

Just as the birth of our first baby inescapably alters our marriage, the arrival of each subsequent child brings additional changes in a family's relationships. Many parents wonder how they will *divide* their love among multiple children (until they come to appreciate that their love actually *multiplies* enough to go around!). By the time we're having our second child, we usually have grown comfortable parenting the first one. We seek, with some apprehension, to repeat what has been largely a rewarding experience. One way many of us mustered the courage to conceive a second child was to imagine that he or she would turn out similar to our first. The fact that we loved our first so much was the very reason we searched for likenesses in our second baby.

I think this practice occurs commonly among parents and may be the original source of subsequent damaging sibling comparisons. The innocent comments that begin as compliments for a second-born child ("She looks so much like her sister, it's like bringing Laura home all over again!"), when perpetuated throughout childhood, can become oppressive life-role scripts. While some comparisons may be harmless or even useful, our emphasis as parents should be on acknowledging and honoring the unique differences in each of our children, rather than on raising siblings according to identified family "themes." The key to bringing out the best in each of our children is to respect their individuality and to resolve to love them unconditionally, simply for being exactly who they are. Only when we discard our preconceived expectations for our children do we truly grant them the freedom of fully expressing their unique potential.

In retrospect, Larry and I admit that we allowed some unspoken "rules of the game" to evolve as we began raising our own five children. Since both Peter and Paige excelled in their schoolwork and seemed to derive great satisfaction in pursuing academic honors, we quickly fell into the trap of expecting the other three children to have the same scholarly aptitudes, interests, and motivation. While they all turned out to be fine students, none of the younger three felt compelled to aim for all A's the way Peter and Paige had done. We spent several awkward years pointing out that the younger children "were capable of doing better" before they collectively insisted that they were perfectly satisfied with their grades and "weren't just like Peter and Paige." Since that time, we have worked hard to avoid implied expectations and to respect the individuality of each child. Fostering a unique sense of self in each of our five children has been my greatest parenting challenge, but over the years I've come a long way in identifying, cultivating, and honoring the special attributes of each child.

Avoid Overt and
Subtle Comparisons

Most parents aren't even aware of how often they compare their children and how destructive this practice can be to a child's self-esteem and individuality: "Kayla isn't even crawling yet, and Nolan was already walking at her age." "Your brother never gives me any trouble; why can't you behave like Landon?" "Wendy's already taller than Johnny was at her age." "Why won't you run for student council? Erika ran last year." Can you glean from these comments that comparisons always imply a more favorable and a less favorable outcome? Such comments provoke sibling rivalry by pitting siblings against one another in our eyes. Comparisons also carry the suggestion that specific conditions exist for parental love and acceptance. Thus, even when one child comes out on top in a comparison, she is left feeling uneasy about the tenuousness of her position and the possibility of faring less well in the next comparison.

Despite the damage they can inflict, most of us would have to admit that comparisons are a regular part of our conversations about our children. It takes a concerted effort to minimize sibling comparisons in our everyday speech. We can practice emphasizing the unique qualities of our child when referring to him or her without always making references to our other children: "I enjoyed watching you hustle on the field today." "I like to see you looking your best." "I'll bet you're proud of the effort this report card reflects."

Encourage Children to Articulate Feelings

When adults review the imaginary scenario outlined earlier in this chapter, most will immediately recognize the legitimate and deep feelings of competition their children experience when they try to share their parents—their ultimate source of protection, comfort, approval, and love—with uninvited siblings. While the feelings are inevitable, specific techniques can minimize their intensity and help children learn to handle the anger that often accompanies sibling interactions.

If put in our children's place, most of us would admit that, at a minimum, we would like our parents to acknowledge the depth of our feelings about our siblings, without making judgments. We'd like them to say, for instance, "I didn't realize you felt that strongly. You're really angry at him," instead of, "Of course you don't hate your brother. I don't want to hear you say that again!"

While we can't allow our youngsters to harm one another, we can permit them to verbally express their anger without fear of reprisal. Young children may need help putting their feelings into words, so you may need to say, "You don't like me to spend so much time feeding the new baby, do you?" to a toddler. But even adolescents appreciate your acknowledgment of their raw emotions; they'll feel understood when you say, "It's embarrassing when your brother calls you names

in front of his friends. I'll bet you're furious right now."
A child who is encouraged to articulate his feelings is
less likely to act them out. Thus, let Ken exclaim to his
brother, "I'm so mad at what you did that my blood is
boiling. Don't touch my things again without my
permission!"

Allowing a child to express her wishes or fantasies
about a given situation usually helps to diffuse anger:
"You wish the new baby didn't have to stay at our
house. You'd rather have Daddy and me all to yourself
again," or "You wish your sister would ask you before
borrowing your clothes. You wish she'd show more
respect."

Teach Children Appropriate
Outlets for Anger

One of the most frustrating aspects of sibling rivalry is
the physical outbursts and actual abuse that can be associated with sibling conflicts—kicking, shoving, biting,
throwing, punching, and damaging toys and property.
These are common but highly inappropriate responses
to anger that begin in childhood and often continue into
adulthood. Learning to handle anger responsibly and
express it creatively, instead of destructively, is one of
the most important childhood lessons you can impart.
Teach your children at an early age to develop creative
outlets for their anger and refuse to tolerate antisocial
violent outbursts. I believe parents' failure to teach children appropriate outlets for anger is partially to blame
for our society's current epidemic of violence.

You tell your toddler she can bang her dolly against
the floor all she wants, but she is *never* allowed to hit
the new baby. Your preschooler can draw a picture of
his angry feelings, or yell as loud as he can, or make
something out of clay and then crush it, but it is *never*

112

okay for him to punch his brother. Your adolescent can describe her angry feelings in her diary, write a poem about her anger, hit a punching bag, play loud music, or write a letter to her sister that she can either give to her or throw away. But she can't trash her sister's room, call her cruel names, or pull her hair. Kids can be taught to use a punching bag, ride an exercise bike, recite some kind of mantra, walk around the block, or just sit in their rooms until they cool off. They should always be congratulated for handling their anger creatively, instead of destructively.

Finally, kids should be taught to work out their differences with one another in constructive ways. They need to learn to confront their siblings directly about undesirable behaviors instead of reflexively exploding over them. In addition to the creative outlets just described for re-channeling angry outbursts, children need to learn how to tell one another in a controlled manner just what behavior has made them angry *and* the way they would like their sibling to act in the future: "It makes me so mad when you go in my room without my permission and take my toys. I expect you to ask me when you want to borrow something of mine."

Help Children Solve
Differences Constructively

The day-to-day sibling problem parents complain about most is frequent fighting and arguing that seem to necessitate parental intervention and mediation: "Stop pinching your sister right now!" "Quit screaming or I'll send you both to your rooms!" "Okay, which one of you started this?" "Stop crying and just tell me what happened. I'll listen to Jonathan's side next." While making each child feel special may diminish sibling squabbling within your family, there is simply no way to eliminate it altogether. And you wouldn't want to extinguish all disagreements anyway. Years of practice in resolving sibling conflicts is a valuable skill that children can use to learn to get along with their classmates, friends, teammates, and college roommates. So how do you manage inevitable sibling fights and yelling matches with the greatest effectiveness and the least stress?

First, the physical safety of each child must be guaranteed. No child should ever be allowed to cause physical harm by biting, punching, pinching, pulling hair, throwing things, or otherwise injuring another person. Parental interference is always called for to protect a child from his sibling.

Many fights can be prevented by avoiding potentially inflammatory situations. If your two-year-old invariably knocks over the elaborate towers your six-year-old labors to construct, consider allowing the older child to erect his structures in your room away from his brother or while the younger child is taking his nap. Try separating your children more than you do now. Give each child his own space and play area, even if he doesn't have his own room.

Except when children are inflicting physical harm, don't jump in right away to mediate all their arguments. Resist the temptation to intervene immediately, to get emotionally involved, to interrogate, lay blame, or mete out justice. By the time the kids are screaming at each other in anger, the sequence of events is probably so complicated you'd have trouble getting to the bottom of the story anyway. Allowing the fight to attract your undivided attention and incite your anger offers the kids a measure of secondary gain by pulling you into their dispute. Instead, let kids successfully solve as many disagreements as possible on their own. State their dilemma, "Both of you want to play with the Barbie doll right now," and express your confidence that they can work out a satisfactory solution. And whenever they do mutually settle a conflict, congratulate them on coming to a peaceful resolution of their differences.

Avoid using one child—typically the older one—as a scapegoat. Many parents automatically accuse the older child when any dispute arises, saying, "You're the oldest; you should know better." "You're too old to let something like that bother you!" "I can't stand that screaming; just give the toy to your little sister." Generalizing blame in this way is infuriating to older children, and many younger siblings take unfair advantage of the practice by deliberately provoking their older brothers and sisters, then running to Mama or Daddy for guaranteed protection.

Whenever possible, assume both children are partially to blame for the fight and provide negative reinforcers that will be mutually unpleasant for both children. For example, if they are arguing over a toy, calmly announce, "You know the rules; if you can't play quietly with something, it gets put away." Then place the toy out of their reach. You might set a timer for three minutes and offer, "If you can reach an agreement about how to share the toy before the timer goes off, I'll let you play with it again. If not, I'll leave it where it is for the rest of the day." In this way, you can reinforce children's willingness to negotiate a peaceful solution. If they are successful in reaching an agreement, congratulate them on their resourcefulness and offer the toy again.

The same approach can be used for other common sources of sibling conflict. If fighting over the television is getting out of hand, simply turn the set off. Again, you can offer one chance at resolving their dispute amicably before a timer buzzes, or else the TV will stay off for the next hour. The idea is to convey to children that it is to their mutual advantage to solve their differences among themselves. In lieu of the traditional "who to blame and who to punish" approach to sibling disputes, you can better foster a spirit of cooperation and joint resolution by focusing on win-win solutions.

Birth Order

Have you ever wondered how an individual child's development might differ depending on whether he is the middle son among three boys, the only son after four daughters, the oldest followed by two younger sisters, and so on? Just how much are a child's personality, talents, or vulnerabilities shaped by his or her position in the family? I am fascinated by the effects of birth order on the outcome of siblings. Perhaps what has piqued my interest in birth order was my own position as the middle child in a family of five children. My two sisters and I were sandwiched between an older and younger brother.

Contrary to popular stereotypes about the undesirability of the middle child position, I thought I was the most privileged of children since I had one of every sibling type—an older brother, an older sister, a younger brother, and a younger sister. As I write this, I have in view my favorite childhood photograph, which sits on the shelf above my word processor. The black-and-white photo was taken when my siblings and I ranged in age from eighteen months to ten years. I was about five and a half at the time. We are seated in a tight stair-step arrangement, lined up from oldest to youngest. Next to this classic picture is a colored photograph of my own kids taken nearly twenty-five years later when my children were approximately the same ages. With a boy on either end and three girls in the middle, I had duplicated in my own family the historic birth order of my childhood, and decided to re-create the memorable stair-step pose a generation later. In the early years of my parenting, this coincidental replication of our birth order sometimes caused me to project onto my children specific traits of the aunt or uncle whose birth order corresponded to their own.

While the effects of birth order on children are not hard and fast rules, generalities do exist to describe common characteristics of firstborns and only children, middle, and youngest children. These are thoroughly discussed in *The Birth Order Book* by Dr. Kevin Leman. Birth order stereotypes are harmful to the degree that they narrow a child's experiences or limit his potential. But simply being aware of the stereotypes can help us avoid placing unfair expectations or limits on our children based on their position in the family.

Firstborns and Only Children

Typical firstborn traits are largely the result of early parental inexperience and anxiety, coupled with higher expectations for the first progeny than for subsequent children. Every milestone of a firstborn is scrutinized, photographed, recorded, replayed, and retold by doting parents to admiring relatives and disinterested friends. Beneath all the dazzling attention, however, is a scripted message of high parental expectation, which can place a lifelong burden on the designated family trailblazer. While subsequent children will strive to keep pace with siblings a few years their senior, the firstborn will always have a seemingly herculean task of emulating his adult parents.

As a result of these circumstances, classic firstborns and only children are highly responsible, perfectionistic, conscientious, organized, individuals. They make serious, compliant students, and they tend to be compulsive and competitive in their work and play. Firstborns and onlies are programmed from an early age to be goal-oriented and high achievers. Their strong need for approval from others serves to hone their people-pleasing skills, and they have a highly developed sense of justice and respect for authority. Because parents often place excessive demands and expectations on firstborns, they typically incur a disproportionate share of household duties or responsibility for younger siblings.

While firstborn and only children are often very gratifying for their proud parents, such children are at risk for growing up too fast, fulfilling the expectations of others instead of their own aspirations, and accepting a "rescuer" role for the family. Ultimately, the combination of excessive parental pressure and adult role models can produce an uptight, overachieving youngster who must struggle to fulfill his parents' agendas for his life. Such children easily can become victims of adult workaholism or get caught in personal bondage to guilt and perfectionism.

You can help shield your firstborn from the limitations of the traditional stereotype by honestly examining your overt and implied expectations for him. If you are exerting excessive pressure on your oldest child, admit it and then back off. Instead of pushing him into sports, music lessons, scouting, and karate, discourage him from taking on too many commitments at once. Support him in saying no when he wants to, without feeling guilty and without worrying about disappointing other people. Avoid comments that force him to act grown up like "You're too old for that" or "You're acting like a baby." Instead, encourage him to be more spontaneous and playful and less structured.

Since firstborns attract attention predominantly as a result of their accomplishments, they may come to believe that parental love is conditional based on their performance. Go out of your way to let your firstborn know that you love him apart from his achievements.

Don't ask your oldest always to play the role of enforcer of the rules and regulations with his younger siblings. And regardless of how pseudomature he may appear, don't succumb to the temptation to dump your adult troubles on your oldest child. While you may end up feeling better, chances are he will lie awake at night worrying about adult problems over which he has no control.

Peter, our oldest, manifested many firstborn traits during his childhood, when Larry and I were relatively inexperienced and ill-informed. Looking back, I can see that we were guilty of many of the parental behaviors that foster perfectionism in a child. Because Peter excelled so often, it became easier to escalate our expectations of him. Without realizing it, I was vicariously experiencing his successes as my own. Essentially, I was stroking my own ego at his expense! Fortunately, as Larry and I gained more insight as parents, we were able to acknowledge many of the ways in which we were fostering the firstborn stereotype in Peter. During his college years and as he has grown into adulthood, I'm pleased that Peter has been successful in extricating himself from some of the external pressures to perform, without compromising his career goals or personal fulfillment. In his last year of college, Peter was accepted into medical school. Much to my surprise and initial reservations, he decided to defer his entrance into medical school for a year, instead accepting a position as a teaching assistant in the chemistry department at the college from which he graduated. During that interim year, Peter lived on his own, worked in the chemistry lab, tutored undergraduates, played several recreational sports, revived old hobbies, acquired new skills, made new friends, and learned to relax. By the time he departed for medical school, Peter was not simply a year older, he was definitely a more satisfied, balanced, and integrated person.

Middle Children

Middle children are far more difficult to stereotype than firstborns or lastborns. The principal generality that can be made about middle children is that they are at risk for receiving less parental attention than either firstborns or the last of the line. As a consequence, middle children often look outside the family for additional meaningful relationships. They are likely to have more friends and stronger commitments to their peer group. They may be the first to leave home, like our middle child, Tricie, who was the first to choose to attend college out of state.

The highly developed social skills of likable middle children often make them excellent mediators. In my own case, being in the middle allowed me to maintain close friendships with the brother and sister at both extremes. Whereas the nine-year age difference between my two brothers seemed like a lot during their childhood, I was separated by only four years from both the older and younger brother. Often my mother would divide us into two groups—the three oldest or the three youngest. I could easily move from one into the other, thereby gaining the privileges or concessions of both groups.

Unfortunately, life may sometimes seem unfair to middle children, some of whom feel like an afterthought to a brilliant older sibling and unable to captivate the family's attention like the darling baby. Yet the middle position offers great training for the real world of lowered expectations, negotiation, and compromise. Middle children who often must break the mold set by an older sibling may thereby learn to challenge family values and seek their own identity.

Middle children are far less predictable than the oldest and youngest stereotypes. They can turn out much like their older siblings, or radically different. Many later-born children choose to follow in the footsteps of their oldest sibling, particularly if they have comparable talents and interests and feel they can compete favorably. Certainly, we can think of families whose children carry out a unified theme, with all the children being distinguished scholars, top athletes, or accomplished musicians. On the other hand, it is not uncommon for later-born children to depart widely from the particular role claimed by their older brother or sister and to carve out a distinct niche of their own, either favorable or unfavorable. Thus, if big sister gets her accolades from academic achievement, younger sister may deliberately seek recognition in the athletic arena instead. Unfortunately, if a subsequent child feels he simply cannot compete successfully with a sterling older sibling, he may resort to acting out in a negative way, just to establish his own identity.

The effect of the middle position on a child can be greatly impacted by her own gender and ability, as well as the constellation of other children. An only girl sandwiched between an older and younger brother will probably not have any trouble gaining special recognition within her family. On the other hand, the middle boy among three sons would be at greater risk of losing his identity. Another difficult middle position could be the second daughter who is followed by a baby brother. She is neither the oldest, the youngest, nor the only child of her gender. If she is unsuccessful competing with her big sister or finding areas of her own in which to excel, she may eventually conclude that the best way to get parental attention is to be irresponsible and rebellious.

In general, middle children can always use some extra parental attention. Go out of your way to regularly schedule one-to-one time with your middle child, and avoid making comparisons with their brothers and sisters. Allow them the freedom to carve out their own identity in a new area, or to share interests with their siblings, without feeling like they need to compete to be recognized.

Youngest Children

By the time their youngest child is born, parents are usually much more relaxed and laid back. The same mother who meticulously recorded every milestone her firstborn achieved will usually summarize the entire developmental history of her youngest by simply stating, "He did everything about the same time as the others." While the oldest is expected to perform and achieve, the youngest is expected to stay cute, cuddly, and lovable. A relaxed parental attitude and lowered expectations often combine to produce a child who is delightfully affectionate, but who may border on disorganized and absentminded. As a child, super-structured Peter always knew when and where his soccer games were each week, which parent was bringing oranges, and who was driving. On the other hand, when Mark was younger, he typically waited until the morning of his game to begin thinking about how he would get there. Unable to locate his printed schedule, he would have to call another player to find out what color shirt his team was wearing.

If firstborns are subject to growing up too fast, lastborns may be forced to remain youthful and cute long after they've matured. Pet names, like Markie or Chuckie, and affectionate phrases like, "He's the baby of the family," can make a lastborn child cringe when used in public. I vividly recall the time Mark announced to the family that he no longer believed in Santa Claus. As it turns out, he actually hadn't believed for some time, but had delayed telling Larry and me because he didn't think we were ready to give Santa up just yet!

Another risk for the youngest is the sense that he is continually living in the shadow of his older siblings and will never be able to measure up. Compared to them, he never quite feels "big enough," "old enough," or "good enough." Even teachers may be quick to announce, "Oh, you're Angela's brother. I remember Angela well; she was such a good student." I have attended many parent-teacher conferences for our younger children that were punctuated with frequent nostalgic references to Peter or Paige, offering me a glimpse of what a younger sibling might experience on a regular basis in the classroom.

The same parents who doted on their firstborn may be less available to their youngest child. Instead, older siblings may spend more time with the youngest than the parents do. Big brother or sister might end up reading him stories, teaching him to tie his shoes, or rehearsing the alphabet with him. As a result, the youngest may continually look to his older siblings to defend him, entertain him, rescue him, or cover for him. Their solicitousness and his continual dependence on them can serve to inhibit his own developing responsibility.

There is a tendency for lastborns to gain the attention they crave by turning on the charm, clowning around, acting helpless, or just cutting up. We may even unwittingly provoke their spontaneous and amusing antics because they provide a refreshing contrast to the serious predictability of the older firstborn. The danger of the lastborn stereotype, however, is that it can limit the youngest from taking himself seriously and being willing to test his true abilities in an area where his older siblings may have excelled. Beneath the funny-guy mask may be an insecure youngster who fears risking, failing, stretching, and recognizing his full potential.

Don't always cover for your lastborn or lower your expectations just because she's the baby. Help your youngest to set and achieve personal goals and to take pride in her accomplishments. Delegate appropriate levels of responsibility to her, and encourage her to participate in activities her older siblings modeled, as well as original endeavors no one in the family has yet tried. Do things alone with your youngest, where she can temporarily escape the powerful influence of the older children.

Twins and Other Multiples

Even under optimal circumstances, considerable effort may be required if parents are to cultivate and honor the unique differences in their children. Twins and other multiples pose even greater challenges to the successful establishment of a unique identity in each child. Since it is emotionally more difficult to form an individual relationship with two children at once, the parents of multiples often succumb to the temptation to treat their twins as a single unit or set. Our society's fascination with twins also tends to encourage practices that foster the blending of twin identities, such as giving twins rhyming names, dressing them alike, insisting the children cannot be told apart, and referring to them as "the twins" instead of mentioning each child by name. Helping children establish separate identities is one of the most important parenting challenges we face, and the issue takes on even greater importance for parents of twins.

To guard against the risk of unitizing your twins, make a special effort to spend time alone with each twin on a regular basis and to allow each twin one-to-one time with other siblings as well. Instead of emphasizing the sameness in twins, identify their unique qualities and foster the development of individual talents and interests. Encourage the children to dress differently, style their hair the way they want, be in separate classrooms, or have their own friends if they desire.

Vulnerable Children

Specific children in a family may be emotionally vulnerable at a given point in time for a wide variety of reasons. For example, the excessive attention society lavishes on twins can completely eclipse a brother or sister, making him or her easily subject to feelings of jealousy or inadequacy. In one family, a handicapped child may be made to feel like an unwanted intruder who disrupts everyone's normal routines. In another family, so much activity may revolve around a "special needs" child that the "normal" siblings can end up feeling like displaced persons whose needs don't count. Worse yet, the healthy children may feel guilty for being well, much like survivors of the Holocaust, who were haunted by the fact that they were spared when other members of their family died.

Thus, in addition to birth order and gender, one's childhood can be deeply impacted by one's own or his siblings' particular giftedness or disabilities. It takes tremendous parental insight and effort to effectively meet the specialized needs of one child without making another feel neglected. I am reminded of a little girl I encountered whose older sister had cystic fibrosis. So much daily attention was focused on the ill sister's inhalation therapy, postural drainage, and medications, that the younger girl announced to me matter-of-factly, "I'm not important; I don't have cystic fibrosis." To young children especially, the amount of attention adults give to something is equated with its importance. Thus the "low-maintenance" healthy child had concluded that she was not as special to her parents as her afflicted sister.

Your best guard against such vulnerabilities is to
spend individual time with each child in your family and
to communicate openly about special family circumstances. Avoid labeling your children or assigning them
family roles, like the "problem child," the "scapegoat,"
or the "rescuer." Instead, go out of your way to foster
latent abilities in vulnerable children, to let usually competent children express their deepest needs, and to identify the successes of your difficult children.

Most children will grow up in families where at least
one other sibling is present. Instinctively, they will compete for parental love and attention, jockey for stature
in the unspoken family hierarchy, hurtfully tease one
another, frequently argue, and sometimes fight. Amid
the complexities of sibling interactions, our parenting
challenge is to convey to each child that she is a person
of unique, infinite worth who is irreplaceably important
to us. If this fundamental requirement is met, chances
are that a childhood with siblings will offer invaluable
lessons about mutual regard and respect, practical experience in the successful resolution of differences, creative opportunities to share possessions and pool
resources, and the privilege of realizing the rewards of
lifelong loyalty and friendship.

ADDITIONAL READING:

Ames, Louise Bates, and Haber, Carol Chase. *He Hit
Me First: When Brothers and Sisters Fight*. New
York: Warner Books, 1982.
Faber, Adele, and Mazlish, Elaine. *How to Talk So
Kids Will Listen & Listen So Kids Will Talk*. New
York: Avon Books, 1980.

Faber, Adele, and Mazlish, Elaine. *Siblings Without Rivalry*. New York: Avon Books, 1987.

Leman, Kevin. *The Birth Order Book*. New York: Dell Publishing, 1985.

Novotny, Pamela Patrick. *The Joy of Twins*. New York: Crown Publishers, 1988.

5

UNDERSTANDING MISBEHAVIOR

No other parenting issue generates as much controversy and misunderstanding as the topic of discipline. The very term *discipline* is often misapplied by people using it to refer to punishment given for misbehavior. But discipline really describes the daily modeling, teaching, and shaping of desired behavior in our children. Too often, we oversimplify all of children's misbehavior as "being bad" and assume that any means we employ to get our children to do what we want is synonymous with successful discipline. But misbehavior is far more complex than mere willful disobedience, and effective discipline has far greater value than the immediate goal of coercing children "to act right."

In the years since *Dr. Mom* was first published, I have had the privilege of addressing thousands of parents and being a guest on radio talk shows in many cities across America. Inevitably, once I offer to accept questions from the audience, the primary concern I hear parents express is that of problem behavior in their children. A parent will ask, "What should I do to stop my child from biting the other children at daycare?" I only wish I could offer a simple two-step program to instantly curtail all biting; it would be wonderful if behavior problems could be diagnosed and treated as conveniently as strep throat is identified and eradicated by penicillin. In fact, I often hear parents extol the merits of their favorite method of discipline or punishment, implying that time-out, spanking, grounding, or bribery will work for all children in all situations. But in fact, there are no cookbook answers to discipline problems—no single technique is universally effective.

Instead, a problem like biting must be viewed in the context of a child's developmental stage, the family dynamics, the daycare setting, the child's self-image, and the discipline approaches that already have been tried. The reasons a child misbehaves are highly diverse and developmentally influenced. While a wide variety of effective methods can be used to modify undesirable behavior, it is also true that inappropriate parental responses can actually perpetuate or even escalate the problem behavior.

For example, one child initially may bite another as an uninhibited act of aggression. After he has been told that biting is unacceptable behavior, we simplistically expect him never to bite again. But, the child may continue biting others for a variety of reasons. The secondary gain he achieves by capturing the undivided attention of his adult caretakers may be more important to him than any punishment he receives. Or the patterns of behavior he witnesses daily in his own family may leave him confused about the appropriate use of aggression when dealing with others. He may hear, "Don't you ever bite anyone again!" but also "There, see how much it hurts when I bite you. So, no more biting!" Or the child honestly may not know an acceptable way to behave when he feels angry and frustrated. Perhaps no one has labeled and acknowledged his angry feelings, by saying something like, "You're really mad! You want to play with the toy Deshawn has right now." Perhaps he hasn't been offered an alternative behavior; perhaps no one has said, "Why don't you hammer these pegs as hard as you can until you calm down?" Or offered an alternate solution to the problem: "When the timer goes off in three minutes, it will be your turn to play with the truck."

Not only is misbehavior irritating and frustrating for both parent and child, but its frequency is often a barometer of the quality of their relationship. Few things erode the mutual affection and respect between parents and their children as much as the failure to understand and respond appropriately to perceived misbehavior. Whether they're dealing with tantrums in a two-year-old or a missed curfew in an adolescent, contemporary parents are hungry for guidelines to help modify their children's behavior in a way that enhances their relationship.

In this chapter you will gain a better understanding of why children behave as they do at certain ages and under certain circumstances. You will gain insight into the immediate or secondary motives children can have for misbehaving. In addition, you will examine how your usual response to your child's actions may be contributing to his undesirable behavior. Once you discover that you have at your disposal multiple strategies for dealing with problem behavior, I hope you will begin to feel confident and in control. Most importantly, however, I expect you will come to appreciate that discipline is far more than getting your kids to mind you. Your consistent praising, modeling, teaching, guiding, limiting, and (sparingly) punishing ultimately will form the cornerstone of your child's own self-discipline and self-concept.

Why Bother to Discipline Children?

No matter how you do it, effective discipline is plain hard work—a parental labor of love. The reasons we bother to discipline appropriately range from concern for the personal safety of our child, to societal expectations, to family harmony and our own emotional needs. At the most fundamental level, effective discipline helps protect our child from physical harm. We remove dangerous objects from the environment of our one-year-old and remove the baby physically when he approaches something harmful. We forbid our three-year-old to play in the street, and we don't leave her unsupervised. We teach our six-year-old not to play with matches, and we don't let him come home to an empty house after school. We expect our sixteen-year-old to abide by traffic rules. These firm limits must be nonnegotiable because our child's very life can depend on adhering to them.

We discipline because we want to raise a responsible child who becomes a contributing member of society. We expect our six-year-old to pick up his toys and our thirteen-year-old to feed her rabbit and clean its cage because we know that responsibilities appropriate to a child's age enhance his self-concept. We don't intend to live with and wait on our child for life, and we recognize that teaching him to take increasing responsibility for his own care is essential to subsequent independent living.

We discipline because we want to raise children with a moral sense of right and wrong. We want our children to develop consciences that will allow them to successfully internalize limits for themselves against the time when we are no longer standing over them. For this reason, we make our five-year-old return to the store a candy bar she takes without paying. And we insist that our adolescent repair the neighbor's mailbox that he vandalized, or else buy a new one.

We discipline because we know our children must learn to appreciate the natural consequences of their behavior. Of course, we would never let our two-year-old run into the street in order to discover for herself the dangers of traffic. But we can let our forgetful ten-year-old run out of clean socks in order to learn that Mom will not wash anything that isn't in the clothes hamper. We might not be willing to let our adolescent miss the deadline for his college application just to teach him to complete things on time. But we might decide to convey the same lesson by having him miss a concert he wanted to attend because the event sold out before he tried to buy tickets.

We discipline because we want our children to experience social acceptance, to have good peer relations, and to be a good friend to others. To this end, we refuse to tolerate biting by our three-year-old, and we patiently help him learn to share his toys and to take turns. We require that our ten-year-old use appropriate table manners, we forbid our adolescent to use offensive language, and we expect our high school graduate to write thank-you notes for her gifts.

Quite honestly, I think we also discipline our children because, to some degree, we fear that their behavior is a reflection of our parenting success. We are mortified when our two-year-old has a tantrum at the checkout counter because he wants the gum he sees on the rack. And we cringe when our twelve-year-old talks back to us while the bridge club is meeting at our house. Fortunately, such unpleasant public outbursts are far less likely when parents have made the effort to discipline consistently in private.

Finally, we bother to discipline to preserve our sanity. Whether your child is four or fourteen, incessant whining, provocative teasing, sibling bickering, and manipulative behavior are hard to take. The best way to minimize these common sources of parental stress is to take the time to establish and regularly enforce acceptable limits of behavior.

Why Children Misbehave

Children who misbehave aren't innately "bad." Actually, most children *want* to please their parents and to behave in a socially acceptable manner. But children are like little scientists in a real-world laboratory. They are highly astute observers of cause and effect, and perhaps what children observe most closely is our response to their behavior. Impressionable children then take their cues about how to behave from these careful observations. For example, most parents dislike whining and would prefer to have their child talk to them in a normal tone of voice. The child scientist, however, in conducting his experiments using different voice inflections, has quickly noted that his parents often withhold their attention when he speaks normally. On the contrary, as soon as he starts whining, his mother stops what she is doing and gives him her undivided attention, loudly lamenting, "What do you want now? I can't stand that whining voice." The little scientist's conclusion: "Grown-ups *claim* they don't like to hear whining, but they listen better when I use a whiny voice."

With this example in mind, let's take a look below the surface of a child's misbehavior and identify some common motivators for children's undesirable actions. Behaviors we are quick to label as "inappropriate" may, when examined from a child's point of view, actually represent highly appropriate means of achieving a desired goal. Bill and Kathy Kvols-Riedler, in their excellent and practical discipline guide, *Redirecting Children's Misbehavior*, outline four misdirected goals that account for a great deal of childhood misbehavior.

The Goal of Attention

Many parents make the mistake of taking good behavior for granted. Their child gets no attention for playing quietly, sharing, going to bed on time, meeting their curfew, or doing their chores. Parental acknowledgments, comments, and actions are reserved for the occasional misdeed. But a child's craving for parental attention is so great that many youngsters actually prefer to take the consequences of overtly negative attention to being ignored.

Look at the world from the perspective of three-year-old Suzie for a moment. She has been playing quietly in her room, looking at picture books for nearly an hour. During this time, her mother has been on the telephone, scheduling appointments, talking to friends, and tending to personal matters. "Read me a story," Suzie implores a couple of times, to which her mother curtly replies, "Can't you see I'm on the phone?" From a three-year-old's point of view, it looks like Mommy would rather give her undivided attention to a relative stranger on the telephone, while ignoring her own daughter in the next room.

Without apparent provocation, Suzie starts ripping pages from her books and throwing them. Her mother abruptly ends her conversation with "Gotta go. Suzie's destroying her books." Then, face-to-face and undistracted, Mommy lectures Suzie about taking good care of her toys and threatens not to buy any more books. When Suzie starts to cry, Mommy feels bad and gives her a hug. "I know you didn't mean it. Here, I'll read you a story if you'll promise to be good." Meanwhile,

Suzie scientist has deduced: "If I do something naughty, Mommy stops talking on the phone. I might get yelled at, but it's worth it in the end when Mommy spends time with me."

A teenage girl, Pam, typically earned A's and B's on her report card. While she was an excellent student with a fine record, Pam felt her parents paid little attention to her grades in comparison to those of an older brother who was a straight-A student and class valedictorian. When Pam got a D in advanced math as a junior in high school, her parents were shocked and disappointed. They both sat and talked with her at length about her poor grade. They scheduled a joint meeting with the math teacher, her counselor, and the school principal to discuss Pam's unexplained difficulties in math. "You know, Mom," Pam casually observed, "you've given me more attention for this D in math than for all the A's and B's I earned this whole year."

The Goal of Control

An excessively authoritarian discipline style can leave a child feeling overly controlled. Such parents make consistently broad commands like "Do it and don't ask questions," or "Because I say so is reason enough!" Traumatic life circumstances that are beyond a child's control, such as parental divorce or a move, can also exaggerate a child's sense of being powerless. As a result of feeling so impotent, a child may outwardly rebel and try to regain some control over his environment by manipulating his parents' behavior.

Misbehavior based on the need for power and control is especially common around the age of two and during adolescence when separation and individuation issues are naturally more prominent. In young children, power struggles commonly emerge around feeding issues. The toddler who cooperatively opened his mouth like a little bird awaiting every bite of solid food at eight months of age now tightly clenches his jaw at eighteen months of age, while his anxious, captive parents try to cajole him to accept a bite. I've seen baby scientists as young as nine months of age discover that they can influence their parents' behavior powerfully at feeding times. In adolescence, these power struggles often center around issues like hairstyles, curfews, clothes, and the parents' need for their teen to have a clean room.

The Goal of Revenge

Many children have a highly developed sense of justice. When they are punished arbitrarily or excessively, or when their feelings are hurt or they are made to feel unloved, they may try to retaliate by hurting us back. They may not even be aware that their misbehavior is an attempt to lash out at us and make us feel as rotten as they already feel about themselves. Whenever you feel particularly wounded by your child's behavior, consider that he may be feeling especially hurt himself and may be trying to get revenge. For example, a three-year-old who is severely scolded and sent to his room for the remainder of the afternoon for spilling his milk at lunchtime may, while confined to the room, get out his crayons and color all over his walls.

The Goal of Avoidance

Sometimes children, particularly those who suffer from low self-concept, will refuse to cooperate with your requests or participate at an expected level of performance. They often whine, speak in a quiet voice, deny their capabilities, and generally emphasize their helplessness. They might insist that they just "can't" clean their room or "can't" do a homework assignment alone. As a result, the adults responsible for such children may feel compelled to rescue them, saying "Here, let me do that for you. I guess you're just not old enough." Although this outcome will satisfy the child's immediate goal of avoiding responsibility and any personal risks, it also reinforces his self-perception of being woefully inadequate. Children who misbehave to avoid being challenged ultimately may adopt the attitude that it is better not to try something at all than to try and fail to perform it perfectly. I suspect that some children become withdrawn like this and develop a self-fulfilling prophecy about their own inadequacy after having been told repeatedly by perfectionistic parents, older siblings, or domineering peers that they "can't do something well enough."

Inappropriate Parental Expectations for Age

I find it outright alarming how little some parents know about normal child development. We don't allow people to drive a car without requiring that they possess a minimum knowledge of traffic rules. A cosmetologist can't cut your hair without being trained and licensed to do so. Despite admirable claims that parenting is the most important job we'll ever do, there are no educational prerequisites for parenthood. In my opinion, if child development were made part of the core curricula for high school students, the next generation of parents would be far better equipped for their role.

It is my personal bias that parental perception of childhood misbehavior is often related to ignorance about appropriate developmental expectations for a child. In fact, parental anger that erupts in a violent rage and leads to child abuse often can be attributed to inexperience about normal childhood behavior. For example, many abusive parents have voiced the tragically mistaken belief that an inconsolable infant should be able to stop crying on command. And many toddlers have been abused following routine toilet training accidents that parents have viewed as deliberate misbehavior.

Similarly, a parent may misinterpret the tantrum thrown at the checkout counter by two-year-old Amanda as being blatant, rebellious misbehavior. More likely, Amanda has been dragged along on a marathon shopping trip so her mother can complete her busy agenda for the day. By the time she explodes in a tantrum, Amanda is probably tired, hungry, frustrated, and bored far beyond the normal endurance of a two-year-old. At this point, while Amanda already feels badly about losing control, her exasperated mother may compound the situation further by spanking, yelling, labeling Amanda a "bad girl," or threatening "I'll never take you to the store again." In retrospect, the most sensible thing would have been to leave a two-year-old home with a babysitter while her mother ran errands all day. Or, if Amanda were going to accompany her, the mother might have broken the trip into shorter excursions. She also might have scheduled the outing after Amanda's nap and brought along some snacks and toys to distract her when she became restless.

Strategies for Preventing Misbehavior

Now that we have identified some of the underlying reasons why children misbehave, I will outline multiple strategies for promoting desirable behavior in children and minimizing misbehavior.

Foster Your Child's Self-Esteem

Chapter 3, "You and Your Child's Self-Esteem," emphasizes the critical importance of helping your child develop a positive self-concept and assuring him of your unconditional love and acceptance. Children who feel good about themselves have parents who seldom struggle with discipline issues, whereas problem behavior is a common manifestation of poor self-esteem. The techniques that follow explain why positive discipline tactics will enhance a child's self-image, while inappropriate methods only erode self-concept further.

Do your best to devote at least twenty minutes each day to each of your children. The time should be spent one-to-one, during which you should give your child your focused, or undivided, attention. Listen attentively while maintaining eye contact. Respond empathetically to any concerns your child voices, and validate his feelings of sadness, anger, jealousy, and so on by acknowledging and accepting them. Don't just assume your child knows you love him; regularly tell him and offer daily physical evidence of your love by touching, patting, hugging, or kissing your child.

Try hard never to link your child's character or worth to misbehavior, regardless of how angry or upset he has made you. Avoid saying "Johnny, you're such a bad boy! Just look what you did! You make me so angry." Instead, let him know that while you detest his behavior, you still love him unconditionally. Explain that what makes you angry is not him, but rather his actions. Use "I" statements to describe how the behavior makes you feel instead of "you" statements that malign his person: "I get so upset when my possessions get broken by carelessness," instead of "You just make me furious when you throw toys and break my things."

Maintain Age-Appropriate Expectations

As already emphasized, make an effort to become as informed as possible about the expected behavior of children at different ages. Avoid derogatory labels that generalize about your child, such as the "terrible twos" or the "terrible teens." It's easy for such descriptions to evolve into self-fulfilling prophecies. Make allowances for some regressive behavior during times of stress, such as the birth of a sibling, a move, or parental divorce.

Establish Clear Limits and Provide Explanations

Most children thrive on structure, routines, and schedules. Appropriate limits are an essential part of the orderly structure in a child's life. Clear limits offer a measure of security and predictability to a child, whose increasing autonomy is alternately gratifying and frightening. Unfortunately, many parents falsely conclude that children dislike limits, simply because they test them so often. In reality, a major reason children repeatedly test our rules is because they seek frequent reassurance that we are prepared to enforce established limits. It can be especially disturbing for young children to experience doubt about their parents' ability to exercise control.

Limits shouldn't be arbitrary or constantly in a state of flux. Children should not be left to guess what the rules are today. Instead, the limits should be clear and consistent. In addition, children should be told the rationale behind each limit. This will help children view parental limits less as personal impediments or restrictive burdens and more as protective, loving guidelines designed to enhance and enrich their lives.

One day recently, I was addressing a group of children, ranging in age from preschoolers to fifth graders. I asked the youngsters to tell me about the kinds of rules their parents made for them. I was pleasantly surprised when most of the children voluntarily cited an explanation along with the rule they chose to mention:

"You can't run in the house, or else you might trip and fall and cut your head like I did. See this scar!" exclaimed a four-year-old advocate of the "no running" rule, brushing back her bangs to show me the visible reminder of a parental limit that made good sense to her.

"I can't turn on the stove unless my mom is in the kitchen," offered a ten-year-old girl who was learning to cook, "because I might cause a fire or burn myself."

"You have to pick up your toys, or else someone might accidentally step on them and break them," explained a five-year-old boy, sounding like he had experienced at least one crushed toy.

"You can't play in the street, because you might get runned over by a car," recited a three-year-old. "And don't talk to strangers!" he added with emphasis.

As children mature, it is important to obtain their input and to establish mutually agreeable, realistic limits. Adolescents, especially, detest arbitrary, overly strict rules. Comments like "Because I said so" and "You'll do as I say as long as you live in this house" only invite conflict and power struggles. When your adolescent has mutually agreed on a reasonable curfew for weeknights, weekends, and special events like the prom, he is far more likely to adhere to his commitments.

Enforce Limits Consistently

Establishing appropriate limits is clearly important, but most parents would agree that consistently enforcing them is a whole lot harder. While our intentions are often admirable, our physical stamina and emotional reserve can vary widely from day to day or even hour to hour. For example, at the end of a hectic day, a fatigued parent might be too depleted to enforce limits consistently, finding it easier to tolerate misbehavior momentarily than to utilize effective discipline techniques with regularity.

In the long run, however, frequent lapses in consistent discipline only encourage children to challenge their limits more often. If a football referee only randomly imposed a penalty whenever he observed "holding," how long do you think it would take before both teams were "holding" with increased frequency? Some parents discipline so inconsistently that their children never fully grasp the "rules of the game." Thus, they resort to provocative parental testing in a frustrated attempt to clarify the ground rules. The more consistently you are able to enforce limits, even when your resistance is down, the less often your children will challenge your rules.

A common time when parental defenses are down occurs at the end of the workday. If you recognize that you are especially tired at that time and your kids are wound up, try to plan ahead to prevent and deal with misbehavior. Begin by minimizing the stresses on yourself and conserving your energy for consistent disciplining. Perhaps you can stop and buy fast food instead of starting to cook when you get home. Don't talk on the phone at length, letting your kids get away with behavior you normally don't allow. Put a favorite children's movie in the VCR or calm them down by playing a board game with them. Remind yourself that taking the time to respond consistently even when you don't feel like it will pay off in the long run.

"Catch 'Em Being Good" *Positive Reinforcement*

One of the best ways to reinforce desirable behavior in your child is simply to offer liberal praise whenever he is acting the way you would like. In essence, you "catch 'em being good" and offer praise and attention for the desirable behavior: "Esther, I like to see you playing so quietly while Davie takes his nap." In addition to verbal compliments, a moment of attention or a physical reward like a hug, nod, or smile will have the same positive effect of promoting more of the desired behavior. This technique is especially effective for those children who misbehave because of the misdirected motive of gaining parental attention.

Despite the confirmed effectiveness and simplicity of this discipline principle, most parents mistakenly take the exact *opposite* approach to their child's behavior. They tend to take for granted desirable behavior, and essentially ignore the child while they are "being good." Instead, they respond to misbehavior and, in effect, give their children attention for the undesirable behavior.

143

Reward

The use of positive consequences, or rewards, represents one of the most effective means of motivating a
person to repeat desirable behavior, yet too few parents
discipline by regularly rewarding their children for good
behavior. Instead, most parents control their children's
actions by overusing negative consequences for misbehavior. Rewarding good behavior will foster your
child's self-esteem and improve your relationship with
him, while excessive use of punishment and focusing
on misbehavior only tends to erode your child's self-
concept and damage your relationship.

A reward can be any kind of compensation your child
receives for good behavior, ranging from a compliment,
smile, hug, favorite activity, to food, gum, candy, to-
ken, toy, or money. For the reward to be maximally
effective, it must be given as soon after the appropriate
behavior as possible. A reward can be either spontaneously offered or specifically promised. For example,
you can simply "catch 'em being good" and praise, hug,
and cuddle your child for his polite behavior in a restaurant. In fact, parental social rewards such as verbal
praise, focused attention, and physical closeness are
among the most powerful motivators of all. Offering
your child your full attention when she talks without
whining is a very effective means of spontaneously rewarding non-whining.

Rewards can also be promised incentives to be given
after specific behavior occurs. For example, you might
offer to reward your child by taking him to the swimming pool if he first cleans his room. In general, the
younger the child, the more essential it is for the reward
to be presented at the time the desirable behavior is
observed. Promising to read your two-year-old a story
immediately after he picks up all his toys will be more
effective than telling him you will take him to the play-

ground next weekend. As children grow older, they can begin to postpone gratification and accept future rewards for present behavior or to accept immediate tokens, like stars on a chart, that can be traded for rewards at a later date. Thus, a five-year-old might receive daily stars for completing her chores and then each week receive a cash reward based on her accumulated stars. Or a ten-year-old might be promised a new baseball glove at the end of the month if he agrees to mow the lawn each week.

Even as adults, we continue to respond to social incentives and tangible rewards. We faithfully may save something from every paycheck in order to take a long-awaited vacation in the tropics next winter. Or we might agree to work late on a big project at the office, either for the concrete promise of overtime pay, or simply to receive a coveted compliment from our boss and a letter of commendation in our personnel file. Similarly, school-aged children will work hard on their assignments, both for the personal satisfaction that comes with earning a good grade, as well as for the parental approval that usually accompanies academic achievement.

Parents often confuse bribes with rewards. A reward is an incentive given for desirable behavior; it's something your child can work toward and feel proud of. A bribe is an advance payoff given either to produce desired behavior or to stop or prevent misbehavior. The crucial difference is that a bribe is given *before* the desired behavior, as when you say, "I'll let you sit next to your friend if you agree not to talk in class." Chances are, the two friends will talk plenty. Bribes given in advance are always less effective than either positive or negative reinforcement that is closely linked to the behavior. For example, once I couldn't find my car keys. "I'll give you fifty cents to help me look for my car keys," I told one of the kids, who gladly accepted the money but didn't look with much enthusiasm. I ended up finding the keys myself and my own search was positively reinforced right away when I was able to drive off where I wanted to go.

When bribes are used to prevent negative behavior— "I'll let you have hot chocolate this morning if you promise not to act up on the bus today"—they place the emphasis on the offensive behavior to be avoided instead of on the desired behavior to be repeated. Whenever you are tempted to use a bribe, ask yourself if there isn't a way to apply positive reinforcement or a reward instead.

Offer Choices Whenever Possible

Often misbehavior represents a power struggle or control issue between parent and child. Such misbehavior can be minimized by giving children age-appropriate control in the form of limited choices. Allowing your three-year-old to choose between having grape or apple juice for breakfast, wearing his yellow or blue shirt, and bringing along his stuffed bear or raccoon may avert a tantrum later in the day when he has to leave the playground against his will. Similarly, your adolescent will be more likely to honor your mutually agreed-upon curfew and complete the chores you've negotiated if she is allowed to pick her own clothes and hairstyle and keep her room the way she wants.

Strategies for Dealing with Misbehavior

Despite your best efforts, all children inevitably will display some problem behaviors from time to time. The following techniques will help you successfully deal with misbehavior when it occurs. Since no single discipline method is universally effective in all circumstances, it should be reassuring to know that you have at your disposal a wide variety of acceptable options to minimize and modify misbehavior. These and other effective discipline techniques are elaborated in Charles Schaefer and Theresa DiGeronimo's helpful book *Teach Your Child to Behave*.

Ignore Misbehavior

A companion technique to praising desired behavior is ignoring misbehavior, especially when you suspect that the motive behind the misbehavior is to gain the parents' attention. Ignoring works best when employed against negative behaviors such as teasing, whining, verbal arguments, cajoling, throwing tantrums, breathholding, swearing, acting silly, or crying. When your child engages in these irritating activities, do not acknowledge him verbally, visually, or by body gestures or grimaces. Simply go about your business without giving any indication that you are affected by his comments or actions. You may need to turn up the radio or TV, play a tape, place a phone call, or go into the bathroom and read (if your child is old enough to be left unsupervised).

Be prepared for the likelihood that the incidence of misbehavior will temporarily increase before it decreases, since your child will probably escalate the activity at first to see whether she can get your attention for it. Consistency and perseverance on your part will soon convince your child that the misbehavior no longer has an effect on you. The technique of ignoring is most effective when it is coupled with frequent compliments for the desired alternate behavior.

Of course, you should never ignore dangerous behavior in your child, such as physically harming her sibling, playing with matches, teasing the dog, or running with a lollypop in her mouth. The technique of ignoring is also inappropriate for misbehavior that provides obvious secondary gain, such as stealing money from your purse, sneaking candy without permission, taking toys from a sibling, or coming home after curfew.

Use Natural Consequences.

Another highly effective discipline technique is letting your child experience the natural consequences of his undesirable behavior. Many parents are convinced that they must protect their child from bad decisions and unpleasant consequences. This belief system gets easily ingrained early in our parenting, as we appropriately rescue our young child from physical harm. We may warn him repeatedly about electrical hazards, but we would never think of deliberately letting him experience an electrical shock just to reinforce our admonitions. Instead, we diligently protect him from such physical harm, while continuing to use verbal cautions. This is not to imply, however, that it is our parental duty to protect our child from all negative life experiences. On the contrary, as children mature, they can benefit immensely from experiencing increasing levels of physical and emotional discomfort that arise as a direct consequence of their own behavior.

Nothing teaches us as powerfully as experience itself, and life inevitably includes some negative outcomes that result from inappropriate behavior. Some of the most valuable lessons our children will ever learn will derive from natural consequences. To allow our children some of these valuable experiences, we must learn to restrain the powerful parental urge to rescue them. Experiencing natural outcomes of bad decisions and feeling some measure of discomfort today may well protect our child from a devastating life experience in the future. For example, an adolescent who has just obtained his driver's license may get behind the wheel of his car with a sense of indestructibility and unrestrained freedom. Getting in a minor fender-bender or being stopped by a police officer for a traffic violation might provide an effective lesson on how quickly and unexpectedly a motor vehicle accident can occur and how easily one can lose the privilege of driving. Letting the teen pay the car repair expenses or traffic fine himself will make it more likely that he will respect traffic rules in the future.

Natural consequences should never be used if they put your child or another person in physical jeopardy or involve gross insensitivity to one's feelings. A mother eagle may push her fledgling out of the nest to teach him to soar on his own, but if he is not yet ready for flight, she will always rescue him before he crashes to the ground. Letting a youngster go hungry at noontime if she forgets her lunch money might be an appropriate natural consequence for a healthy child, but it would be both inappropriate and medically dangerous for a diabetic child.

The punishment incurred through natural consequences should be sufficient to convey the lesson in point, without the need to levy further punishment. For example, ten-year-old Fred was required to pick up the neighbor's trash that was ripped open and scattered by Duke, because Fred was the person who let Duke out of the yard on trash day. When twelve-year-old Katie absentmindedly set her purse down in a store and later found it had disappeared, her mother sincerely empathized with Katie's financial loss, but decided it was best not to replace her missing money. Katie's mother had reminded her on numerous past occasions to guard her purse and recognized that Katie needed to experience the consequences of her carelessness. By losing the money she had been saving to buy a sweater, Katie learned a valuable lesson that ultimately taught her to better protect her personal property throughout her life. Had her mother felt compelled to rescue Katie by replacing all her lost funds, she may have robbed Katie of a major learning experience.

Seventeen-year-old Kristi received a car from her father, with the stipulation that she would be required to pay for insurance, license plates, gas, and maintenance. Kristi began saving money to pay for her license plate renewal, but she underestimated the magnitude of this expense. Furthermore, just before the renewal deadline, she saw a pair of shoes she wanted and bought the shoes, using some of her designated car funds. When she was short on funds to pay for her license plates, she appealed to her father to make up the difference. Instead, he elected to enforce the terms of his original agreement with Kristi. He let the plates expire and grounded Kristi from driving until she was able to pay the renewal fee on her own. In the meantime, Kristi almost lost her part-time job because she lacked dependable transportation. Thereafter, she carefully budgeted money for her car expenses before she bought clothing or personal items.

Offer Warnings

Many children who overstep a limit will respond promptly to a simple warning. Warnings are most effective among younger children, who will often abort misbehavior after being reminded about a particular rule and the consequences of breaking it; "Shayna, I've told you not to hit your truck with your wooden hammer. If you do it one more time, I'm putting the hammer away for the rest of the day." Such brief warnings can work well to interrupt undesirable behavior, thus eliminating the need for more elaborate and time-consuming disciplinary measures, like time-out. For young children, the threatened consequence should occur promptly in relation to the misbehavior, but as children mature, your warnings can refer to more remote consequences, as when you say, "Matt, I'm reminding you that if you miss your curfew again this week, you'll be grounded the whole weekend and not allowed to attend the concert on Saturday."

To be effective, a warning must be specific in nature, and you must be absolutely willing to carry through with the consequences it promises. Don't resort to shouting, getting angry, or becoming emotional. Rather, articulate in a matter-of-fact tone the familiar limit and the outcome of continued misbehavior: "Ricky, I'm warning you, if you hit Bobby again, we're leaving his house and going straight home."

Although most parents use warnings regularly, too few apply them appropriately. Instead, we often threaten in anger, exaggerate grossly, and fail to be specific. "Just wait until your father comes home; you'll be sorry then" is an inappropriate warning because the consequence is nonspecific and too delayed. Exaggerated threats like "Knock that off right now, or you'll wish you never were born!" or "Do that again and you're grounded for life!" are seldom effective because children quickly learn that you do not really intend to carry out the promised consequence. And "I'm warning you, that's the last straw!" is vague and often meaningless to a child.

In reality, enforcing a warning may seem more inconvenient to you at times than to your child. One parent, for instance, said, "Courtney, you know you're not allowed to throw sand. If you do it one more time, we're leaving the beach and returning to our hotel room." At the moment, it may seem easier to keep on warning Courtney and to give him second and third chances than to pack up your things and leave the beach. However, your prompt compliance with the terms of the warning will quickly convince Courtney that you mean what you say. In the long run, your whole vacation is likely to go smoother than if you remain on the beach voicing periodic idle threats, such as "I really mean it this time, Courtney"; "This is the last time I'm telling you"; "We're never coming back here if you don't shape up"; "You're really going to get it next time."

Consider the common scenario of siblings being disruptive in the car. Eight-year-old Cody and ten-year-old Tyler were loudly bickering in the backseat while their mother was driving them to baseball practice. Initially, they seemed oblivious to their mother's exasperated emotional outbursts: "If you two don't knock it off, I'm going to drive into a tree!" or "I swear I'm never taking you anywhere again if you don't stop that incessant fighting!"

When the boys' mother remembered how to formulate an appropriate warning, she calmly announced: "If you don't stop your fighting within fifteen seconds, I'm going to turn the car around and drive back home. You realize if you miss practice today, your coach won't start you in Saturday's game. I'm counting now . . . one, two, three, four . . ." Cody and Tyler were so stunned at their mother's uncharacteristic announcement that they looked at each other and immediately fell silent. Her warning was highly specific and was stated deliberately, leading them to suspect that she had every intention of carrying it out.

Scold

Verbal scolding is one of the most widely used penalties for misbehavior. A scolding is very similar to a warning, except that a scolding takes a little longer because it should include an explanation about why the misbehavior is undesirable to the parent. In addition, a scolding offers a substitute appropriate behavior.

When used appropriately, a scolding can be both effective and instructional. Far too often, however, scoldings are delivered inappropriately and contribute to undermining children's self-esteem, while doing little to enhance desired behavior. The most common error parents make when scolding is to link their child's whole person or character with their misbehavior, saying, for instance, "Shame on you, Jared, you're such a bad boy. Only bad boys throw food on the floor." Inflicting shame and heaping excessive guilt on children can be highly destructive to their self-esteem and emotional development. Don't scold by shaming, using phrases like "Shame on you," "You should be ashamed of yourself," or "I'm so ashamed of you." Instead, when scolding, the emphasis should always be on the undesirable behavior, not the child. Thus, you say, "Hitting people is bad"; "It's wrong to take things that don't belong to you"; "Swearing isn't polite." Or you can simply state the unacceptable behavior that must be corrected without passing judgment: "Don't throw rocks." "Put your brother's game down." "Quit splashing water."

Other common scolding errors are to verbally chastise a child for a protracted period of time. Children have short attention spans. At best, a lengthy verbal assault will be ignored; at worst it will erode your child's self-esteem and breed resentment toward you. Effective scoldings are not measured by duration; they are characterized by brevity.

Begin by stating the misbehavior; then offer an explanation for the limit: "Leave the dog alone; I'm afraid he might bite you." Whenever possible, do this with an "I" message that diverts attention away from your child's negative behavior and onto your own reaction to the behavior. In a fit of anger, we are tempted to blurt out something like "Shame on you for coloring on the walls, Buck. You know better than that. You make me so furious when you ruin our walls." Instead, take a deep breath and pause a few seconds to think about how to phrase your scolding more effectively and sensitively. Try something like "Don't color on the walls, Buck. I get angry when I see crayon marks spoiling our nicely painted walls because it means a lot of work for me to clean off the marks."

Continue the scolding by enforcing the established consequence of the misbehavior: "You know the rule; when you color on the wall—you have to help me wash it off and you can't use your crayons for the rest of the day." Or you can decide to issue a warning with your scolding: "Don't drive the car over the newspaper again, Shawn. It makes me angry to find the paper torn up because I can barely read it. If you run over the paper again, I'll ask you to walk to the corner newsstand and buy me another paper, and you won't be allowed to drive our car for the rest of the day."

An effective scolding is not complete without offering an alternate acceptable behavior, such as "Buck, I expect you to color in your coloring books," or "Shawn, I expect you to pick up the newspaper before backing the car out of the driveway." Be sure to scold with clarity, so that your child understands the undesired behavior, the consequences that will be levied, and the expected substitute behavior. Finally, end the scolding on a positive note, with a compliment, hug, smile, or other affirmation of your continuing affection for your child.

Putting the whole sequence together, an effective

brief scolding might sound like this, "Mark, do not stop at someone's house to play on your way home from school. I worry about your safety when you aren't home on time, and I don't like spending my afternoons trying to locate you. The next time you aren't home by three-thirty, you won't be allowed to play outside our yard for the rest of the week. If you want to play with a friend after school, I expect you to report home first and ask my permission. Are you clear about what time I expect you home and what will happen if you are late again? Thanks, Mark. I appreciate your cooperation."

Time-Out

In recent years, the use of time-out for misbehavior has gained widespread popularity, particularly among parents of preschoolers, as an effective, nonviolent alternative to spanking. Time-out involves briefly removing a misbehaving child to a quiet, subdued setting where he can regain control of his behavior.

Because a young child's attention span is so short, time-out must be implemented as soon as the undesirable behavior occurs. It should not be viewed as a delayed punishment, like after-school detention; you don't want to find yourself saying, "This evening you're going to sit in time-out for half an hour! That ought to teach you a lesson." By evening, your child won't even remember his afternoon antics. Rather, time-out represents an immediate and compassionate means of helping a disruptive child regain his composure. It allows both parent and child to cool off, calm down, and start over in their interactions.

A good rule of thumb for time-out is one minute for each year of age. Leaving a child in time-out for prolonged periods does no more to improve behavior than brief time-out; it only causes a child to forget why she is being punished and to feel resentful, inviting subsequent misbehavior for the misguided motive of revenge. Set a timer for the appropriate number of minutes. If your child repeatedly asks you how much longer, emphasize that the buzzer will go off when three minutes are up. Your child will be more likely to accept the objective limits imposed by an impersonal timer than your seemingly more arbitrary regulation of his confinement.

Your child's time-out chair should be conveniently located, but removed from the mainstream of activity, creating a sense of relative isolation. His bedroom is not a suitable location, as a child's bedroom should be a sanctuary for him, not a site of punishment. Kitchens and bathrooms pose too many hazards to a child's safety, and scary places are definitely not suitable. Because time-out should represent temporary loss of freedom, it's important not to let your child read a book, watch TV, or play with a toy while in time-out.

I often hear parents complain that they have tried time-out but had to give it up because their child would not stay seated in his time-out chair. At first, you may need to stand near your child during time-out. Every time he gets up before the timer goes off, escort him back to his chair. Try not to create a big fuss or react in such a way that you reward your child with your attention. Be prepared to return him to the time-out chair dozens of times if necessary, without getting angry or emotional. Once he learns you have every intention of *consistently* enforcing this limit, he will stop getting up.

Time-out is not meant to be used as your sole disciplinary technique. You shouldn't use time-out for every infraction, and your child shouldn't have to go to time-out several times every hour. Instead, pick a few problem behaviors, particularly ones that infringe on the rights of others. Time-out in isolation is an especially appropriate punishment for antisocial behavior, since it requires a child to leave her family or friends when her behavior is unacceptable and allows her to rejoin the others once she can control her impulses. Thus, time-out is well-suited to abort disruptive behavior like temper tantrums, biting, kicking, hitting, breaking things, or calling people names. On the other hand, time-out isn't very effective when used to threaten a child in order to get her to do something: "Get in the car right now, or you'll sit in time-out."

Loss of Privileges

Another type of penalty that can be used to modify offensive behavior is loss of a privilege. When the punishment is logically matched to the specific infraction, loss of privileges can be both instructional and effective in curtailing undesirable behavior. Punishments should never be levied in anger or revenge; instead, the purpose of punishment should be to teach a lesson and to shape behavior.

To a young child, time-out represents a temporary loss of the privilege of freedom. Grounding, which is an extension of loss of freedom, is a commonly applied penalty for various abuses of freedom in older children, like going somewhere without permission, missing a curfew, sneaking out of the house at night, or taking the car without asking. But just as time-out should not be used for all misbehavior in a young child, grounding should not be the only form of punishment used for an adolescent. Yet I know parents who ground their children for every violation, from forgetting to take the garbage out to failing a subject in school. I think punishments make the most sense to children and seem most fair when they directly relate them to the "crime."

It is also important that penalties not be too severe.

Grounding for months at a time or losing TV privileges for a semester, or shelving a skateboard indefinitely can make a youngster feel hopeless and deeply resentful.

Remember that the ultimate purpose of discipline is to enable a child to internalize limits and learn to behave in an acceptable way even when no one is around to enforce the limits. Excessive punishment breeds resentment and actually provokes a child to rebel more.

In the real world, the penalties we incur for offenses often are quite logical ones: if I miss payments on my car, the vehicle will be repossessed; if I drive while under the influence of alcohol, I will lose my license; if I commit fraud on my income tax statement, I will pay back taxes plus a penalty and interest; if I am frequently late to work, I will lose my job, and so on. Parents can help prepare children for responsible adulthood by imposing logical penalties. Thus, if Joey consistently fails to feed his rabbit, we can return it to the pet store. If Robin rides her bike in the street, she can lose the privilege of riding her bike for the rest of the day. If Pat and Jason keep fighting over which TV program to watch, the TV can be turned off for the next hour. If Cindy is cited for speeding after getting her driver's license, she can be required to pay the fine for the ticket and be restricted from driving for a week. If Brian misses an agreed-upon curfew, he can be grounded the following weekend. If Danny fails his first semester of college because he is partying all the time, his parents can refuse to pay further college costs until he makes the semester up at his own expense.

Many parents believe that every offense requires a penalty and that misbehavior is not resolved until a punishment has been levied. As already discussed, however, sometimes the natural consequences of a child's behavior will be punishment enough. For example, ten-year-old Kip was warned not to tease the neighbor's dog. He disobeyed and received a painful bite, necessitating a visit to the emergency room and a tetanus booster. At first his parents considered grounding Kip to "teach him a lesson." Upon reconsidering the matter, they agreed that there was no point to imposing any loss of privileges on an already traumatic experience. Instead they discussed with Kip the real dangers of approaching and teasing strange dogs.

Making Restitution

One of the most logical punishments of all is to require a child to make restitution, whether by apologizing for rude behavior or paying for damaged property. This type of penalty is very effective in teaching children about the effects of their behavior on the rights of other people. Apologies can be very humbling experiences, but most children will feel better about themselves after making things right with another person. Requiring children to make restitution can be likened to the adult practice of performing court-mandated community service. Frankly, I think children are benefited greatly whenever they are required to consider the rights and feelings of others.

About Spanking

No discussion of discipline would be complete without commenting on the sensitive issue of spanking. The older I get, the more convinced I am that spanking is not only an ineffective form of discipline, but an insensitive, illogical, and destructive practice. No matter how you disguise it, spanking is an excuse for a large adult to hit a small child. It is the only circumstance in our culture where hitting another person is socially acceptable.

Because spanking is often done in anger, it creates a potentially explosive situation. Thousands of times each year, spanking escalates to the outright physical abuse of children who are powerless to protect themselves.

Spanking profiles an inappropriate way for a child to vent their own anger. Even when no physical harm occurs, spanking can inflict emotional harm on a child and cause damage to a child's self-esteem. It is degrading, frightening, and enraging to be struck by another person. Children who are often hit by their parents will reflexively duck when they misbehave, assuming someone will slug them. They also mimic their parents' behavior by hitting their dolls and their playmates.

Instead of teaching a logical lesson, spanking is highly confusing to many children when physical violence is used to correct aggressive behavior, as in (Smack) "Don't you ever pull your little sister's hair again," and (Whop) "I told you not to bite people." Much of the material presented in this chapter has focused on modeling and encouraging desired behavior, treating your child with respect, aborting misbehavior with sensitivity, and using consequences that make sense. The next time you are tempted to spank your child, stop and ask yourself just what message you want to convey and whether physical punishment is the best means to modify your child's misbehavior. Can you think of even one circumstance where physical punishment would naturally guide a child to choose acceptable behavior over misbehavior?

Finally, ask yourself how you would feel if you ever lost control and inflicted permanent physical harm on your child. As long as spanking remains part of your discipline repertoire, a very real risk exists that you could lose control and hurt your child. No one who hits their child is ever immune from the possibility of hitting too hard. It can happen to anyone. My message is simple: if you don't ever hit, you won't ever hit too hard!

Most people who spank do so because they are frustrated and can't think of a better way to manage their child's behavior. My hope is that the information presented in this chapter will give you a variety of effective discipline techniques that will not only encourage acceptable behavior in your child, but enhance your mutual relationship and self-esteem.

Attention-Deficit Hyperactivity Disorder (ADHD).

Although the discipline techniques outlined in this chapter are effective for most children, a significant number of youngsters have Attention-Deficit Hyperactivity Disorder (ADHD), which causes them to be more active, impulsive, and inattentive than others. ADHD is one of the most common developmental disorders of childhood, with boys being affected several times more frequently than girls. It has been estimated that two to five percent of school-age children have ADHD, causing them to have some of the following problems: restlessness, fidgetiness, poor concentration, distractibility, impulsivity, disorganization, disruptive behavior, emotional immaturity, and non-compliance. In some instances, these characteristics can result in a constant state of family disruption and a daily struggle to maintain discipline.

A parent of an ADHD child might easily assume their youngster is being willfully non-compliant. In fact, the child may be unable to comply with parental expectations because of a limited capacity to control his easy distractibility and impulsive behavior. Parents need special understanding, extra patience, and specific techniques to assist them in improving the behavior of a child with ADHD.

161

Fortunately, sixty to eighty percent of ADHD children are helped by stimulant medications, such as Ritalin or Dexedrine, which have been shown to improve attention span and to decrease impulsiveness and hyperactivity. Behavior-modification programs supervised by a pediatric psychologist or developmental pediatrician also can be very helpful in controlling the behavior of young children with ADHD.

If you suspect your child might have ADHD, share your concerns with his teachers and his pediatrician. Standardized-behavior rating scales, which allow parents and teachers to compare a child's behavior with that of normal children the same age and sex, can be helpful in making the diagnosis of ADHD. Children who grow up with unrecognized and untreated ADHD are at great risk for low self-esteem, poor peer relations, and unsatisfactory school performance. Early recognition, coupled with parental information and support, special educational strategies, behavior-modification techniques, and medication can greatly improve the outcome for children with ADHD.

Children Without a Conscience

In a chapter on children's misbehavior, I would be remiss if I didn't acknowledge that a few children suffer such serious psychological pathology that their behavior cannot be controlled by any of the techniques just described. Dr. Ken Magid has provided a thorough and shocking discussion of psychopathic behavior among unbonded children in his book *High Risk: Children Without a Conscience*. As the title suggests, such children feel no remorse whatsoever, even when their behavior is outrageous. They are unable to give and receive affection or to make long-term friends; they display cruelty to other people and often torture or kill animals; they fly into uncontrollable rages and vandalize property and start fires; they are manipulative, superficial, conniving liars.

The severe pathological behavior in these children is the result of their failure to attach to a primary caretaker, or mother figure, during their infancy. Often, these children were orphans or abused babies whose early emotional needs were never met. With no one to cuddle, hug, hold, or coo at them, they failed to form a bond with a loving caretaker. This fatal flaw in their early life prevents them from later making bonds of affection and from developing a conscience. When an unbonded child is unknowingly adopted by an altruistic family, the adoptive parents may be convinced they can make the child right simply by loving him enough. In reality, these children are emotionally "broken," and they make life hell for everyone around them.

Fortunately, unattached, or unbonded, children are not common, but I have described these youngsters because it is so essential that they be identified early and referred for professional guidance and supervision. In some cases, controversial therapies have proved effective, but many of these children bounce from one foster home to another before becoming adult sociopaths. The greatest emphasis must be placed on preventing increased numbers of such children in our society by supporting mothers who wish to remain at home with their young children; campaigning for longer maternity leaves before employed mothers return to work; teaching working parents how to obtain adequate substitute caretakers for their children; preventing teenage pregnancies; interrupting the repetitive cycle of child abuse; strengthening family unity; and teaching parenting skills to caretaking adults.

ADDITIONAL READING:

Christophersen, Edward R. *Little People: Guidelines for Common-Sense Child Rearing.* Kansas City, Mo.: Westport Publishers, Inc., 1988.

Cline, Foster, and Fay, Jim. *Parenting with Love and Logic.* Colorado Springs: NavPress, 1990.

Dinkmeyer, Don, McKay, Gary, and Dinkmeyer, James. *Parenting Young Children.* Circle Pines, Minnesota: American Guidance Service, 1989.

Hayes, E. Kent. *Why Good Parents Have Bad Kids: How to Make Sure That Your Child Grows Up Right.* New York: Doubleday, 1989.

Kirshenbaum, Mira, and Foster, Charles. *Parent/Teen Breakthrough.* New York: Plume, 1991.

Kvols-Riedler, Bill and Kathy. *Redirecting Children's Misbehavior: A Guide for Cooperation Between Children and Adults.* Boulder: R.D.I.C. Publications, 1979.

Magid, Ken, and McKelvey, Carole A. *High Risk: Children Without a Conscience.* New York: Bantam Books, 1987.

Popkin, Michael. *Active Parenting.* HarperSanFrancisco, 1987.

Schaefer, Charles E., and DiGeronimo, Theresa Foy. *Teach Your Child to Behave: Disciplining With Love, From 2 to 8 Years.* New York: New American Library, 1990.

Wyckoff, Jerry L., and Unell, Barbara C. *Discipline Without Shouting or Spanking.* New York: Meadowbrook Press, 1984.

Wyckoff, Jerry L., and Unell, Barbara C. *How to Discipline Your Six to Twelve Year Old Without Losing Your Mind.* New York: Bantam Doubleday Dell Publishing Group, 1991.

6

INSTILLING VALUES IN CHILDREN

One of the compelling reasons many of us choose to have children is to diminish the reality of our own mortality by creating a new being that is an extension of ourselves. We fantasize that the best combined traits from ourselves and our partners will be concentrated in a new life that approaches perfection. In fact, one of the most positive interactions parents initiate with their newborns is the identification of physical and personality traits attributed to each parent:

"He's got Dave's eyes and my mouth."

"Another classical musician! Look at those piano fingers!"

"He's going to be real assertive, just like me; you should hear him wail when he's hungry."

"He's so even-tempered, like Rachael."

"We're hoping for a redhead this time. Someone in the family has to inherit Bev's carrottop."

"Check those hands; he's a basketball player for sure."

As a young intern, I underestimated the influence of this innate desire to see our distinctive qualities replicated in our offspring. Only a week or two into my internship, I examined a newborn whose right ear was malformed and the right side of whose mouth did not move symmetrically with the left. I knew I had to go to the mother's bedside and inform the family that their infant had a physical imperfection. Like many physicians tend to do, I already had projected onto this family the disappointment that I would have felt if I had just delivered a baby with a defect, however minor. This would be my first experience telling new parents that their baby had a malformation of any kind and I was dreading the scenario. I'm afraid I bungled it badly.

"Hi, Mrs. Barnard," I began, "have you seen your baby?" I opted for this vague opening, fully expecting her to immediately articulate her concern about the misshapen ear. Surely, it was all she could think about.

"Oh, yes," she replied. "Isn't he beautiful?"

"Have you seen his ear?" I asked incredulously. Obviously, she must have overlooked the deformity if she had described her baby as "beautiful."

Just then, Mr. Barnard started beaming radiantly and pulled out his wallet. I noticed his asymmetric smile and the underdeveloped ear on the same side. "It's a family trait," he was actually bragging. "See, here's a picture of Grandpa Barnard. He passed it on to me. This new boy's a Barnard, all right!"

I felt so ashamed. I had said all the wrong things, things that could have undermined this young couple's perception of their newborn. I had focused on an isolated and minor deformity, instead of seeing the whole little person they had created. Fortunately, they seemed oblivious to my inappropriate comments, and I quickly retreated from the room before inflicting any more damage. I left them alone with their new son, indelibly stamped with the family genes.

I have been impressed that parents feel as strongly about instilling their personal values in their children as they feel about passing on physical traits. We want our youngsters to appreciate the things that have brought us joy and have given increased meaning to our life. More often than not, we want our offspring to embrace our spiritual faith, work ethic, monetary values, attitude toward marriage and family, sexual mores, educational standards, appreciation of the arts, career aspirations, athletic interests, interpersonal relations, and recreational outlets.

For some of us, having a child who follows in our footsteps feels like the supreme validation of our own life choices and makes us feel successful as parents. On the other hand, to have a child repudiate our personal and professional values feels like the ultimate rejection and implies parental failure.

Recognizing Your Governing Values

Your values are the guiding principles or ideals that govern your daily actions by prioritizing the competing interests in your life. My own definition of personal success might differ markedly from that of my neighbor, who operates under a different value system. For one of us, success might be measured largely by the acquisition of material possessions, personal appearance, societal status, or career advancement. The other person may place the greatest premium on the attainment of athletic superiority, academic excellence, or musical, artistic, or dramatic preeminence. Others may value most their interpersonal relationships with family and friends and the preservation of their personal integrity and character.

Most of us would agree that parenting makes us examine our values more carefully, as our children provide an inquisitive audience wherever we go, scrutinizing both our actions and the motives behind them. To begin clarifying your own values, try asking yourself some questions like these:

- Who are the *people* for whom you would put your life on the line?

- What are the *principles* for which you would risk your life?

Once, a college youth was heard to protest compulsory draft registration by shouting, *"Nothing's* worth *dying* for!" Well, if nothing is worth dying for, is anything worth *living* for? If we can't identify anything or anyone we would give our life for, then perhaps we have failed to find real meaning in life and to have little regard for ourselves or others.

Our values are the freely chosen precepts that help guide our daily decisions and actions, thereby giving increased meaning and direction to our lives. Values are cherished worthwhile beliefs that enable us to affirm and respect ourselves and others. Identifying and adhering to our personal values is a process of self-awareness that deepens our commitment to our lifetime goals and thus enables us to grow into better persons. By helping us live in harmony with our beliefs, values enable us to lead more satisfying and productive lives.

Typically, people with firmly held values want to campaign for them publicly and to act on their beliefs. Such individuals can find joy and fulfillment through their fervent dedication to a higher cause even in the face of adversity. Conversely, people who don't cherish anything in their lives experience apathy and lethargy, often finding little meaning in life and suffering from depression.

After contemplating the beliefs, people, or principles for which you would risk your own life, consider the following sample questions, which might prompt you to do some additional clarification of your values. Value clarification does not tell us what our values ought to be; instead, the process provides the means for discovering what values we actually live by.

- What would you do if you learned your sixteen-year-old son was sexually active?

- What would you do if you learned your sixteen-year-old daughter was sexually active?

- Would you move your family to a distant city or accept a promotion requiring frequent travel?

- Would you move your family to a distant city so your wife could continue her graduate education?

- If you were in a financial bind this month, would you defer paying your MasterCard bill or your church pledge?

- Would you accept a lucrative out-of-town speaking engagement that fell on your daughter's birthday?

- What would you do if you found a wallet with two hundred dollars in it?

- Would you take a cut in pay to spend more time with your troubled teenager?

- Would you give money to a homeless beggar who appears drunk?

- Would you enter your attractive three-year-old in a Tiny Tots' Beauty Contest?

169

- Would you encourage your striking adolescent to explore a career in modeling?

- How soon would you go back to work full-time after having a baby?

- What would you do if your elderly parents could no longer live alone?

- What would you do if your spouse of ten years became permanently disabled?

- How would you react if you learned your child were gay or lesbian?

- What would you do if your son's soccer play-offs fell on the same day as your daughter's debate tournament?

- How would you feel if your son wanted to marry a woman of another race or another religion, an unattractive woman, a disabled woman, an obese woman?

- Would you have amniocentesis to detect a genetic abnormality in your unborn child?

- Would you obtain an abortion if your unborn child were found to have a genetic abnormality?

- How did you react when Ted Bundy was executed?

I'm not suggesting that there are any right or wrong answers to questions like these, but your responses are sure to reveal something about your values and priorities. Such hypothetical questions might also point out where your day-to-day decisions and actions sometimes differ from the values you espouse. Do your answers reveal double standards in your value system? For example, do you value boys more than girls, husbands more than wives, healthy babies more than babies with birth defects, people like yourself more than people different from you? Do you value money more than integrity or peace of mind?

How Values Become
Ingrained in Children

A couple I know, Tanya and Phil, were especially pleased when their five-year-old son, Alan, announced one day that he wanted to become a doctor. Phil was a social worker and the young couple were struggling financially on his meager salary. In addition to serving others, their religion was central to their lives, and grounding their child in a spiritual faith was a paramount parenting goal for them. Alan's announcement about becoming a doctor was particularly gratifying to his parents.

"Why do you want to be a doctor, Alan?" they asked. "Is it because you want to help people?"

"No, don't you know doctors like Uncle Leroy make a lot of money?" Alan explained.

Tanya and Phil were surprised and disappointed. Why was Alan, at his young age, so preoccupied with money? They certainly didn't think they had emphasized money as an important value in their lives. In fact, Phil had taken a marked salary cut when he left a lucrative career in real estate to become a social worker. They gave a full tithe to their church even when it meant making personal sacrifices.

From Alan's perspective, however, money was extremely important. In fact, he perceived it to be one of the central themes in his parents' lives. His mother complained about not having enough of it almost daily. At times, she would chide her husband for having left his previous profession. Repeatedly, she had told Alan that he couldn't have something because it "cost too much money."

Alan's Uncle Leroy was a bachelor surgeon in a neighboring community. He often bought new clothes and toys for Alan and gave money to his mother to help make ends meet. Alan's mother explained that Uncle Leroy had more money than they did because he earned more money as a doctor.

Tanya and Phil repeatedly *told* Alan that money was not important for happiness. On the other hand, Alan *had witnessed* a different reality almost daily: lack of money made his mother unhappy. His good-natured Uncle Leroy brought smiles to everyone's face when he spent money on them. For Alan, understanding was simple: Having money was a good thing and not having enough money put a damper on life.

We've all heard stories about rebellious children who seemed deliberately to reject their parents' most fundamental values, such as:

- the preacher's daughter who becomes promiscuous and professes to be an atheist

- the son of two doctorate-level college professors who receives failing grades in high school, dropping out to work in a fast-food restaurant

- the child prodigy of musician parents who reaches adulthood and refuses to play the piano again

We wonder how children raised by "good," conscientious parents could turn out this way. We point to a "weak genetic constitution," or unalterable external influences by peers and the media. We refer to outcome odds in childrearing, as if parenting were a blind gamble.

In fact, regardless of how much we verbally espouse

certain values, our children will be influenced more by how they see us act than by what they hear us say. Thus, outright rejection of parental values can stem from a child's perceiving hypocrisy between our stated beliefs and our daily performance. Or, some children, feeling intolerable pressure to please, and insufferable doubt about parental love, may rebel against inflexible parental control around certain issues.

On the other hand, it's no measure of success to have produced overcompliant children who passively mouth parental values, who are too inhibited to rebel against the overpowering demands on them. Dependency fosters the *acceptance* of values imposed by others, which is very different from the *conscious choice* of a certain value from among several alternatives. The appropriate exploration and questioning that accompany the free choosing of values will necessarily be stifled in children who automatically adopt the values of their parents out of a desire to please and be accepted.

Some parents, disappointed by their own unmet hopes and dreams, try to relive their lives vicariously through their children. Many submissive children have entered adulthood still trying to fulfill parental expectations. Such individuals find themselves marrying, entering the seminary, going to medical school, or having children, solely in fulfillment of imposed parental values. Ultimately, no one can be happy under such an arrangement. The children are likely to harbor a deep sense of resentment toward their parents, whose love they had to buy with their accomplishments. And the parents may never achieve their own identity or fully accept themselves as long as they are preoccupied with living someone else's life.

How, then, can we parents best attempt to instill values in our children? Typically, values are initially transmitted verbally (which involves *preparation*) and reinforced by our daily modeling of our beliefs through our actions (or their *presentation*). As children mature, they will have increasing personal experience putting their values into practice in daily living (the process of *application*). Inevitably, they will be exposed to contrasting values, through their peers and the media, and will ultimately have to sort out which parental values they will accept for themselves and which will be rejected (the process of *assimilation*).

Our various life experiences will cause our values to grow and evolve accordingly, as we continue to learn just what brings us personal satisfaction and what does not.

From the outset, we need to acknowledge that our children are unique individuals who will ultimately establish their own value systems through the process just outlined. While they will undoubtedly incorporate many of our own priorities into their value system, they are almost certain to reject others. We cannot allow ourselves to be threatened by the inevitable fact that each of our children will make some life choices that we will disagree with. If we expect our children to become replicas of ourselves, they will be stifled and unhappy. On the other hand, if we fail to ground them in some of the solid principles we esteem, they may be powerless to resist peer pressure and media messages that promote superficiality, promiscuous sex, drug use, or violent behavior. Let's review the major steps involved in the transmission of values.

Preparation

Our everyday speech conveys a great deal to our children about our values. Both overt and subtle messages about priorities and relative worth are communicated in our language:

"Lying is wrong." "We don't tell lies."
"That guy's a bold-faced liar!"

"Drugs are bad; don't ever take drugs."
"He's nothing but a low-life druggie!"

"Premarital sex is a sin; nice girls wait until they're married."
"She's a slut; she sleeps with her boyfriend."

"He's class valedictorian—a total brain."
"He's sure to succeed in life."

"Stop gossiping. If you can't say anything nice, don't say anything at all."

"She's a naughty girl!" "Let's try to be a nice boy!"

"We really can't afford to buy it. Oh, well, I'll just charge it."

Our family's "doctrines" are introduced through spoken "creeds" of behavior. Occasionally, these creeds are transmitted through deliberate conversations, such as a "birds-and-the-bees" discussion, where our personal beliefs are presented like a formal catechism. More often, however, our values find repeated expression in our everyday casual conversation. These unstructured verbal explanations are often a child's initial exposure to his family's belief system. For young children, stories, fables, and message-laden movies like *Bambi* provide fertile material for prompting discussions about values.

Presentation

For most children, a wide discrepancy exists between what they hear communicated verbally and what they observe in practice. The well-worn cliché "Actions speak louder than words" is a truism. We can tell our child about the dangers of drug abuse, but the effect of our words is diluted when they witness us mixing a martini after work each night or drinking a six-pack of beer in front of the TV. Many children observe their parents using medications daily to alter the way they feel. Countless parents take pain pills to relieve minor discomforts, sleeping pills to fall asleep at night, tranquilizers to calm them, and caffeine to stay awake. A frightening number of parents actually have used illicit drugs in front of their children and even offered drugs to them! Many parents watch television programs and movies depicting explicit drug use as their children sit nearby. Their failure to comment may be interpreted as implied condoning of such behavior.

Thus, it does little good to "preach" if we don't reinforce our words by "practicing what we preach." To preach one message and act out another is confusing to a child; it is also the height of hypocrisy. Don't be surprised when your child does exactly what he was trained to do by your modeling! You can expound on the virtues of honesty all day, but if you ask your thirteen-year-old son, who is small for his age, to pretend he is under twelve so he can get into the movies for a child's price, the message that gets transmitted is that money is valued more than honesty, especially when dishonesty can go undetected. In a way, we "apprentice" children into values. They learn by watching us and other adults they respect over long periods of time.

We can harp all we want on the subject of our preschooler's controlling his temper, but if we don't model appropriate ways to handle anger ourselves, our lecture will fall on deaf ears. When we smack Johnny and shout, "Don't ever hit your brother again!" Johnny learns that hitting people is the best way to get their attention.

A well-known study was conducted a number of years

ago to determine the relative influence in our communication of our words, tone of voice, and body language. The results showed that only 7 percent of what we communicate to one another is based on the specific words we speak. Another 38 percent derives from our tone of voice, while a whopping 55 percent of what we communicate is a direct result of our body language. When I say one thing, but do another, is there any question which message is communicated best?

I've heard parents of delinquent adolescents insist they would give one hundred thousand dollars to have a moral child. Yet too often, the behavior modeled by these parents conveyed to their child that a few dollars are worth more than telling the truth. How much would you be willing to pay to have your child value honesty? Three extra dollars at the movies? Try to think of specific techniques to transmit to your child that honesty is worth more than money. For example, a young man explained that his father modeled integrity for him by scrupulously adhering to the limit whenever he went fishing.

A teen I know once accompanied his father to select individual tents for the children for Christmas. The final price rung up at the register seemed too low, even considering that the tents were on sale. After the man had exited the store, he scrutinized the sales slip in the presence of his son and determined that he had been charged for only two tents instead of four.

"Great!" his son exclaimed. "Everything is so overpriced anyway. It's about time we got a good deal on something."

"No," the father protested. "It's wrong to take something for nothing. The sales clerk will probably get in trouble. I won't feel right until we correct the mistake and I pay the difference."

He walked back to the store and pointed out the mistake. The clerk was extremely surprised and grateful that the man had been so honest. He told the manager about his action, and the manager arranged to give the father a 10 percent discount on the purchase price. When father and son reached their car, the son was still irritated.

"Gee, Dad, you could have saved over fifty dollars. I don't see why you had to be so honest."

"Well, son," he explained, "my integrity is worth a lot more to me than fifty dollars. I hope you'll understand that someday."

An essential component of modeling desired behavior for our children involves being honest about our imperfections, admitting our own moral failings, and acknowledging inconsistencies in our behavior. For example, children have a strong sense of justice and they are intensely aware of circumstances in which they are owed an apology. Six-year-old Sarah was wrongly accused by her mother of stealing a bracelet from another child at school. While her mother urged her to admit the theft, the child insisted the bracelet had been a gift. Ultimately, after the facts vindicated Sarah, she still wouldn't drop the subject.

"Aren't you going to apologize to me for accusing me, Mommy?" she asked insistently. For Sarah, the conflict was not just about distinguishing right and wrong; it represented a self-esteem issue for her as well. Sarah needed to know she was important enough to warrant an apology from her mother.

Application

After hearing about values and watching us model them in our daily lives, children need to experience putting their beliefs into practice. At this point, we can serve as "consultants" when asked, offering our advice and guidance as children directly apply their values. Trust me: you won't have to worry about setting up these experiences for your child. Life offers countless opportunities for us to clarify our values by examining the moral dilemmas that arise daily.

My oldest son, Peter, did not have a steady girlfriend in high school and he seldom dated. He had a distant crush on a classmate, but the girl already had a serious relationship with a college freshman. Late in his senior year, Peter acknowledged that he would like to attend his senior prom, but he was realistic about the probability that the evening would not be a Cinderella–Prince Charming type of event. Determined to go to the prom and have a good time, he invited Lisa, a junior girl he knew casually and whose company he thought he would enjoy.

Much to Peter's surprise, forty-eight hours later, the girl he had "loved from afar" broke up with her boyfriend and asked Peter to take her to the prom. Meanwhile, Peter was aware that the girl he already had invited had purchased a dress.

Peter discussed his dilemma with Larry and me, beginning with, "If only I had waited forty-eight hours before inviting Lisa." We didn't tell Peter what to do, but we talked about the probable consequences that would result from each course of action. We asked how he thought he would feel about himself if he *uninvited* Lisa, how she would feel, and how his peers might react. We also raised the distinct possibility that the second girl would make up with her boyfriend before the prom and leave Peter without a date.

After we talked, Peter elected to keep his commitment to Lisa and to maintain a positive attitude. He did not want to make her an innocent victim by escorting her grudgingly or making her feel uncomfortable. He determined to enjoy himself at the prom and to explore a relationship with the "admired girl" afterward. In the end, the second girl did make up with her boyfriend and went to the affair with him. Peter and Lisa had a fun and memorable evening, and he was proud of his decision. One of his friends "dropped" an invited girl at the last minute to go with a new fling. As he recounted this to Larry and me, we could tell Peter's own self-esteem was enhanced by the knowledge that he had chosen to treat his date with respect.

Assimilation

One day President Lincoln posed the question "How many legs would a sheep have if you called its tail a leg?" After a moment, someone replied, "Five." Lincoln quickly retorted, "No, it would only have four." Calling a tail a leg does not make it one."

Parents need to prepare children to interpret for themselves the unsubstantiated claims they can expect to hear from their friends and in the media. Children need to learn that calling something safe, or desirable, or "cool" doesn't necessarily make it so:

"It's not really wrong. Everyone does it."

"You can't get pregnant the first time."

"You'll really enjoy it. It can't hurt anything."

"I'm nothing without him. I'll just die if he leaves me."

"You've only had a few drinks. It can't affect your driving."

"You don't really need an education."

Children can be taught not to take everything they hear and see at face value, but constantly to examine issues for themselves and to draw their own conclusions.

Help convince your child that, while her peers and the media may "call a tail a leg," she has the necessary skills to assess for herself whether a given assertion is true. This process can begin even with preschool-aged children, for example, by pointing out the difference between the way some toys are depicted in a TV advertisement and the way they look in real life. My brother-in-law, Chuck, took my six-year-old niece, Jenny, to buy a birthday present for her younger sister, Becca. They selected a doll the girls had seen promoted on TV. After Becca had opened her gift, Chuck asked, "How do you like the doll Jenny got for you?"

"I like it fine," replied Becca, "but why didn't Jenny get the one with the sparkles?" Further questioning revealed that whenever the doll was depicted in a television ad, an aura of lights had flashed around it. Consequently, Becca had believed that the doll came with flashing lights intact.

As children strive to integrate the conflicting messages to which they will be exposed, our most successful method for minimizing the influence of peers and the media is to frequently discuss with our children their reactions to values that contrast with our own. By communicating without judging, conveying our unconditional love, and continually showing our acceptance, we have the best chance of avoiding deliberate rebellion in our children and helping them identify and cultivate personal values that will reflect appropriate concern for themselves and others.

When individuals successfully assimilate certain moral values into the fabric of their lives, they become more decisive and confident about ethical dilemmas. In the past, absolute moral values were routinely instilled, beginning in childhood. Sadly, in today's society, situational ethics all too often replace traditional, time-tested values. In a popular movie a few years ago, *Indecent Proposal*, a happily married couple is offered

$1 million by a fabulously wealthy man if the beautiful young wife agrees to spend a single night with him. After much deliberation, the couple decides to accept the unconventional proposal, confident that the marriage can survive a monetarily motivated one-night stand. In the end, it cannot. If the value of marital fidelity had been assimilated fully into their lives, the bizarre offer could have been declined without any weighty deliberations. "I don't do adultery" means not for $1 million, not with Robert Redford, not under any circumstances. Similarly, although 80 percent of U.S. high school students admit they cheat, those who have assimilated the values of honesty and integrity into their lives don't have to weigh the risks of getting caught against the academic stakes involved. They simply choose *not* to cheat—every time.

The assimilation of values inevitably involves the challenging of parentally ingrained values by peers and the media. Initially, we expose our children to our personal values and beliefs, and we reinforce our words through our daily behavior. Then we support and guide our children as they apply these beliefs through personal experience. To some degree, however, we must also permit our children to explore other value systems, restricting them only when their safety is threatened. Some childhood precepts will stand up well to exposure to conflicting values, while other childhood values will change over time. Some of the changes in our children's values will disappoint us, while others might actually reflect a more mature view of the world than our own.

For example, many children who witness their parents' ugly bigotry will refuse to be intolerant of others. And children of highly sexist parents may deliberately choose more nontraditional roles when they start their own families. Children of alcoholic parents may vow to be teetotalers, while workaholic parents may beget offspring who reject their parents' work ethic in favor of a lifestyle that makes them available to their families.

Recently, Peter and Paige were discussing their future families and medical careers. Peter admitted he would prefer that his wife not work outside the home when their children were small. Paige immediately interrupted with, "What does that say about what Mom did? She worked when we were babies, and it didn't hurt us any. I'm going to do the same." For some reason, Paige felt she needed to defend and validate my values by embracing them as her own. Peter, on the other hand, was processing all available sources of data to make the best-informed choice for himself, even though it differed from my model.

Examining and Transmitting Specific Values

In the following section, I have selected a few representative values and offered some guidelines for clarifying our own beliefs and transmitting them to our children. The same introspection can be conducted for countless other personal values, including our beliefs about education, marriage, drugs, recreation, work ethic, family life, and patriotism.

Natural Consequences

I believe one of the greatest legacies we can leave our children is the recognition that "I am the consequence of my own actions." Whether the issue is oversleeping on a school day, smoking, being sexually active, or missing dinner, children should be taught to do a cost-benefit analysis for each of their decisions. When consequence training begins at an early age, children are

183

better prepared to make good judgments during adolescence. Instead of always being rescued by us, even young children can be allowed to experience a variety of natural consequences of their actions that will make lasting impressions without causing them physical harm. For example, if eight-year-old Jared doesn't wear a jacket to school despite your admonitions about the weather report, he may be uncomfortably cold while waiting at the bus stop (obviously, we wouldn't allow him to get frostbitten during severe weather conditions just to prove a point!). The result is that the next time you advise Jared to wear his coat, he's more apt to listen.

During a recent discussion with a group of teens, one girl candidly admitted she had been sexually active with her boyfriend. Initially, she insisted that she felt good about her decision because she had been "in love" with the boy. Later in the conversation, however, she mentioned being distressed because the boy had gossiped about her to his friends and had damaged her reputation after they had broken up. As we engaged in dialogue, she began to appreciate that her tarnished reputation was not just the result of the boy's inappropriate gossip; it was a direct consequence of her own decision to have sex with him.

From the time our children were small, I often discussed magazine or newspaper articles with them at the dinner table, emphasizing the consequences of someone's actions. Many of these discussions centered around personal safety. For example, I might point out that the people who had died in a car accident were those individuals who had not been wearing a seatbelt. Or I might explain that a house fire had been started by faulty wiring on a Christmas tree, or that a hitchhiker had been assaulted by someone from whom he had accepted a ride.

Other times, I focused on issues of character, perhaps

citing the example of a successful lawyer who had been permanently disbarred because he was convicted of selling drugs, or the case of a celebrity who was publicly disgraced when caught shoplifting, or that of a schoolteacher who was sent to prison for molesting children. In each instance, I was trying to establish "cause and effect" through these personal tragedies, in hopes of equipping my own children to make better decisions for their lives. Several of my kids have since told me that the lessons they learned from the newspaper scenarios I presented helped them weigh personal decisions later.

Integrity

Many children do not appreciate the value of their personal integrity until they have been caught in a lie and then have found that people do not take their word again. Few things are more frustrating than sincerely telling the truth and not having people believe you. Parents who doubt that their children are telling them the truth have almost always been lied to in the past. Thus one's integrity is the reward for a long history of consistent truth-telling.

From a young age, children should be congratulated for telling the truth, even if they are admitting misbehavior: "Jose, what you did was wrong, but I really respect you for telling me the truth about it." I also find it helpful to offer children examples of how one lie inevitably spurs additional lies to perpetuate the cover-up. As Sir Walter Scott has said, "Oh what a tangled web we weave when first we practice to deceive!" If a child does tell a lie, we can help him recognize that dealing with the consequences of a single lie is always preferable to complicating the situation by a network of lies. Unfortunately, many contemporary examples are available to portray the devastating effects of compromising one's integrity, from Watergate and research fraud to scandals among TV evangelists.

Often the ways a child compromises his or her personal integrity is obscured by other issues. For example, a youth who smokes in private may find it necessary to shield her behavior from her coach in order to play on the soccer team, thus compounding her smoking by deceit. I know a girl who abstained from smoking while on a camping trip with her boyfriend's parents to keep the couple from discovering her secret habit. Similarly, the girl hid her smoking from her teachers, her grandparents, coaches, and other significant adults, for fear that knowledge of her habit would lower their opinion of her. Thus, her smoking was compromising her own integrity and undermining her self-esteem by the daily need to maintain her cover-up.

Spiritual Faith

Many parents insist that they want to imbue their children with spiritual faith, either because the parents' own religion has held importance to them, or perhaps because the absence of spirituality in their lives has left a void. The very miracle of new life and the awesome responsibilities of parenthood prompt many adults to renew their religious faith in order to buoy their human inadequacies. Religious rituals like a baptism, christening, bris, or naming ceremony can offer gratifying reassurance to new parents, through the promise that a supportive community of believers will help share responsibility for the precious child welcomed into their midst.

The most effective way to transmit your spiritual values to your child is to take your family with you to your church, temple, synagogue, or mosque. I know parents who "send" their children to Sunday school, but remember, children evaluate what is important to you, not by what you say, but by how you spend your time. You may claim that your religious faith is an important priority in your life, but unless your children see you act out your faith, or "walk your talk," they will not believe your words alone. Thus, modeling our beliefs has the greatest impact on our children—reserving "family night" each week; spending time at Bible study, choir practice, or visitation; adhering to Sabbath restrictions, church doctrine, or dietary laws. These behaviors will demonstrate to our children that our spiritual faith is an important aspect of our daily life.

In my own family, our children witness me teaching Sunday school, they see Larry attend choir practice, and they observe both of us going to a couples' Bible study each week. Each of our children has enjoyed attending church camp in the summers, and Tricie returned to work there as a camp counselor. I try to be faithful in my daily time of prayer and study, my car radio is tuned to a Christian station, and I am comfortable telling my children and their friends that I am praying for them about something. I also try to offer frequent examples of God's answer to prayer in our daily lives and of how He works good out of our misfortunes.

It is our sincere hope that our children will derive comfort, strength, and encouragement from their religious faith and will continue to cultivate their spirituality throughout their adult lives. Thus, we make a conscious effort to present our religion as positively and supportively as possible. We want our children to know God as a loving Father who seeks the best for us, who forgives our wrongdoing, and who wants to draw us into relationship with Him. We do not want our children to be filled with guilt or to fear a wrathful, vengeful God of punishment or judgment. We try to make Sunday mornings as pleasant as possible by going to brunch as a family after attending church. The kids are always encouraged to invite their friends to come along. If they balk against going to church on a given morning, we have elected not to coerce them or to threaten them, in order not to provoke even more anti-religious rebellion. The weekly invitation to Village Inn still stands. By keeping our approach positive, we have found that, more often than not, the kids attend church and look forward to breakfast together afterward.

My personal goal for my children's spiritual faith has been to model the importance in my own life of my relationship with God. Next, I have strived to present God as a loving Creator and Father and to introduce them to a supportive community of other believers. As they mature, I will continue to pray that each child will maintain positive feelings about God that will foster the growth of their personal relationship with Him. Ultimately, my burning desire is that my children will develop a spiritual faith that will serve as a source of strength in this life and a source of hope for the next life.

Money

Examine carefully which financial values you want to transmit to your child. Do your daily actions suggest that money is universally a source of happiness or that lack of money always means misfortune? Does your behavior imply that money is valued more than time with your family, integrity, friendships, or recreation? Is hoarding your money more important to you than spending it in ways that bring you pleasure? Is spending all your money valued more than saving for your future security? Do you model the belief that your money is only to be spent for your own enjoyment? Or do you consider it a privilege and joy to share your resources with others?

The mismanagement of money is a universal source of personal stress and family conflict. The challenge to live within our budget is difficult both for single parent households and for dual-income families. Whether it's a used car, a new home, or a company jet we can't afford, all of us are vulnerable to the luring temptation to overextend ourselves financially. Even our small children are exposed to compelling commercial messages that insist that happiness depends on owning, eating, wearing, and playing with specific products. From youngest to oldest, our citizens are bombarded by advertising campaigns urging them to possess material things and to crave more and more.

Few people fully appreciate that our possessions ultimately own us. The new house with the big mortgage payment must be furnished, heated, cleaned, and maintained. The big yard must be landscaped, fertilized, mowed, raked, and weeded. Every piece of equipment from the swing set in our yard to the recreational vehicle in our garage must be serviced and maintained. Contrary to the way we've been socialized, more isn't necessarily better; it's just more.

When I was a little girl, I read a book about migrant workers called *Cotton in My Sack*. The poor family upon which the book was based lived in abject poverty until each payday, when they had money in their pockets for a brief time. Instead of budgeting their meager wages or saving for essential expenses that would improve their lifestyle, however, the family would spend all their earnings within a few days and then do without the rest of the month. Many of us are like that migrant worker family, spending recklessly when we have some money and then being unhappy when our money is gone.

I am convinced that one of the greatest gifts we can give our children is to teach them to budget their money and to spend within their budget. Giving children a regular allowance is one way to help teach them to prioritize their personal needs and wants and to make realistic short- and long-term spending plans. Because the main purpose of an allowance is to help a child learn to manage his money, you may prefer not to tie a child's allowance to the performance of chores. The amount you give will depend on your own financial resources, the age of your child, and what you expect him to pay for with the money. If you expect your child to purchase lunch, clothes, school supplies, or sports equipment out of his allowance, you may need to give more money than if your child is required to pay only for entertainment. Sit down with your child and establish an appropriate allowance amount based on a mutually agreed upon budget.

In order to determine an appropriate amount for your child's allowance, I think it is important to address both short-term expenses, as well as to include an amount to be saved toward a long-range goal. As early as you deem appropriate, open a savings and/or checking account for your child to help her save more effectively and feel responsible for her money. A child will experience little control or joy over her money if you insist that all of it go into a college account for the distant future. On the other hand, she will learn little about budgeting or saving if she is permitted to blow her whole allowance the day she receives it and then hounds you for an advance all week.

It is very instructive to expect your child to designate some money to the welfare of others. This can take the form of a weekly church pledge or a regular gift to a foundation or charity. No one is so destitute that he can't identify someone else in greater need. Recognizing, empathizing, and responding to the needs of others contribute to elevated self-esteem and is one way to teach children to identify and cultivate their own strengths. Let your child select a worthwhile cause to which he can contribute a regular amount of money, such as feeding the homeless, preserving the environment, or finding a cure for a disease that has afflicted a family member or close friend.

One way to help a child stick to her budget is to provide separate envelopes for each area of expense. The available amount of money for each spending category is then put into a labeled envelope, such as school lunches, savings, charity, Christmas club, and so on. The only discretionary money available is that which is left over after budgeting for all essential categories. For large purchases, like a bike, you might consider contributing half if your child can earn or save the other half. Your contribution will feel very supportive to your child, and the requirement of providing a portion will help him assume responsibility for the item. Even if you can afford to purchase a car for your teen, requiring that he pays for the insurance or help with repairs, for example, can help him appreciate how much is involved in maintaining a vehicle.

Failure

Think carefully about what you want your child to believe about failure. Too many parents portray failure as something to be avoided at all costs. Children who view every failure as a humiliating and painful experience will be unwilling to venture outside their comfort zone in any arena and, thus, will never reach their full potential. Fear of failure and fear of rejection are what keep children from trying out for cheerleading, running for office, asking a girl for a date, or applying to graduate school.

Instead, children should be taught that periodic failure is essential to personal growth. Thomas Edison failed thousands of times before he invented the lightbulb, but he viewed each "failure" as the "successful identification" of a method that wouldn't work. Babe Ruth established the record for the most strikeouts in the same year that he set the record for the most home runs. Many millionaires, including Walt Disney, have gone bankrupt several times on their way to becoming incredibly rich.

A highly admired and accomplished mentor was once asked by a younger apprentice, "How did you become so successful?"

"Good decisions," was all the sage, older man offered.

"But how did you learn to make so many good decisions?" the young man pressed. "Experience," his counselor explained in a word.

"And just where did you get the right kind of experience?" the hopeful beginner pressed on. "Bad decisions," his learned guide responded. You see, informed, examined experience is the best training for life, and it's often the examination of our mistakes that teaches us the most.

Fearing rejection and failure isn't abnormal and it isn't harmful; we all harbor such fears. Our role as parents is to model for our children what it's like to feel the fear and then "go for it" anyway. No one ever fails without learning something valuable. Thus, all failures constitute unique opportunities for "major learning experiences."

So, whether it's a theater audition or an entrance exam, children should be encouraged to set personal goals, try out, risk failing, learn something about themselves, work on self-improvement, and then try out again. When Paige was in junior high school, she was determined to be a cheerleader. But the first time she tried out she didn't make the cut; she didn't make it the second time, either. My heart ached to witness her disappointment (bordering on devastation), and a part of me wanted to shield her from such pain. Fortunately, Paige has an unconquerable spirit, and she kept bouncing back after each failure. Right away, she would identify the strengths and weaknesses evaluated at her tryout and begin working on a new routine. (She even convinced me that she would be more likely to be selected if I would let her shave her legs!) Eventually, Paige did make the team, and being a cheerleader brought her enjoyment throughout much of her high school and college years. Although the tryout process involved the uncomfortable experience of initial failure, cheerleading ultimately brought Paige a lot of personal fulfillment, and she would agree it was a goal worth striving for.

Sexuality

Many parents think of children's sexuality in terms of specific heterosexual activities associated with dating, like kissing, petting, and having sex. They may see their role as delineating for older children acceptable limits of behavior and making threats to enforce the limits. But sexuality is much more than sex acts, and our parental role in this area actually begins at birth, not at puberty.

To begin with, some parents place different value or expectations on their children, depending on their gender. A child of the less-valued sex will suffer damage to his or her self-esteem and will be permanently burdened with the parents' disappointment over something beyond the child's control. Similarly, sex-role stereotypes are potentially harmful and always place artificial limits on a child's development. Thus, our values about sexuality should begin with the unconditional acceptance of our child's gender and the shedding of restrictive sex-role stereotypes.

Next, we need to transmit to young children our full acceptance of all parts of their bodies. Many parents have told me that they are immediately uncomfortable if their infant reaches for his genitals during a diaper change. Yet the same parents usually express obvious delight when their infant grabs his toes. As soon as a toddler begins naming body parts, he will promptly detect the differences in his parents' responses when he points to his nose or when he grabs his penis. Preschoolers readily appreciate that body parts given accurate names are neutral areas of their bodies ("knee," "elbow," "earlobe"), while those parts described by code words are emotionally charged, "dirty," or "bad" areas of their anatomy ("wee wee," "pee pee," "chi chi").

When children are taught that *penis* is a naughty word, they may assume that their penis is a bad part of their body. Then a child may feel guilty about the inevitable pleasure he derives from touching his penis. Making a child feel embarrassed or uncomfortable about certain areas of their body contributes to lowered self-concept and also may place a child at increased risk for sexual exploitation. If youngsters can't mention their vagina or scrotum without upsetting you, how likely are they to confide that someone touched them in a private area? On the other hand, children who are comfortable with their bodies and have high self-esteem will be less likely to confuse sex with love or to let others take advantage of them sexually. Consider whether you have adequately empowered your child to "just say no" to uncomfortable sexual pressure.

Let's say you hold strong beliefs about premarital virginity. In this case, you certainly should discuss those beliefs with your child. You can tout the advantages of chastity and point out the natural consequences of premarital sex when you hear examples of them, such as teenage pregnancy, sexually transmitted diseases, loss of self-esteem and reputation. But keep in mind that your teen will weigh your comments and what you have modeled against widespread societal acceptance and heavy peer pressure to have sex before marriage.

Regardless of your own values, you can't effectively "forbid" your child to have sexual intercourse. If you make premarital sex so taboo that your child can't talk with you about her pressures or feelings, you may indirectly provoke the activity you have forbidden. In addition, you may unwittingly transmit to your child the idea that you have lost respect for her if she engages in the behavior you oppose.

Although sexual mores are among the most emotionally charged values we espouse, we must take care not to transmit such extremely rigid views about this topic that our child feels unable to bring it up without inciting our anger. When sex is made a taboo subject, a teen may feel she has nowhere to turn for accurate information about birth control or sexually transmitted diseases. When youth are confident they can talk openly with their parents about their sexuality, they will be more likely to keep communication channels open and to feel good about themselves.

Allowing Children to Establish Values of Their Own

When our children were quite young, I gave little thought to the eventuality that they would be independent from me someday. I suppose I simplistically expected to be there always, making life decisions for them and protecting them from their own mistakes. But just as my children have matured, so have I. And one of the most important lessons I've learned as part of that maturation process is the necessity of letting go— letting go not only of my need to protect my kids, but also of the temptation to make their decisions for them.

One thing that has helped us make the transition has been the realization that we can best serve our children as they develop if we place less importance on making them believe precisely as we believe and greater emphasis on helping them formulate their own values and ideals. History has repeatedly confirmed that each successive generation invariably repudiates many of the values of the preceding generation. While we can expect our children to buy into some of our beliefs as they mature, it is only reasonable to assume that they will reject many others.

Rather than locking horns with our children over differing values, we need to focus on finding effective ways to help them frame their own beliefs and to learn to live by them. One of the most loving things we can do for our children is to nurture them to the point where we can eventually let them go, secure in the knowledge that we have helped them recognize the values by which they will organize and periodically re-examine their unique view of the world.

ADDITIONAL READING:

Bennett, William J. *The Book of Virtues*. New York: Simon and Schuster, 1993.

Dyer, Wayne. *What Do You Really Want for Your Children?* New York: Avon Books, 1985.

Ekman, Paul. *Why Kids Lie*. New York: Charles Scribner's Sons, 1989.

Eyre, Linda and Richard. *Teaching Your Children Values*. New York: Fireside, 1993.

Glenn, Stephen, and Nelsen, Jane. *Raising Children for Success*. Fair Oaks, California: Sunrise Press, 1987.

Lickona, Thomas. *Raising Good Children From Birth Through the Teenage Years*. New York: Bantam Books, 1983.

McDowell, Josh. *How to Help Your Child Say "NO" to Sexual Pressure*. Dallas: Word Publishing, 1987.

7

ENRICHING YOUR FAMILY LIFE

Family Traditions

When you examine your own childhood memories, you probably recall first those special events celebrated with your family—holidays, vacations, school performances, graduations, birthdays, family reunions, religious observances, weddings, moving to a new home, and getting a pet. Children *love* the reassuring familiarity and sense of identity that accompany family traditions.

Traditions provide the social glue that bonds one generation to another. They create a sense of family continuity through the "security of the known." Especially in today's fast-paced world, children derive comfort from the assurance that some cherished past experiences will continue to occur with regularity. Since you and your partner will bring unique life experiences to your parenting, you will need to negotiate and evolve your joint family traditions. The specific ones you choose don't really matter—what *does* matter is that you create some islands of predictable behavior to which your children can anchor themselves through the storms of life.

One Christmas season, our office personnel celebrated with a potluck dinner. As we dined together, one by one we shared our past childhood and present family Christmas traditions. Each staff member recalled the Christmases of her youth with hints of childlike wonder, contrasting those memories with the way in which her own family now celebrates the holiday. My then-twenty-year-old secretary explained with mock seriousness that she was forced to reconsider her marriage plans when she learned that her fiancé's family opened presents on Christmas Eve instead of Christmas Day! Fortunately, this matrimonial incompatibility was reconciled before the wedding, and the young couple ultimately preserved some old and initiated some new traditions with their own little children.

Traditions can be based on ethnic or national heritage, religious affiliation, community identity, or on the family's own predilections. The American school-year calendar is based on traditional American holidays (and Judeo-Christian religious observances). The American workweek is predicated on the religious significance of the Jewish Sabbath and the Christian Sunday. Afternoon tea and the morning coffee break are cultural traditions that shape the workday here and abroad. In Islamic countries, by contrast, an individual's activities are structured around the Moslem call to prayer occurring five times daily. A given family can be expected to embrace multiple traditions of diverse origins, arising from their ancestral heritage, their ethnicity, their religion, our American holidays, and their extended family and nuclear family observances.

We can think of traditions in terms of annual events, like a family reunion, vacation, or holiday celebration. Or we might think of weekly routines, such as Sabbath observances, church services, "family night" activities, or weekend time spent with a noncustodial parent. Some of the most meaningful traditions, however, are routine daily activities that children find reassuring, like reciting grace before meals, enjoying a snack after school, dining together each evening, and being tucked into bed at night. From an early age, most children appreciate the security and stability provided by familiar daily routines. For example, toddlers often adopt elaborate bedtime rituals to help them settle down and fall asleep each night. Saying the Pledge of Allegiance, singing "America the Beautiful," giving the weather report, and having "Show and Tell" are predictable, familiar activities that a kindergartner finds comforting. The reassurance provided by dependable routines simplifies a child's life and imparts a sense of timing, predictability, and control in an often unpredictable, uncontrollable adult world. In this way, traditions help a youngster venture into the unfamiliar with some measure of confidence.

When I was nine years old, my father was transferred to the naval air base on Guam. We sailed from San Francisco on the USS *Barrett* and spent fourteen days crossing the Pacific Ocean to reach the Marianas Islands. I had left my friends on the East Coast while school was still in session, and our family of seven had taken ten days to drive across country, staying in a different motel each night. We were moving to a tiny Pacific island that promised sweltering heat, drenching humidity, seasonal typhoons, and alien boondocks. The first day at sea was so rough that only my father, older brother, and I managed to show up for dinner that evening. At night, the ship and surrounding ocean were so dark that if I awakened and opened my eyes I could see absolutely nothing. I would briefly imagine that I had gone blind. During the trip, several lifeboat drills were held, raising the frightening possibility of something happening to our ship, leaving my family adrift in a tiny lifeboat on the huge expanse of ocean that extended as far as I could see in every direction.

Despite all these anxieties, I loved every minute of the voyage, and part of what made the experience so enjoyable for me was the highly structured daily routine that we followed. We were awakened by ship's chimes at the same time every morning, and I played shuffleboard until we were called to breakfast. We were assigned to the same table at each meal and were served by the same waiter. All the children on board met after breakfast to sing together and participate in arts and crafts activities, and we played Ping-Pong the rest of the morning until lunch was served precisely at noon. Every afternoon, a feature movie was shown, and a shuffleboard tournament continued until dinner was served. Evenings held either a dance, talent show, beauty contest, or other entertainment. Thus, my fears were soon tempered by the familiar routine of shipboard life. I thrived on the regular activities, actually placing second in the shuffleboard tournament. (I had been randomly teamed with a talented man.)

Because children of all ages enjoy routines so much, an isolated activity quickly can become ingrained as a "tradition." I heard a counselor for troubled youth share a heartwarming story during a radio interview. The man supervised a group home for delinquent boys and was always looking for ways to enhance interaction among the youngsters. Discouraged because so few words were spoken at dinner, he tried innovative ways to encourage communication among the boys. One night, he announced at dinner that they were going to play a new game. He began by naming a car that started with A—Audi. The boy next to him was to name a car that started with B—perhaps BMW—and so on, around the table. The boys named their cars in monotones—Cadillac, Dodge, Edsel, Ford—but no bustling conversation was spurred. In fact, there was no convincing indication they had even enjoyed the game. The next night, the counselor resolved to try again. This time they would each name an animal, beginning with A—alligator, B—barracuda. Again, the boys participated, but with little display of emotion. The counselor was so discouraged by the boys' apparent lack of enthusiasm that he decided to abandon the dinnertime game idea. Besides, the next night he needed to hurry through dinner to make it to a meeting on time. When he got up from the dinner table early and announced he had a meeting to attend, one boy immediately protested: "But we haven't played the naming game yet!"

This has certainly been my experience with my own kids. Several years ago, I found I wasn't spending as much time with my teenagers as I would like, so when one of them asked if we could go out to breakfast after church one Sunday, I decided it was a good idea. The next week was my birthday, and we celebrated by having Sunday brunch together. The third Sunday, when I left for church, Heather asked if we were going out for breakfast afterward "like we always do." Thus, our Sunday brunches became a tradition and served as one of the key times during the week when we were all together and focused on one another.

To some extent, many of us remain creatures of habit as adults. For the fifteen years that I was a student, resident, and faculty member at the University of Colorado School of Medicine, it was my routine to start the day at morning conference and to end the week by attending grand rounds each Friday afternoon. These regular conferences provided the framework around which my day and my week were structured. They also served to remind me that the acquisition and dissemination of medical information was the core mission of a school of medicine and the essence of being a faculty member.

I believe that traditional family activities can strengthen a child's sense of individuality, family identity, and cultural heritage. Our traditions are a part of who we are. I have a good friend who married into a family of Polish descent. It had long been a tradition in this family to hold an open house on Christmas Eve and serve Polish dishes. Several of her new aunts taught my friend to make potato pancakes, kielbasa, sauerkraut, and fried desserts, and for several days the entire family works to prepare the traditional foods. From 5 to 9 in the evening on Christmas Eve, they open their home to friends and relatives. I can't imagine going to that much trouble the day before Christmas, but the look on the boys' faces when they greet guests at the door makes it clear that this elaborate family tradition will continue for at least another generation.

Ten years ago we moved to a large, new house. The preceding ten Thanksgivings had been rotated among multiple relatives, and we had hosted only one that I recall. The year we moved, we invited more than thirty relatives to our home. By moving the furniture out of the living room and placing three Ping-Pong tables end to end and using folding chairs borrowed from the church we were able to seat everyone at our makeshift dinner table. We provided the turkey, stuffing, potatoes, and gravy, while the relatives contributed all the side dishes and desserts. It was a lot of work—and wonderful fun. As everyone was leaving, someone asked expectantly, "Are you going to do this again next year?" We have now hosted ten consecutive Thanksgivings at our home, and I think it's safe to say the annual event is a deeply ingrained tradition. One year, fifty-two people were present, representing four generations of Neiferts and numerous unrelated friends. A core of about forty people can be counted on each year. It's also certain that some college students who can't be home for Thanksgiving will be present. One year we had a Bangladeshi student, another year a Norwegian business intern from Larry's office; we've even hosted a faculty advisor from our son's college.

We don't send formal invitations, because it is understood that a standing invitation is extended to everyone.

We don't even organize what dishes people bring any-more because everyone has a permanent assignment. If Aunt Eleanor doesn't come, we know there won't be any freshly baked zucchini bread that year. If Aunt Marg can't make it, we'll be short on candied sweet potatoes. Aunt Betty not only brings a relish tray and her famous cherry dessert, but she always arrives early enough to help in the kitchen and to bring an assortment of pots and pans, salt and pepper shakers, paper cups, and cornstarch. She starts saving empty plastic bowls and lids weeks before Thanksgiving so I'll have storage containers for leftovers. Like clockwork, Betty calls me before leaving her house to see if I've forgotten anything or need a pep talk.

Since so much of the occasion is a Neifert affair, I felt the need to interject an Egeland tradition from my own childhood. Chestnut stuffing became my original contribution to the event. My father always made chest-nut stuffing at Thanksgiving, and I have continued the tradition. I ritually call my parents the night before to review the recipe. As we enumerate each ingredient, I feel I have carried a little of my own childhood holiday into the present.

The aunts hover over the gravy and help with the final meal preparations. Our cousin, Pastor Bob, says the grace, and then everyone is served buffet style. After dinner, the aunts and I remain seated while the younger generation cleans everything up. It's an un-spoken agreement that I get all leftovers as compen-sation for hosting the event. After talking awhile, the aunts and uncles gather around the piano and Aunt Marg plays hymns by request while everyone sings. Eventually, Aunt Betty takes over, and with a little persuasion from Aunt Helen, she starts playing by ear some boogie-woogie and songs from their childhood. Meanwhile, the youth migrate downstairs to watch foot-ball or movies on the VCR and to play pool. The small children have fun exploring in my children's rooms, which are supposed to be off-limits. Small groups that change composition periodically can be overheard discussing everything from the serious to the mundane. Everyone senses when it's time for dessert and a dozen pies, cakes, and other goodies appear. Several new concoctions can be found among the staple of annual standbys, and we sample as many different desserts as possible.

While most things stay constant from one year to the next, new routines are sometimes added to the tradition. Recognizing that many of those present see each other only once a year, we decided to ask each individual seated around the table to stand and share some highlights from their year and state something they were thankful for. This activity turned out to be so meaningful to everyone that it was established thereafter as a new tradition. Engagements, pregnancies, career changes, and personal crises have been announced at the Thanksgiving table. Even the youth stand up to share something important in their lives, like playing a sport or getting their driver's permit. Until Grandma Neifert died, she was the central figure, smiling and nodding over conversations she couldn't hear, filled with unabashed pride at being directly responsible for all these descendants.

One year, I was particularly tired, busy, and overwhelmed. As Thanksgiving neared, I mumbled something about how much trouble it was. "Why can't someone take me out for a holiday meal just once? How much longer do I have to keep hosting this event?" I whined. Before long, I had my children complaining too about cleaning the house, about babysitting second cousins, and about having their rooms messed up by roving munchkins. "Maybe we just won't hold Thanksgiving this year," I suggested. "But it's a *tradition*!" Mark defended. Traditions don't just happen; they require great effort, but they're worth it. Ultimately, we pulled ourselves together and had the best occasion ever.

Thanksgiving is, in fact, a lot of work for me and my family, and a big expense. It's also one of the most meaningful gatherings of the year, and I know our children will remember these family reunions all their lives. Several generations are brought together, and family pride is engendered. For a few brief moments, each individual present becomes the focus of attention. We review family history, remember deceased relatives, and get a glimpse of how we want to look and act years from now. Perhaps most important, we learn to like people we didn't choose to be related to but who have become a permanent part of our history.

In addition to our annual Thanksgiving ritual, we have another near-sacred tradition. We take a family vacation at the same time and same location every summer. We have gone camping at a lakeside in Nebraska ever since Mark, our youngest, was born. We started with five little kids who slept in bunk-cots in a huge Army surplus tent over a four-day weekend, during which most of the first and last days were spent setting up and taking down camp.

As the children played happily at the water's edge, safely strapped into their life preservers, I would be sprawled on a lawn chair, novel in hand. But my eyes would be glued to the water, as I recited methodically, "one-two-three-four-five, one-two-three-four-five," accounting for every child virtually every moment. Thankfully the younger ones took a nap each afternoon and for a few carefree hours, I could actually read and relax. A few years later, Peter would buy me a button that asked, "Are we having fun yet?" as a reminder to claim those precious hours every day.

I sometimes regret that our family has never been to Disneyland or Disney World. We've never camped in

Yellowstone, seen the Grand Canyon, or driven across country. We've never taken a ski trip together, flown to Mexico, or traveled to Canada. Instead, every year we elect to return to our familiar summer respite on the edge of a beautiful lake and perpetuate this family tradition. The year Peter graduated from high school, Mark asked anxiously whether he would still come to the lake while he was in college and after he married. The children all vowed to return with their own families after they have grown and left home. I don't know whether or not the tradition will continue, but I am confident that it has strengthened our sense of family for more than fifteen years.

We have traditional camping food and we pack traditional camping supplies every year. We not only bring ingredients to make "s'mores" for ourselves, but it has become a tradition for neighboring campers to join our campfire for songs, companionship, and the sugary concoctions. We sing the same familiar songs each year, while Larry plays the guitar and I accompany him on the harmonica. After our Irish setter had been along twice, her attendance also become traditional. Despite the inconvenience of taking an oversized dog on a long car ride, we couldn't imagine leaving Shannon at home. When the girls reached their teens, they asked if some friends could accompany them. Now it is a tradition to bring at least five additional guests on the trip. It would be simply unthinkable to go by ourselves now, without our favorite neighborhood youth making preparations and joining us.

Once, when we arrived at our usual campsite, someone else was already settled in our spot. The children were indignant that someone was using "our" campsite. I was about to explain that we didn't "own" any lakeside property at the state park, but was confident we could manage to have a good time camped elsewhere this particular year. But no comments were ever necessary.

As soon as eleven teens and a huge dog piled out of four vehicles, and we started unloading ten days' worth of food and erecting six tents on the adjoining campsite, the middle-aged couple on "our" spot quietly packed up and drove their R.V. to another location.

Over the years, we have experienced a litany of vacation woes associated with our annual trek to the lake. We have encountered tornado-force winds, blinding sandstorms, drenching rain, flat tires, broken-down vehicles, loss of property, and minor injuries. But every year, we declare it was our best vacation ever. Why do we treasure this trip so much? I am convinced it's because our usual lifestyle is so hectic and high-tech that we all relish being together for ten whole days, without intrusions by television, telephones, pagers, or fax machines. Our life is simplified to daily necessities—like preparing, eating, and cleaning up three meals together, making storm preparations, refurbishing supplies, raising the boat sails and taking them down, and just having fun together. For as long as we live, our lakeside campsite will be synonymous with family and friends, rest and relaxation, spectacular scenery, resourcefulness and resilience, constancy and commitment.

Not only have traditions enriched my nuclear family life, they have helped me remain connected with my extended family in a deeply meaningful way. Because I travel so frequently, I have made a commitment to combine business trips with visits to my parents and my siblings' families whenever possible. The value of the relationships I have cultivated with young nieces and nephews more than compensates for the extra effort I expend and the additional time I am away from home each year. It has been a distinct privilege to have been present when Dana, Jenna, Jenny, Becca, Tommy Jr., Jeff, and Matt were integrated into their families. Though I regret that I was preoccupied with tiny children of my own when Karin and Drew were born, I

have worked hard to get to know these exceptional
youths as unique individuals with whom I share some
genes. It touches my heart to find the words "Ant Mari
comes" written in a child's hand on the calendar at my
sister's house or to hear that two-year old Jeff called
out Aunt Mari's name and continued looking around
the house for me after I had gone. I urge you to invest
some emotional energy in your own extended family.
It has been a most gratifying dimension of my family
life!

Pets

Pets have had such an important influence on my own
children that I feel compelled to talk about the valuable
lessons children can learn from caring for and being
loved by pets. While one or more pets are part of childhood memories for nearly all kids, it seems we've had
more than our fair share.

About ten years ago, when my kids were in elementary and junior high school, several employees at the
university became infected by a rare virus isolated from
some sheep housed in a research laboratory. All staff
members who worked in the vicinity of the animal research lab had to have their blood drawn to screen for
possible exposure to the infection. When it was my turn
to be interviewed prior to the blood test, the physician
researcher inquired if we had any pets in our home.
"Yes," I replied, "we have a dog, and a cat . . ."
"Okay," he interjected, assuming I had finished. ". . .
and a parrot, a parakeet, a gerbil, two rabbits, a ham-
ster, a turtle and three goldfish," I concluded. "I think
that's all." The physician stared at me, pen in hand,
suspecting I might be joking. I realized with some em-

barrassment that most people probably didn't have as many pets as we did.

Over the years, we've had six dogs, two cats, dozens of rabbits (including dwarf bunnies, lop-eared bunnies, and Dutch rabbits), numerous gerbils, hamsters, guinea pigs, chickens, ducks, white mice, parakeets, finches, a parrot, countless goldfish, exotic saltwater fish, lizards, salamanders, crawfish, hermit crabs, frogs, turtles, and garter snakes. As I write this, Tricie reminds me that we never had a monkey—"the only animal I ever *really* wanted," she adds with a grin. (We also managed without a pig or a pony.)

Starting when they were in first grade, peaking somewhere in the elementary years, and continuing into high school, my kids were always asking for a new pet, and I could usually be persuaded to bring home some cute, furry, baby-something, complete with cage, water bottle, feeding dish, and other animal sundries. For several years after my last child was born, I was especially vulnerable to any remotely convincing argument about why we needed a new animal. I had been bringing babies home regularly for so many years, and part of me still longed for a new baby, even if only a baby animal.

We visited a pet shop almost every weekend during this period. After all, we needed pet supplies. Once in the store, the kids would be drawn to the cages of puppies, kittens, bunnies, and other small irresistible furries. Inevitably, rational explanations degenerated into emotional cajoling and pleading: "I promise I'll feed and clean its cage *every day*." "This is the last bunny I'll ever ask for." "See, it likes me; it's so cuddly." "It's the smallest one; I've always wanted one just like this!" "Daddy won't mind." (Daddy would end up minding a lot!) "Pleeeease!"

At least half the time, we left with the cute baby furry who grew (overnight it seemed) into a huge, not-so-cute, defecating, urinating, copulating, eating-machine.

The child who had solemnly vowed to regularly feed, water, love, play with, and clean up after this essential creature would require daily reminders of his or her responsibility. Nevertheless, my children would admit that pets have taught them a lot about life and brought them a great deal of joy.

Responsibility

A pet is totally dependent on others for its feeding and care and provides an ideal opportunity to teach your child about responsibility. Too often, however, parents grow weary of consistently enforcing or supervising pet duties and end up assuming sole responsibility for the pet themselves. While this route may seem easier in the short term, it runs the risk of conveying to children the unrealistic message that others will cover for them when they shirk their responsibilities, that someone else will look after Munchie even if they don't.

Depending on your child's age, he should be expected to take partial or full responsibility for feeding, holding, walking his pet or cleaning its cage. Initially, you should expect to closely supervise your child until it is clear he independently can perform each step involved in his pet's care. Obviously, you will need to take charge of veterinary needs, but your child can accompany you to gain an appreciation of the importance of having his pet immunized, spayed or neutered, clipped, groomed, or licensed.

A child who is successful in carrying out her commitments to her pet will benefit in several ways. First, she will experience enhanced self-esteem from knowing she is competently caring for a pet who depends on her. Your periodic praise and comments, such as, "Muffy is lucky to have such a responsible owner," will add to her feelings of self-confidence and pride. Being responsible in "little things" will better equip her to assume responsibility for weightier matters, such as handling her own wardrobe in her early teens and owning and maintaining a car in her late teens.

One child explained to me that caring for her small pet reminded her of just how much daily care and maintenance she required from her own parents, "the ultimate pet owners." Owning a pet had given this young girl increased appreciation for the magnitude of sacrificial love and physical care her parents provided for her.

Unconditional Love

One of the most rewarding aspects of owning a pet is the exchange of affection that occurs between animal and owner. Whether referring to a fish in a bowl, a gerbil in a child's hand, or a puppy on his lap, the exclamation "See, he likes me!" reflects the feelings of unconditional love and acceptance that a child can experience through a pet. A pet can be a source of solace in times of sorrow, an attentive listener when a child pours out his heart, a ready companion who won't reject him, and a trusted, faithful friend.

As soon as my car begins to nose up our long driveway at the end of the day, our Irish setter, Shannon, comes over to greet me. Eleven years ago, as a lanky, playful pup, she would come bounding up to me. Today, at the sound of my car approaching, she raises herself with great effort and lumbers over, both tail and body wagging "hello." She's done this literally thousands of times without expecting anything in return. Whether I acknowledge her with lavish praise or ignore her presence altogether, Shannon still welcomes me with renewed enthusiasm each day. Before I've hit my doorstep, I've already experienced total acceptance by a very good friend who has uplifted me unconditionally.

Nurturing

Caring for a pet provides an ideal opportunity for children to develop nurturing behaviors toward others. Young children are by nature very self-centered, focusing most closely on "me" and "mine." Dolls and stuffed animals are usually the first recipients of young children's emerging nurturing tendencies. A pet offers the chance for boys and girls to feel love for something alive and to express their affection by talking to, holding, caressing, and kissing—without risking rejection.

Most pets respond to the "law of the harvest," whereby children discover that they generally reap what they sow. With rabbits, for example, my children quickly learned that the more they regularly held and cuddled their bunnies, the more responsive the animals became. If they ignored a rabbit and left it in its cage for several weeks, it tended to try to bite them and wriggle away when they decided to take it out and hold it. Our most personable dwarf bunny, Sassie, was a docile, white cuddly bunny, owned by Heather when she was ten years old. Not a day passed without Sassie contentedly being held and petted while Heather watched TV or did her homework. The bunny clearly trusted Heather and rested comfortably on her arm while being carried about the house from room to room. In the history of our family, no other rabbit received such loving daily attention, and none was ever as domesticated as Sassie.

As I wrote this, my usually standoffish cat jumped onto my lap and entreated me to pet her. At first I didn't want to be bothered, but as Pippy rubbed her head against my arm solicitously, I stopped my typing

to stroke her lovingly. Immediately she began to purr
with contentment, stretching her neck to show me
where she wanted me to place my hand. Her motoric
hum of appreciation was my instant reward for a reluctant gesture of tenderness. As we nestled for a few
moments, I was glad I had paused to show her some
affection and to feel hers returned so openly. Whether
housebreaking a dog, brushing a cat, or teaching a parrot to talk, children soon recognize that the more they
invest in their pet, the greater the personal satisfaction
they will receive.

Aging

Raising a pet can offer a child insightful glimpses of the
stages of life, as a fluffy, romping puppy grows into a
sleek, vibrant adult dog and, ultimately, to a slow-
moving, hearing- or vision-impaired, aged animal.
Thus, the immutable life cycle is condensed to the span
of a few years or a decade when seen through the life
of a pet. A child can learn to be sensitive to the special
needs of the aged when they recall the former youthful
vigor of their now arthritic old dog. I know that Shannon has allowed my own children to experience the
truth in the Japanese proverb "The sun setting is no
less beautiful than the sun rising."

Death

Although death is an inevitable part of life, many parents try to shield their children from experiencing the
loss associated with the death of a loved one. These
misdirected efforts often cause parents to avoid talking
about death or to use euphemisms like "Grandpa's gone
to sleep" or "She passed away." They may try to mask

their own grief at the loss of a relative in hopes that their child won't think anything is wrong. Instead children have the right to know about the reality and permanence of death and to have these concepts presented with sensitivity and in age-appropriate language.

For many children, the death of a pet will provide their first experience with the death of a loved one. The death may result from animal euthanasia, old age, or being run over by a car; and occasionally a pet may die from neglect. I've heard of parents trying to substitute a look-alike pet for the deceased animal in order not to traumatize their child. Or other parents belittle the death, saying, "Oh, come on, Buffy was only a gerbil. They don't live forever, you know."

The best approach is to use honesty in explaining how the pet died and to be empathetic about the child's loss. Buffy might have been only a gerbil, but she was Suzie's good friend. Let your children talk about their dead pet, and listen attentively while they retell favorite stories, look at pictures, and express their sadness. Most children will want to bury their animal and hold some type of funeral service. We had a veritable pet cemetery in our yard during our peak pet-owning years!

If a pet's death results from negligence on the part of its young owner, you will want to make the tragedy a learning experience, without letting your child wallow in guilt. This can be an opportunity to teach about consequences, such as, "You sprinkle only a little bit of fish food into the bowl every day. If you dump in the whole box of food, your fish might die." "If you let your rabbit loose in our unfenced yard, you have to watch it at all times, or else the neighbor's dog might come over and get your rabbit when you aren't looking." Children who have made such errors in judgment need to know that you aren't angry with them and that you are confident they won't make the same mistake again. Explain that we all make mistakes, and that learning from our mistakes is how we mature and grow. Acknowledge that you realize they really loved their pet and that they will have other opportunities to take better care of an animal.

Reproduction

Just as pet life offers valuable parallels about love, aging, and death, it may also spur conversations with your child about sexuality, reproduction, and family life. The reasons for neutering or spaying a pet provide opportunities to talk about birth control with older children. And the major responsibility associated with raising a litter of animals helps introduce children to the long-standing responsibilities of parenting.

As soon as my daughters owned several bunnies, they began to ask permission to mate their rabbits. Eventually, we agreed to let them raise several litters of dwarf bunnies. It was truly heartwarming to watch thirteen-year-old macho neighbor boys "oohing" and "aahing" over tiny, helpless, nursing newborns only a few inches long. The kids were fascinated with the birth process, nursing, and the speed with which a rabbit can get pregnant again!

Humor

There's no doubt that pets provide a ready source of fun and laughter. What pet owner can't relate a funny story about one of her animal's antics? Shannon has a terrible sweet tooth, and she finds chocolate irresistible. One Valentine's Day, Larry bought me a huge, ten-pound, heart-shaped box of See's Candy. Within a few days, we had eaten the entire top layer, but someone carelessly left the box within Shannon's reach. The next day, when the kids got home from school, they discovered the box of candy on the floor and Shannon nearby, looking guilty and sheepish. She had consumed a large portion of the remaining candies! (I know this isn't purely funny, as dogs can overdose on chocolate, but Shannon was certainly a sight!)

As we reminisced about pets while I worked on this chapter, Paige couldn't stop laughing when she recalled the time I accompanied Heather to our favorite pet store to sell the last dwarf bunny in our litter. While I transferred the bunny to the storeowner and collected the eight dollars he customarily paid, Heather was busy inspecting the other rabbits on sale. As I was prepared to leave, she approached me carrying a tiny golden rabbit, about the size of the one we were selling. "Look at this bunny, Mom. We've never had one this color. We'll never find one like this again. He's so cute. Can't we get him?" I don't know what came over me. I had come to sell the last bunny in our litter, and for some unexplainable reason, I left the pet shop with a new twenty-dollar bunny . . . plus a cage, water bottle, feeding dish, and salt lick!

Guidelines for Selecting and Keeping a Pet

Safety

No pet has value above a child. That statement sounds obvious, but countless parents have jeopardized their own child's safety by harboring a dangerous pet. We've all heard stories of pit bulls who mauled toddlers. In other less common scenarios, a boa constrictor has crushed an infant, a ferret has chewed off a baby's ears, and exotic pets like tigers have been known to turn on people. Although you may be tempted to obtain an exotic pet to enhance your self-esteem, please put your own ego needs aside and select a safe animal that best serves your child's needs. It should go without saying that the paramount consideration in selecting a pet has to be *safety* once there is a child in your family.

If you have a pet that poses any danger to a child, such as a dog who has bitten in the past, I urge you to find a new home for the animal today.

Age of Child

If your goal is to have your young child begin to learn responsibility by assuming some of the care of a pet, I'd suggest starting with something like fish or a low-maintenance caged animal, such as a gerbil. Once your child has proven herself capable of performing daily pet duties, as well as showing attention to her animal, then she will be ready to assume the increasing levels of care required for a cat, dog, or pig. If you give your six-year-old a puppy for Christmas, chances are you will find yourself trying to housebreak Rufus, cleaning up his "accidents," teaching him not to chew tennis shoes apart, immunizing, deworming, and bathing him. If you are prepared to take on such responsibility, you may decide to go ahead with your plans. It's probably reasonable to expect your child to be responsible for feeding and walking the dog daily. Think about whether you prefer that your child assume most of the care for a small animal or just a piece of the care for a larger pet.

Lifestyle

You may always have wanted an English sheepdog, but you'd better pick another breed if you and your partner both work outside the home and you live in a high rise. The darling puppy you bring home today may turn out to be an unmanageable commitment a few months from now. Be realistic and think ahead about how an animal would fit into your life.

Interestingly, parents-to-be often acquire a dog shortly before their baby is born. I think it's a sort of nesting instinct and a subconscious desire to "practice parenting" with the puppy. Actually, I did this myself. I was given a wire-haired terrier pup late in my first pregnancy, and I presented it as an "early birthday present" to Larry when he arrived home from the West Pacific just before Peter was born. I realized what a ridiculous idea this was when we brought Peter home from the hospital and found his nursery confining a high-strung, attention-seeking puppy and the floor covered with soiled newspapers. It was immediately evident to Larry and me that this "gift" dog had appeared at the wrong time in our lives and would need to be transferred to new owners with different priorities. I'm happy to say that Skoshi found a suitable home where he was appropriately celebrated as the "new baby."

Like all relationships in life, loving a pet involves emotional risk-taking. Several years ago, our girls were in the habit of taking Shannon jogging after dark. We had admonished them incessantly about the dangers of not being visible to a passing motorist and the risks of being hit by a car. One Sunday night, shortly after the girls had left to jog, Heather came running into the house, breathlessly announcing that Shannon had been hit by a car.

I raced to the scene of the accident and found Shannon lying by the side of the road, motionless except for her barely perceptible breathing. As a car had approached, the girls had veered to the side of the road, and Shannon was crossing the street to join them when she was struck by our neighbor's vehicle. I suspected she had life-threatening internal injuries, and I feared she had been paralyzed or would go into shock. We covered her with a jacket and tried to calm her. "At least she is still conscious," I rationalized. The girls were nearly hysterical, sure that Shannon would die, and the neighbor whose car had struck her in the dark was feeling bad. Larry arrived with our Suburban and a large piece of plywood to slide under Shannon's body so we could lift her into the car with the least disturbance.

Someone called the vet, who agreed to meet us at the clinic twenty minutes away. Seven very concerned Neiferts piled into the Suburban, talking tenderly to Shannon and urging her to keep breathing. We arrived just as the veterinarian's car pulled up to his office. I'm sure he was a bit taken aback as all of us paraded into the clinic bearing a ninety-pound dog on a board.

The vet quickly shaved a spot on Shannon's leg and started an I.V., scrutinized the whole time by fourteen watchful eyes. "Is she going to die? Is anything broken? Will she be all right?" we asked. After checking her vital signs and evaluating the color of her tongue and mouth, the vet determined that Shannon was not in shock. X rays revealed no obvious fractures. Only then did we dare to hope that Shannon just might live. The tension was permanently broken when Larry announced facetiously, "When will the hair grow back on her leg? You know we're showing her next week." The reason we all burst out laughing so hard is that Shannon has always been a mass of tangled, ungroomed fur, and the prospect of "showing her" was absolutely ludicrous.

The relief from tension that our laughter provided was just what we needed.

As it turned out, Shannon sustained only lung contusions in the accident. She required oxygen the several days she stayed at the animal hospital. We went together to bring her home, showering her with love and attention. She was stiff and slower-moving for many weeks, and some of us think she has never been quite as active since the accident. Nevertheless, we feel immensely grateful that our beloved pet was given a new lease on life—and we were given a lesson in guarding that life.

If you were to ask my kids, they would say that pets have taught them that life is fragile and that you need to express your appreciation for your loved ones daily. Over and over again, we look at Shannon and recall that we almost lost her—which forces us to recognize that we could lose another loved one at any time. Shannon has been our all-time favorite pet, a loyal friend, and an integral part of our family. Not only is she aged, but we have just learned that she has cancer. The fact that her death may be only a few months away has made us appreciate more than ever the transient nature of all our relationships and the importance of living fully in the present.

Holiday traditions, family vacations, and beloved pets are an integral part of the special memories each of us cherishes from our childhood. These uniquely personalized experiences will enrich your family life and provide a lasting heritage for your children. The intimacy and familiarity of the traditions you establish can strengthen your child's sense of identity and his connectedness with his immediate family, his past roots, and his culture.

ADDITIONAL READING:

Curran, Dolores. *Traits of a Healthy Family: Fifteen Traits Commonly Found in Healthy Families by Those Who Work with Them*. New York: Ballantine Books, 1983.

Robinson, Jo, and Staeheli, Jean Coppock. *Unplug the Christmas Machine*. New York: William Morrow, 1991.

Rogers, Fred. *When a Pet Dies*. New York: Putnam Publishing Group, 1988.

Tarrant, Bill. *The Magic of Dogs*. Emigsville, Pennsylvania: Lyons and Burford, 1995.

Zeitlin, Steven J., and Kotlin, Amy J. *A Celebration of American Family Folklore: Tales and Traditions from the Smithsonian Collection*. New York: Pantheon Books, 1982.

8

CHILDREN OF DIVORCE

Divorce is not just a personal matter; it is a societal issue that touches everyone. If we acknowledge the institution of the family as the fundamental unit of society—the original source of a child's nurturance, socialization, validation, and hope—then it must follow that the present rates of divorce and family discord represent serious threats to our idealized notion of unconditional family acceptance and unity. In this sense, every contemporary family feels the impact of the divorce rate.

Whether or not your own marriage is presently intact, the specter of family breakups haunts us all. Words like *partner* and *significant other* creep into our vocabulary to replace words we once used unthinkingly, like *spouse*. School forms are modified to provide sufficient space for demographic information on both custodial and noncustodial parents. Routine correspondence from school begins, "Dear parent(s) . . ." A kindergarten-aged veteran of divorce is overheard discussing the two boys she likes best in her class. "Mike is going to be my husband," she explains, "and Jeff can be my boyfriend." A couple in their forties take their teenage son and his new girlfriend to breakfast. "Do you have any brothers and sisters, Marilyn," the man inquires, striking up a conversation. "Yes, two brothers," she replies, "but they don't live with me. They live in Michigan with my real dad."

So, if you are thinking about skipping this chapter because it doesn't sound relevant to you, please reconsider. Assuming your own family won't be affected by divorce is as naive as believing you aren't impacted by the national debt or aging. Actually, I can think of no one in contemporary American society whose life hasn't been touched, either directly or indirectly, by divorce. Children of divorce are found in every classroom, scout troop, sports team, daycare facility, Sunday school class, and extended family. If you aren't divorced yourself, chances are you have nieces and nephews who have experienced parental divorce. Or your grown children may divorce someday, forcing you to change your pattern of grandparenting overnight. And who hasn't had their friendship with another couple thrown into chaos by an unexpected divorce? Even children from intact families are acutely aware that divorce could conceivably occur to their parents. No one dares smugly boast, "It could never happen to me." Indeed divorce does come, whether predictably or unannounced, to both patently unstable and seemingly ideal marriages. For countless children, the divorce of their parents will be the single most traumatic event of their entire childhood. For others, the pervading fear of parental divorce will hang like a dark cloud over their youth.

According to recent government reports, the rate of divorce in America has doubled since 1970 and tripled since 1960. Estimates are that 40 percent of current marriages will result in divorce, and approximately 30 percent of children born during the 1980s will experience a parental divorce before the age of eighteen. Presently, more than one million youngsters each year in the United States will face the consequences of marital breakup, and one in seven children will endure this stress more than once. Certainly, we each need to show compassion and understanding to the adults and children in our lives who experience divorce.

Because divorce is such an intimate personal decision, I would not presume to make judgments about an individual couple's decision to divorce. Yet we must acknowledge that any divorce, even a "good" divorce, represents a loss. Divorce is inevitably traumatic for all parties involved, and it can leave permanent emotional scars. Obviously, I would urge every couple to commit to trying to make their relationship work, giving it the considerable time and attention it requires if it is to flourish. A marriage needs to be lovingly nurtured, fertilized, watered, pruned, and shaded like a delicate plant; neglected, it will surely wilt and wither.

The idealistic part of me would like to believe that love is never lost; it just gets temporarily misplaced. The marriage bond is so precious that it is definitely worth spending time and money to preserve. Marriage counseling and family therapy can be immensely successful in resolving many family problems that might otherwise culminate in divorce.

On the other hand, I am also a realist. I recognize that often one partner has no control over the matter of divorce, that sometimes irreconcilable differences are present, and that an abusive situation may leave no alternative. While the finality of a divorce may be non-negotiable, certainly many creative options exist to handle the process of divorce sensitively. This chapter discusses the impact of divorce on children and offers practical strategies for parents and other concerned caretakers to minimize its potential negative effects.

Sadly, I have seen that, all too often, divorce brings out the worst in parents. Their inappropriate behavior can allow an unsettling situation for a child to escalate to a nearly intolerable one. Themselves under extreme duress, many parents make fundamental mistakes in relating to their children, thereby causing the divorce to be unnecessarily painful. With a little information and sufficient support, however, parents who must face divorce can learn to minimize the emotional trauma their children will experience and to continue proper parenting after the marriage dissolves.

Impact of Divorce on the Marriage Partners

For most people, the greatest of all fears is the fear of rejection, of losing the love and approval of others.

It comes as little surprise, then, that many adults in the throes of a divorce are emotionally vulnerable and may have little reserve left to support their children. Initially, divorce often undermines self-esteem and leaves parents feeling utterly worthless, hopeless, depleted, depressed, and angry. Often divorced parents feel they have failed miserably and find themselves engulfed by loneliness, self-pity, guilt, and anger. Preoccupied with regrets about their past and anxiety about their future, they may be temporarily out of touch with their children's feelings and unable to offer sufficient empathy or understanding.

Recalling that it's impossible to love someone else more than we love ourselves and that we nurture others from our own emotional overflow, it's easy to see why parents going through a divorce may be emotionally ill-equipped to support their own children adequately. Since children so often mirror their parents' psychological health, it is little wonder that divorce can have harmful effects on a youngster's psyche.

Impact of Divorce on Children

While parents experiencing divorce understandably may be preoccupied with their own grief reaction, a moment's reflection will confirm that a child's life is immediately and permanently altered by the often unilateral decisions of his parents. A child who deeply loves both parents essentially gets no vote about continuing to live with them. Instead, because the parents have stopped loving one another, the child is told he can no longer share his home with both of them. In an instant his world may be turned upside down, and he is made to feel, all too accurately, that he has no control in the situation.

Since the average marriage ending in divorce lasts about six years, many children experiencing divorce are very young, and thus highly impressionable, extremely dependent on their parents, and unable to seek outside support on their own. Even a "good" divorce can have a lasting impact on a child's development, and an unnecessarily traumatic family breakup can be associated with devastating psychological consequences.

Less Involvement of the Father

Unfortunately, divorce usually means that children see less of their father. While their times together may take on added meaning and while children can certainly have close relationships with the noncustodial parent, the reality is that most children of divorce don't see their fathers as often as they did when the family was intact. Statistics show that divorced fathers spend even less time with daughters than with sons. In fact, many children of divorce seldom see their fathers again.

Decline in the Standard of Living

Because maintaining two households is far more expensive than keeping one, divorce usually means that both parties experience a lower standard of living. While many exceptions exist, the mother most often retains custody of the children, while the father is awarded visitation rights. Typically, the mother experiences the greatest decrease in her standard of living, so the children are forced to learn to get by with less.

Less Involvement of the Mother

With the father's absence, a child can be expected to need the support and understanding of his mother more than ever. Chances are, however, that she is now less available, both physically and emotionally, than she was before the divorce. If the mother has been a full-time homemaker, she may be forced to seek outside employment in order to make ends meet. Because of her increased responsibilities at home, her work schedule, dating patterns, or school classes, the mother may have little remaining time to spend with her child. Ironically, the child struggling to adjust in the aftermath of divorce usually ends up seeing less of both parents.

Move from Familiar Surroundings

To add further insult during an already unsettling time, the financial strain imposed by divorce may result in the need to move from a once-cherished home to a less-expensive housing arrangement. The child may be expected to leave trusted friends and classmates, supportive schoolteachers, and his familiar neighborhood. Perhaps even a beloved pet must be left behind in the wake of parental decisions that often exclude input from the child.

Thus the scenario might be similar to what junior high students Todd and Dane experienced when their mother, Eileen, left their father after a fifteen-year marriage troubled by alcoholism. Taking only a few possessions, she and the two boys abruptly moved from their spacious house to a small apartment in a nearby city. Eileen enrolled the boys in a new school; she supported the three of them by working outside the home for the first time. A full year later, Todd still had not adjusted well in his new school, was often sullen and withdrawn, and had few friends. He requested to live with his father in his former community. Dane remained with Eileen, but he missed the companionship of his brother and spent his afternoons alone after school.

For Eileen, the resolve to break out of her enabler role in a destructive relationship ultimately enhanced her own self-esteem. Pleased with her success at achieving self-sufficiency, she soon decided to fulfill her life-long dream of going to dental school. Ten years after the divorce, she was a successful professional, had recently remarried, and was happier than she had been in many years. However, Todd and Dane, who were finishing college and entering early adulthood, admitted they still bore deep resentment about having their lives turned upside down during their emotionally vulnerable junior high years.

"If I had it to do again," mused Eileen, "I would have tried to maintain more stability in the boys' lives during the upheaval of the divorce. I would have given more consideration to keeping them in their school and close to their network of friends," she elaborated. "I guess I was in so much emotional pain myself that I instinctively did what seemed best for me, without fully appreciating how much the divorce and sudden move would affect Todd and Dane."

Assuming Blame for the Divorce

Two pervading emotional responses occur almost universally among children whose parents divorce. The first is an irrational belief that the child is somehow to blame for the breakup of the marriage. Young children, especially, are likely to assume that their misbehavior prompted the divorce, and the perpetuation of this misbelief can be extremely harmful to a child's self-esteem. Eight-year-old Natalie explained her situation to me this way: "My dad would say something bad about my mom. Later I would tell my mom what he had said. Then she would bring it up to my dad and a fight would start. If I hadn't said anything to my mom, maybe they wouldn't have fought so much. It was all their fighting that finally led to the divorce, so I guess, in a way, I'm partly to blame."

Even older children who know intellectually they are not responsible may retain fantasies about their role in the divorce. Staci, at sixteen, recalled with sad nostalgia the extended time her father, Doug, spent with her before he divorced her mother four years before. Doug had always coached her soccer and softball teams, and the father and daughter had spent long hours happily working side-by-side in their big yard. Doug had helped Staci with her homework each night and regularly attended all her school functions.

After the divorce, Doug moved across town to live with his girlfriend; he seldom initiated visits with Staci, becoming more involved in the lives of his girlfriend and her small daughter, Julia, instead. When Doug would invite Staci over, his girlfriend and Julia would invariably be present. Instead of interacting with Staci, Doug seemed preoccupied with Julia, playing with her the way he had enjoyed romping with Staci when she was younger. "My dad doesn't know how to relate to me anymore, now that I've grown up," Staci complained to me. "Nothing about our relationship is the same as I remember it, and I'm so jealous of all the attention he pays to Julia. I know it's illogical," she confided, "but I sometimes think that maybe the divorce was my fault because I couldn't remain a little girl. I grew up, and we grew apart. Now my father shows more interest in Julia than in me."

Fantasizing That the Parents Will Reunite

A second emotional response, almost universal among young children, is the fantasy that their divorced parents will someday get back together. Even older children can tenaciously cling to the magical belief that their parents will eventually reconcile and remarry. Typically, children selectively forget the marital discord that prompted the divorce and imagine that all will be well again if their parents will only reunite.

Eight-year-old Chris told me that he prayed every night for his parents to get back together. He further admitted that their reconciliation was his silent birthday wish when he blew out his candles each year, and whenever he pulled on a wishbone, threw coins into a fountain, or wished on a falling star. Although the divorce was prompted by Chris's father, who had become romantically involved with a co-worker, it was Chris's mother who ultimately remarried first. Chris deeply resented his mother's decision to remarry and was overtly hostile to his new stepfather, who represented an insurmountable obstacle to Chris's obsession with reuniting his parents.

Children's Physical and Behavioral Responses to Divorce

The stress of divorce manifests itself in children by a wide variety of behaviors and symptoms. Unfortunately, both parents and physicians may fail to recognize the association between the child's medical or behavioral symptoms and the emotional trauma of the divorce. Physical complaints, such as recurrent headaches, stomachaches, or insomnia, may linger for months and even years, especially when parental conflict continues.

Infants and toddlers may react by regressing developmentally, by resuming thumb-sucking after the habit had been outgrown, for example, or by beginning to wet or soil themselves after having been potty trained. They may become clingy and resist separating from the custodial parent. Sometimes feeding or sleeping difficulties arise. Preschool children may respond to parental conflict by displaying aggressive behavior around other children, such as hitting, biting, or throwing frequent tantrums.

Arnie was three and his sister, Trudi, was five when their parents divorced and their world turned upside down. Trudi and her mother moved across town to an apartment, while Arnie was sent temporarily to live with his maternal grandparents. Although the older couple did their best to lavish love and attention on Arnie, he developed bedtime fears of the boogeyman and insisted on sleeping with his grandparents each night. Despite having been toilet trained for eight months before the divorce, Arnie started urinating in his closet or the yard when he thought no one was looking. Previously a good-natured, amicable child, Arnie began to display physical aggression toward his sister whenever she accompanied her mother to visit. He would hit Trudi with his toy hammer, throw rocks at her, pull her hair, or push her down.

Arnie's mother lacked insight into the origin of these undesirable behaviors and repeatedly admonished Arnie to "act more grown up now that Daddy's gone." In fact, all of Arnie's misbehavior could be tied to the deep rejection he felt as a result of his father's leaving the family and his mother's sending him to live with his grandparents. His overt hostility toward Trudi was a convenient outlet for the anger and resentment he felt toward his mother for not keeping Arnie with her. His insistence on sleeping with his grandparents stemmed from his heightened fear of abandonment by another set of caretakers. Even peeing in a forbidden place was nothing more than an attempt on Arnie's part to exercise some measure of control in a little boy's world that had gone out of control.

Reactions in young children range from hyperactivity to chronic sadness. Bed-wetting, school phobias, or a decline in school performance may occur. Young children may worry excessively about the physical well-being of the custodial parent, having already "lost" one parent through divorce. Six-year-old Danny recalled a day when his estranged father was verbally harassing his mother, following her from room to room. Finally, in exasperation, she left the house and drove off in the car. After she had been gone two hours, Danny admitted that he began to fear she might never come back. Now, whenever his mom is gone longer than expected, he still worries that something may have happened to her.

Older children and adolescents may experience depression, loneliness, low self-esteem, and shame about the divorce. Their schoolwork may decline and they may act out in a delinquent manner. Often they express embarrassment about their parents' overt sexuality and reveal secret fears about having a failed marriage of their own in the future. Although they may know friends whose parents are divorced, they may not openly discuss their own family situation.

Adolescents also worry whether financial limitations created by the divorce will impact their chances of going to college, having a car, or maintaining their wardrobe. Brad and Andrew's parents have just separated; the boys expect they will divorce in the near future. Brad, a senior, says he is worried that the divorce will mean he can't get a letter jacket, go to the prom, or finalize his college plans. Andrew, still a freshman, tells me he is hopeful that his mother will remarry before he graduates. In that way, he reasons, money will less likely be a problem when he is ready for college. Right now, however, he fears he may not get into college since his grades have fallen dramatically because he "just can't concentrate." When I asked whether his teachers were aware of his parents' impending divorce, he replied flatly, "Most of my teachers I don't even like well enough to tell them about the divorce." Although he is now failing math when he previously had been doing C work, Andrew confides that his teacher hasn't yet inquired whether any life stresses might be interfering with his performance.

As a result of divorce, many children harbor intense anger toward their parents, which can periodically erupt in a variety of age-related outbursts, including temper tantrums, shouting matches, flagrant disobedience, or excessive demands. Shortly after his father moved out, thirteen-year-old Craig's teasing of his little sister greatly escalated. Several times each day his mother would blow up at him for provoking his sister without apparent cause. Often, she would call Craig's father and insist that he reprimand Craig over the phone.

As a rule, if your child is making you feel angry, he is probably very angry himself. Encourage your child to ventilate his angry feelings instead of keeping them bottled up. Explain that turning one's anger inward can result in depression or self-destructive behavior, like substance abuse, excessive risk-taking, or school failure. You can convey acceptance of your child's angry and enraged feelings at the same time that you make it clear that lashing out at others or destroying personal property is never an appropriate outlet for anger.

Instead, try to create an emotionally safe environment for your child, one in which he can verbally articulate his feelings without fearing your judgment or reaction. Once Craig's parents began exploring his reaction to the impending divorce, he was able to tell them how angry he was about the marital break-up and the fact that he no longer saw his dad every day. As Craig began to feel safer about expressing his disappointment and pain, he stopped picking on his sister and spent more time talking things out.

A child can be encouraged to share his feelings with a formal therapist, or to talk openly with a school counselor or peer counselor. If some of his friends have experienced parental divorce, your child may feel comfortable articulating his feelings in a rap session with his peers. You might also suggest that your child express his feelings in a poem, write them in a journal, or put them in a letter to one or both parents. Often, writing the letter produces such catharsis that sending it becomes unnecessary. Children also find creative outlets for their anger through participation in music, sports, arts, crafts, games, or vigorous exercise.

What's most important is your nonjudgmental acknowledgment and acceptance of your child's feelings. If she hasn't expressed any feelings, don't be deceived into thinking she doesn't have any. You may need to prod her to open up; you may need to say something like, "This divorce has probably been pretty hard on you, Deborah. Do you want to talk about it?" or "I'll bet you've got some strong feelings about all that's happened around here lately. I'd like to hear what it's been like from your point of view." Then be prepared to listen without interrupting.

The Impact of Parental Conflict on Children

Mounting evidence indicates that a child's maladjustment after parental divorce is due not to parental separation, but rather to parental conflict. The single most helpful thing parents can do to minimize the distress their child will experience as the result of their divorce is to avoid conflict in their own relationship. Unfortunately, the parental conflict present in the marriage may not stop once the divorce is final. In many instances, conflict actually increases after the divorce, as ex-spouses continue to argue, sometimes for years, over finances, visitation, childrearing issues, and intimate relations with others.

There are many possible explanations for the fact that parental conflict is associated with maladjusted children. Certainly, parental conflict is likely to be a stressor for a child, who easily gets caught in the crossfire between angry, vindictive parents. The unpredictability of parental outbursts can cause a child to be chronically anxious and guilty. The child learns to "walk on eggshells" at home, constantly fearful that his perceived misbehavior or personal needs might provoke a parental battle.

Also, children tend to imitate their parents' inappropriate behavior. Because their parents have failed to model appropriate techniques for conflict resolution, the children tend to become highly conflictual in their own relationships with siblings and peers. Furthermore, frequent parental conflict usually disrupts consistent discipline practices, making behavior problems more likely. Some children actually may develop emotional problems or personal crises as an extreme means of distracting their parents from their own conflict.

The available data about the ill effects of parental conflict on a child imply that, for some families, divorce might actually have a beneficial effect on the adjustment of the children. If divorce results in greatly reduced levels of parental conflict, children may have fewer problems than those who grow up in a home where parents argue. It is essential that parents recognize how significantly their own behavior and interactional style will affect their child's long-term adjustment to divorce. For the sake of your child's emotional well-being, I urge you to make every possible attempt to reduce the amount of conflict in your interactions with your ex-spouse.

Practical Ways to Minimize the Negative Effects of Divorce on Children

Communicate Honestly with Your Child

Don't keep vital information from your child about an impending divorce, naively hoping he won't suspect something is about to happen. Remember, fear of the unknown is almost always worse than dealing directly with reality. As soon as you are certain that one parent will be moving out, your child needs to be told, provided he is able to understand the situation. Don't insist that the separation will be only temporary if you know that is not true. I recall one school-aged child who claimed that the hardest thing for him to accept about the family breakup was the fact that his parents had lied to him by repeatedly assuring him they would never divorce.

Be honest and forthright about how the divorce will affect your child's daily life. Explain that "Daddy will be going to live in an apartment by his office," rather than "Daddy will be going away." Tell your child when he can expect to see his father again, and reassure him that he will continue to live with you in your home and go to the same school (if this is true). Above all, reassure him that both parents still love him very much, even though they have chosen to stop living together.

A young child may worry that if her parents can stop loving one another, they just might stop loving her someday too. Fear of abandonment is one of the greatest childhood fears of all, and this fear often surfaces when one parent leaves. The child may fantasize that if she misbehaves or does something terrible to lose her parents' love, she might be put out next. Children often rationalize that if one parent can be asked to move out, the other parent might decide to leave someday, or that something bad, such as an accident or illness, might befall the remaining parent. Make it clear to your child that you will have custody of her and will take care of her. If you need to begin working outside the home, explain exactly who will watch her in your absence.

If it is true, explain to your child that you made every effort to preserve the marriage before deciding to divorce. You might mention, for example, that you sought counseling and tried hard to work out your differences with your spouse before separating. Because your child's life is so greatly affected by your decision to divorce, it is important for him to know that you made every reasonable attempt to avoid the marriage breaking up. Acknowledge that it may be difficult for your child to adjust to the divorce and that it must seem unfair that he didn't take part in the decision. At the same time, you can emphasize that eliminating conflict in the family will be a positive outcome of the divorce.

Try to convey a receptive attitude that will make your child comfortable talking about the divorce. Be prepared to repeat explanations as often as necessary in the coming months. Don't make the mistake of assuming that a child who doesn't ask questions is handling the divorce just fine. More likely, the child is struggling to contain his questions, anger, and anxiety because he can detect that you are unreceptive.

Fifteen-year-old Ted told me with feigned indifference that his mother, who was suffering from depression, had left the family eight weeks earlier and moved to an apartment downtown. Neither Ted nor his younger sister had dared to discuss their mother's absence with their father. They had no idea whether the separation would be temporary or permanent and both children were still trying to pretend it was "no big deal." When I inquired further about why Ted had failed to broach the subject with his father, Ted confided his fear that "his dad would break down and cry, and I don't know if I could handle that." Sadly, Ted's father so seldom talked openly with his children or displayed any emotion that Ted found it too scary to try to communicate with his dad about one of the most important events in his life.

While children certainly don't need all the sordid details of marital discord, they are definitely entitled to know about family changes that will impact their lives. It is only natural for them to have some curiosity about such events, to want to share their own feelings in a supportive, nurturing environment, and to try to understand and empathize with your feelings. If your child is not asking questions, consider whether you may be giving nonverbal signals that say, "Don't ask." Do your best to cultivate a climate in which children feel free to comfortably raise the subject of divorce and ask questions openly.

A potential backlash of your receptivity is the possibility that your child will make painful accusations about who is to blame for the divorce, suggesting that "You drove Daddy away with your nagging" or "You broke up our family by cheating on Mom with another woman!" When such comments do occur, resist the temptation to become defensive, to feel guilty, or to lay blame. Instead, count yourself lucky that your child is comfortable telling you just what he feels or fantasizes. Remember, you can deal best with what you know is on your child's mind. Remain calm and explain that divorce is never a simple matter. You can acknowledge the truth about your nagging or your extramarital liaison, while reminding your child that there were many other issues contributing to the incompatibility between his parents.

Reassure Your Children That They Had Nothing to Do with the Divorce

Young children are naturally self-centered, and they tend to believe that most things happen as a result of their own actions, wants, or needs. Most children will assume that they caused the divorce in some way—they were "too naughty," made too many demands, or were "too much" or "not enough" for their parents. Children with handicaps or chronic medical problems may be even more prone to believe they are responsible for the divorce. It is essential that you make it absolutely clear to your child that she had nothing to do with the divorce. No matter how upset you become with your child later on, don't let yourself ever succumb to the temptation to blurt out a devastating comment like "You're so bad you drove Daddy away" or "We'd still be together if you hadn't been born." These "silver bullet remarks," screamed in anger and haste, can scar a child's ego for life. Your child needs to hear emphatically and repeatedly that the divorce had nothing to do with her, and that there is nothing she could ever do that would cause either parent to stop loving her.

Communicate the Finality of the Divorce

Both parents need to explain repeatedly that the divorce is final and permanent. It's okay to empathize with your child's wish that you and your ex-spouse will reconcile, but it is important not to feed his fantasies in any way. Help your child understand that reconciliation will not happen, even if he wishes very hard for it.

Unfortunately, parents cannot effectively convey this message unless they have accepted the finality of the divorce themselves. All too often, one partner initiates the divorce, and the other resists it vehemently. The parent who has not come to terms with the reality of the divorce himself is likely to transmit his own fantasies about reconciliation to the child. The child may continue to cling to the unrealistic hope of reconciliation out of loyalty to the parent who refuses to accept the divorce. If you just cannot acknowledge the finality of the divorce, seek professional counseling, both for your own benefit and for that of your child.

Avoid Derogatory Remarks About the Other Parent

The emotional pain and feelings of rejection and hurt that accompany divorce can be so strong that parents may lash out in anger at one another inappropriately.

You may wonder how you ever married your ex-spouse in the first place, and perhaps you'd like nothing better than to erase him or her from your life forever. But there is a fundamental difference between your severed relationship with your former spouse and your child's lifelong relationship with both his parents. Your child probably shares genetic material with the partner you may now despise. Someday you may expect to find another wife or husband, but your ex- is the only biologic or adoptive mother or father your child will ever have. No matter how much you would like to, you simply cannot expect your child to divorce his other parent just because you have divorced your marriage partner.

Making degrading comments about your ex only lowers your child's self-esteem, since your child carries many of his or her traits. Such put-downs, designed to demote your former spouse in your child's eyes, only serve to lower your child's estimation of you. Sheila, now in her thirties, is married today and the mother of two elementary school children. Having experienced parental divorce herself at the age of nine, Sheila shared a vivid childhood image from her regular visits with her father, who harbored deep resentment toward her mother long after the divorce: "He would be driving me home after we had had a wonderful weekend together. Then, as we approached my mother's house, everything would be suddenly spoiled as he started his verbal assault on my mom. Those last five minutes would ruin the whole weekend for me."

Somehow you must make yourself appreciate the necessity of your child's having a positive relationship with the other parent, even if you don't. Don't allow yourself to negate the interactions and experiences your child has with her other parent. Instead, allow that parent to enjoy some of your child's affection and loyalty. Just as you have ample ability to love more than one child in your family, your child is capable of loving her other parent without detracting from her love for you.

Don't Force Your Child to Take Sides

Parents going through the trauma of divorce may try to soothe their own bruised egos by enlisting recruits for their side in an embittered fight. Each might expect to find strong loyalty among their own parents, co-workers, or close friends. Certainly the relationship established with a professional therapist or counselor offers a highly supportive alliance. Thus buoyed by a few trusted allies, many parents will be sufficiently emotionally supported to allow their children and mutual friends to claim neutrality. Unfortunately, however, some parents do succumb to the temptation of trying to win the allegiance of their children. This ploy is highly inappropriate and is greatly resented by children.

Being forced to take sides puts a child in an uncompromising position and inevitably creates guilt feelings. Almost always, the child will fear alienating one parent or hurting a parent's feelings. If coerced enough, he may appear to acquiesce during your verbal assault on your ex-spouse, but chances are he will feel very conflicted about the situation. If he defends the other parent against your accusations, he risks hurting your feelings; if he agrees with you, if only by his silence, he is sure to feel guilty afterward. More than likely, the child forced to choose sides will agree with each of you in the absence of the other. While this may temporarily bolster your own ego, in the long run, your child will probably harbor resentment about being placed in such a predicament and unnecessarily burdened by guilt.

A child's reluctance to choose sides can be so strong that she will be unable to answer honestly when asked with whom she would like to live. Some children have confided that they would prefer their parents to decide where they will live, so they won't feel responsible for hurting one or the other parent's feelings. Children have actually been known to choose the parent they thought "needed them the most," thus placing the parent's perceived needs ahead of their own. If two daughters choose to live with their mother, the only son may feel compelled to say he wants to live with his father. A fourteen-year-old boy, Nigel, explained to me how he handled the dilemma of choosing sides. He told his parents that he didn't care whom he lived with and that he wanted them to make the decision. He only insisted that he remain in his same home so he would attend the same school and keep all his friends. "I'll live with whoever decides to stay in the house," he announced.

Avoid Using Your Child as a "Spy" or Go-Between

Unresolved anger and continuing fear cause some parents to use the child as a messenger to deliver information between ex-spouses who refuse to communicate directly with one another. This is highly inappropriate and makes the child feel guilty and used. Worse yet is asking the child to become an informant for either parent by reporting on the activities of the other parent. For example, after visitation with the noncustodial parent, the child may be pumped for information about financial purchases or dating patterns. Sometimes the information acquired is used against the other parent— for example, to raise child support payments—but at other times the spying represents a futile attempt to maintain the relationship with the ex-spouse. Again, this is inappropriate, and children resent being placed in this uncompromising position. Give your child per-

mission to verbalize his discomfort when either parent
tries to put him in the untenable position of juggling
conflicting loyalties. If he says, "Please don't ask me
who Dad dates—it makes me feel like a spy," listen.
In the long run, you'll be happy you did.

Avoid the "Disneyland Syndrome" During Visits

Often, the noncustodial parent feels guilty about the
divorce and about not seeing the child as often as the
custodial parent. He or she may be fearful of losing
the child's love and, thus, may try to compete with the
custodial parent by constantly buying gifts for and going
places with the child. Overly concerned about showing
the child a good time during visitation, noncustodial
parents often end up structuring every minute of a
weekend visit—eating out, going to an amusement
park, and seeing a movie. The custodial parent, as daily
disciplinarian, enforcer of routine chores, and long-
range financial planner, can easily become threatened
when a child's weekend with the ex-spouse sounds like
a trip to Disneyland.

In reality, such activities may initially seem like fun,
but eventually the routine can become a drudgery, with
the child simply craving to spend some quiet time alone
with the parent. Often, the "good time" parent inad-
vertently discovers that he and the children actually
have more fun washing the car together, going to the
laundromat, cooking spaghetti, playing a game, plant-
ing a garden, or tossing a Frisbee in the park.

Spend Individual Time
with Each Child

If you have more than one child, don't assume that they are handling the divorce in the same way. Each child's response to divorce is individual and depends on many factors, including age, gender, developmental level, relationships with both parents, underlying psychological makeup, support systems, and reaction to continuing parental conflict.

To emphasize this point, let me share some of the differences I observed among three siblings whose parents had separated several months earlier. Russ was thirteen, Heather was eleven, and Trevor was eight when I interviewed them alone over dinner one evening. While all three readily agreed that the separation had promptly achieved a dramatic and most welcomed reduction in parental conflict, their individual concerns about the impending divorce actually differed widely. Heather assumed some blame for parental fights that preceded the separation, while Trevor and Russ denied feeling any responsibility. Trevor and Heather were confident the separation was permanent, but Russ still retained hope that his parents would reunite, mostly on behalf of his father, who had reluctantly moved out at the mother's insistence. Trevor was embarrassed by the separation, denied knowing any classmates whose parents were divorced, and had told only one close friend. Heather, claiming "all her friends' parents were divorced," had shared the news of the separation easily. Trevor and Russ couldn't even entertain the possibility of their mother remarrying someday, whereas Heather thought a future stepfather would be okay, "especially if he was rich." All three kids answered in unison that they would be unwilling to move from their home or go to a new school, although the possibility had been raised because of financial constraints.

Parents are often surprised to consider that their children may be experiencing their divorce very differently. Try to spend even a few minutes alone with each child daily in order to evaluate how he is adjusting to the divorce, to answer his questions, and to reassure each that you love him uniquely. If you are the noncustodial parent, do your best to give each child some individual attention during visitation, or periodically schedule activities alone with each child.

Don't Thrust Your Child into an Inappropriate Role

While you may understandably be lonely and anxious after a divorce, don't expect your child to step in and fill the role of your ex-spouse. Don't require that your young boy suddenly become "the man of the house" or your daughter the chief cook and housekeeper. Your own emotional neediness surrounding the divorce may tempt you to foster such role reversals, expecting your child to parent you in some ways. Children who are overly worried about how their parents are adjusting to the divorce are especially vulnerable to trying to meet their parents' needs. It is important that you guard against the tendency to thrust your child into the overwhelming role of confidant or companion with whom to share your adult problems. Instead, join support groups, seek out a therapist, or enlist your adult friends and relatives to fill these needs. Let your child feel confident and secure that you are capable of taking good care of him. It is an unrealistic burden for your child to feel responsible for you in a crisis.

Avoid Disrupting the Child's Lifestyle

Whenever possible, it is preferable for a child to have as many aspects of her life as possible remain constant during the upheaval of a divorce. Thus, if the child can stay in her home, enjoy the sanctuary of her familiar bedroom, attend the same school, keep her network of friends, attend her regular church or synagogue, and participate in her usual activities, she will be better equipped to cope with having one parent move out of the household. Older children, especially, will handle the divorce more easily if they aren't forced to accept multiple life changes at once.

If a move is unavoidable, make an effort to keep as many things as possible consistent in your child's life. Don't try to deny the impact of a move—avoid saying, "Oh, what are you complaining about? We moved every couple of years when I was a kid, and it didn't hurt me any." Instead, express your empathy and understanding about your child's reluctance to move away: "I know that this is hard on you and that it must be frustrating not having any choice in the matter. I'm sorry it has to be this way, and I'm sure it must make you angry at times." Do what you can to soften the blow: "I'll bet we can have Anna fly out to see you for a couple weeks this summer."

Maintain Regular Visitation and Other Commitments

One way to restore some measure of predictability to a child's life during the often unpredictable transition of divorce is to make every effort to keep your commitments. The noncustodial parent should try to maintain a schedule of regular visitation and to be on time.

Our children measure our love for them by the amount of time we spend with them and by how much of a priority we make them. Failing to show up when promised conveys a strong message that something else was more important at that moment than our child. After divorce, more than ever, a child needs to be confident that he is still valued by both his custodial and his non-custodial parents and can depend on both of them to keep their word and meet their commitments.

Parental commitment applies to many diverse issues, including child support payments, a child's spending allowance, and his chauffeuring needs. Before her parents divorced, thirteen-year-old Karrie received a weekly allowance of ten dollars from her father. After her parents separated, her father started paying only sporadically, explaining, "You'd better make this stretch because I don't know when I'll be able to pay your allowance again." Karrie complained to me that she was unable to budget realistically or predictably plan whether she could go to the movies with her friends. "I wouldn't even care if he lowered my allowance to five dollars a week, so long as I could count on it regularly," she conceded.

Another teen, Barry, explained that he didn't like to ask his mother for rides to soccer practice anymore, although she had always taken him in the past. "She seems so sad and unavailable most of the time that I try not to count on her for anything right now . . . and I don't even tell my dad when my games are anymore," he added, "because it hurts too much to hope he'll come and then not have him show up after all."

Remember Special Activities, Birthdays, and Holidays

Holidays can be especially difficult for divorced families, as memories of happier times re-surface and children are shuffled between households. The young child may long for both parents to be present at his birthday celebration or fantasize that a reconciliation will occur. An older child may worry whether one parent will be lonely or depressed during the holiday. It is important that children not be kept in the dark but be informed well in advance about the specific arrangements for each holiday. Communicate openly with the noncustodial parent to assure that he will remember the child on his birthday, be present at special school performances, scout ceremonies, and the like. Don't set up your ex to look bad at your child's expense—"I'll bet your dad forgets your birthday again this year." Occasionally, both parents, in a spirit of cooperation, will agree to be present at the child's request. At these times, more than ever, your child will appreciate your putting your differences aside so he can enjoy a special day with both his parents unmarred by conflict.

Keep Discipline Consistent

A common complaint following divorce is the mother's difficulty maintaining discipline when the father is absent from the family. Children often vent their anger toward the custodial parent by increased acting-out behavior, tantrums, talking back, or complaining. Regression is also common in the aftermath of divorce, especially among younger children. It is important not to feed into such behavior by losing control, screaming, starting arguments, or overreacting in other ways.

Don't call your ex-spouse in hysteria and expect him to discipline the kids by telephone.

The best advice is to make the rules of the house clear to everyone from the outset and enforce the limits consistently, even when you are tired and vulnerable. Let your child express himself without interrupting, and indicate that you understand his feelings. Avoid needless confrontations and power struggles provoked solely for the sake of "winning control." Instead, limit your battles to the most important issues, and be flexible enough to try to work out a satisfactory resolution whenever feasible. When punishment is warranted, attempt to make it age-appropriate, commensurate with the offense, and instructional, when possible. Above all, remain calm and objective and let your child know you expect him to be responsible for controlling his behavior.

If One Parent Will No Longer Be Involved with the Child

I have written this chapter with my personal bias that most parents have good intentions and sincerely want to do what is best for their children. With sufficient information and support, most parents will strive to meet their children's needs and even to put them above their own.

I also recognize, however, that a few parents have emotional deficits so severe that they are unable to show love appropriately to their children. A few parents are intentionally abusive; some abandon their children or use them to serve their own needs. Fortunately, such parental disturbance is rare, but admittedly, it does occur.

If your ex-spouse is incapable of showing love to your

child, it is best to be honest about this fact. If the parent will not be involved in the child's life, let your child know she should not expect to see the parent again. It is preferable for your child to grieve the loss of the desired parental relationship and then get on with her life than to continue to hold out futile hope that an emotionally disturbed parent will reform.

Explain repeatedly that the other parent's inability to express love for the child has nothing to do with the child's worthiness of love. Emphasize that many other people, including yourself, love the child and that she will establish many loving relationships in the future.

Acknowledge the depth of your child's legitimate sadness over not having two loving parents, and encourage the essential grief work that will enable him to accept the emotional loss of a parent. At the same time, help your child appreciate that anger is a useful emotion only when it can effectively help him achieve something he needs or wants. For example, telling his sister it makes him angry when she takes something from his room without permission might prevent her from taking his possessions in the future. But prolonged, useless anger toward a parent who is incapable of change serves no purpose at all. Such chronic anger just gets turned inward in the form of depression and loss of self-esteem. Explain that, for some things in life, it is best simply to accept the situation instead of continually stewing about it. Then do all you can to help your child cultivate meaningful relationships with other loving adults in his environment and, above all, keep emphasizing that he is lovable, capable, and a worthwhile person, even if one of his parents is unable to show him love.

Beyond Divorce

Divorce is not necessarily always or all bad. Children can learn many valuable lessons in life through experiencing parental divorce. From a young age, our children look to us to gauge their appropriate response to life events. When our toddler loses his balance and falls, he searches our face to see how he should react. If we suddenly look alarmed and act worried that he may be injured, he complies by scrunching up his face and letting out a wail. If we brighten our eyes and announce cheerfully, "Uh-oh, Jason fell down. Jump up, jump up!" he springs back to his feet, face beaming.

Similarly, as our children grow older, they study our reaction to life crises such as divorce, loss of our job, or dealing with a handicap. If we allow ourselves to feel worthless without a mate, wallow in rejection, refuse to accept any responsibility for the breakup, continually denigrate the other partner, or be unable to move beyond the divorce, we convey to our children a variety of negative messages about the inevitable traumas of life. We transmit an unhealthy and pessimistic view that an isolated negative event can "ruin our life," that our self-worth is determined by others, that we have no control over our own destiny, and that happiness is based on outside circumstances rather than our inner attitude.

Conversely, when divorce is handled well, children gain the opportunity to see each parent accept partial responsibility for the failed relationship and successfully resolve emotionally charged issues with mutual respect and self-control. They learn that a crisis or perceived failure can simultaneously represent a challenging opportunity for exciting personal growth. They may witness their mother achieving new levels of self-sufficiency or their father assuming an expanded nurturing role.

They can appreciate that time, and perspective can change negative events into positive outcomes. Most important, they can learn that happiness is a state-of-mind and not a set of circumstances. Successfully adapting to parental divorce can give a child confidence that he can effectively handle and even grow from any life experience that awaits him.

ADDITIONAL READING:

Baris, Mitchell A., and Carrity, Carla B. *Children of Divorce*. De Kalb, Illinois: Psytec Corp., 1988.

Bernstein, Anne C. *Yours, Mine, and Ours*. New York: Charles Scribner's Sons, 1989.

Brown, Laurene. *Dinosaurs Divorce*. New York: Little, Brown, 1986.

Francke, Linda Bird. *Growing Up Divorced*. New York: Ballantine Books, 1983.

Friedman, James T. *Divorce Handbook: Your Basic Guide to Divorce*. New York: Random House, 1984.

Gardner, Richard A. *The Boys and Girls Book About Divorce*. Dunmore, Pennsylvania: Aronson, 1992.

McCoy, Kathleen. *Solo Parenting: Your Essential Guide*. New York: New American Library, 1987.

Newman, G. *101 Ways to be a Long-Distance Super-Dad*. Palo Alto, California: R&E Publishers, 1981.

Prokop, Michael S. *Divorce Happens to the Nicest Kids*. Warren, Ohio: Alegra House Publishers, 1986.

9

MANAGING THE STRESS OF PARENTHOOD

Written by Larry Neifert

No book on contemporary parenting would be complete without addressing the impact of stress on family life. Because stress management is an area in which my husband has developed particular expertise, I have asked him to share his knowledge and insights by contributing this chapter. Larry, my parenting partner, has conducted more than two hundred seminars, workshops, and presentations on stress-related topics over the past ten years. I'm confident you'll appreciate his unique perspective.

I look back on my own experience of becoming a parent with a curious mixture of wonder and panic. Wonder at the awesome miracle that was born of an intense love. Panic because Mari and I felt so ill-prepared to bear sole responsibility for our newborn son. Much to our amazement, we survived our early fumbling attempts at parenting, despite our youth, inexperience, financial worries, social isolation, and unique lifestyle. Perhaps because my own introduction to parenthood seemed unnecessarily stressful, I am particularly committed to helping you minimize the stress in your parenting experience.

I vividly remember pulling into Pearl Harbor on March 1, 1968, aboard the USS *Goldsborough*, the guided-missile destroyer on which I was stationed. We were returning home from a tour of duty off Vietnam, and every sailor aboard pressed against the ship's rails, looking forward to reunion with his family and loved ones. As the ship eased into its berth, I excitedly scanned the crowd of hundreds of wives and children gathered on the dock, looking for the familiar figure of my young wife who had tearfully waved good-bye from this same shore six long months ago.

The moment my eyes fell upon Mari remains frozen in my memory. It was the instant I first came face-to-face with the reality that I was about to become a father. Certainly, we had planned for this child, and I had followed Mari's pregnancy in an endless stream of letters. But I had left behind a young wife still in her teens, barely "showing" the pregnancy that had been confirmed only weeks before my departure. Standing before me now on the brink of motherhood was a woman who would deliver our son in a week. My initial shock was soon eclipsed by the sweetness of our reunion, known only to those who have tasted the emptiness of forced separation.

We had barely a few days in which to begin re-establishing our relationship, however, before Mari went into labor. We drove to the hospital to confirm whether this was the "real thing," neither of us realizing that once Mari disappeared behind a pair of swinging doors, we would not be allowed to see each other again until after our baby was born.

The father's waiting room on the maternity ward at Tripler Army Hospital was a drab and lonely place just before midnight on March 7, 1968. I began my ritual of methodically pacing the empty room, having no idea how long labor would last. As the first hour stretched into two and then three hours, I began to crave a cup of coffee. Someone advised me that I could find a coffee machine in the basement, but I knew intuitively that the moment I left the floor, my son or daughter would be born. "What kind of father would I be if I wasn't there when the nurse brought out my baby?" I reasoned.

Finally, after pacing the floor alone for ten hours, I could stand it no more. I was dying for a cup of coffee, desperately fighting sleep, and hungering for any human contact. Having decided to make a dash for it, I scrambled down the hall, commandeered an open elevator, and shot to the basement. I frantically located the coffee machine, dropped in my dime, pushed "extra sugar," and flew back to the elevator without spilling a drop from my open cup. I quickly rose through the building to the maternity floor and slid back into the waiting room, checking my watch. I proudly noted that the entire trip had taken me only two minutes and forty-seven seconds. There, awaiting me, was an impatient nurse who inquired accusingly, "Where on earth have you been? We brought your new son out to show you, but you were nowhere to be found!"

Within twenty-four hours, however, our immense joy was clouded by the announcement that Peter had developed severe jaundice due to a blood incompatibility. While babies were brought to the other mothers in Mari's four-bed ward, we were advised that Peter had to remain in the nursery. We were allowed to view him through the nursery window only once each day and had never even held him when we were asked to sign permission for an exchange transfusion to be performed late at night on his fourth day of life. Mari and I had exaggerated fears that Peter would die during the procedure or that he might be brain damaged afterward. We had never met any of the military doctors on whom his life depended, and we had no relatives within thousands of miles.

We were relieved beyond words when Peter came through the exchange transfusion without problems. By the next morning, his jaundice was markedly diminished, and we were permitted to hold our son for the first time. Although he looked robust enough, we had been so frightened by his medical problem that we handled him as if he were made of glass.

On the way home from the hospital, we had to stop at a department store to pick up the crib we had ordered a few days earlier. We owned barely any baby supplies and had little idea what a newborn would require. Mari resumed her daily college classes from 8:00 A.M. to 1:00 P.M. only two days after bringing Peter home. I took a second week of leave, during which we jointly learned to care for our baby and began restructuring our lives around his needs. In the midst of everything else facing us, Mari learned to drive that week and got her license, and we hired another sailor's wife to babysit Peter each morning.

Since there was no way we could meet the added expense of a baby on my seaman's salary, I had to take a part-time job in the evenings to make ends meet. None of these events was individually beyond our ability to cope, yet the cumulative effect of all of them happening within a few weeks was incredibly stress-provoking. One night, about two weeks after Peter was born, he cried excessively without explanation and nothing we tried seemed to console him. I've always felt a twinge of guilt because, exhausted and frustrated, I actually asked Mari half-seriously, "Isn't there some way we can just give him back?"

A parent seldom gets to a low point like that as the result of a single event. Single events are seldom the cause of breakdowns or stress-related illnesses. What eventually *can* defeat us, however, is a whole series of events piled one upon another and experienced within a compacted interval of time.

The "final straw" is often little more than just that—a straw. We seem to find a well of hidden strength when it comes to dealing with the major traumas in life. A sustained series of smaller stressful events, however, may quietly empty the well, without our realizing how depleted we have become. Once our reserves have been exhausted, our capacity for effectively dealing with stress is dramatically diminished, and we ourselves become prime candidates for physical and/or emotional illness.

In a famous study examining the health effects of various life changes, Drs. Holmes and Rahe* demonstrated that multiple life changes occurring in a short period of time place an individual at increased risk for contracting a stress-related illness. They developed a list of forty-three life-change items, known as the Social Readjustment Rating Scale. Each item was weighted in importance based on its frequency of occurrence among heart attack victims. Both pregnancy and gaining a new family member are among the items found on their scale. Also listed are numerous modifications in lifestyle that often accompany pregnancy and new parenthood, such as, change in financial status; change in eating and sleeping patterns; change in social activities; change in type and amount of recreation; change in level of sexual activity; change in job status; move to a new home. These changes associated with new parenthood are superimposed upon all the other life changes that would normally be happening even if you weren't gaining a new family member, thus placing new parents at particular risk for stress-related illness. And unfortunately, parental stress doesn't end with the initial adjustment to a new baby. For a variety of reasons, every stage of parenthood is associated with its own unique stressors, producing excess wear and tear on our bodies and minds.

* Thomas H. Holmes and Richard Rahe, "The Social Readjustment Rating Scale," *Journal of Psychosomatic Research* 11 (1967):213–217.

Definition of Stress

Hans Selye, M.D.—considered by many to be the father of stress research—has defined stress as *the nonspecific response by the body to any demand made upon it*. I want to dissect this definition and elaborate on it because understanding what stress is and what it does to us is critical if we are to develop effective ways to combat it.

Stress is *nonspecific* in that it affects different people in different ways. One person might react to prolonged, unrelieved stress by developing an ulcer, while the next person gets high blood pressure, and still another has a heart attack without warning. Or too much stress may manifest itself in less catastrophic ways, such as heightened irritability, sleep disorders, loss of sexual interest, tension headaches, or lower back pain.

Next, stress is a *response by the body* and is, therefore, physiologic in nature rather than being purely psychological, as is commonly presumed. Stress results from *any demand* made upon the body, regardless of whether that demand is perceived as bad or good.

Two types of stress can be identified—"distress" and "eustress." Distress is viewed as "bad stress" and occurs as an adverse reaction to the world around us. It's what enables us to survive real or perceived threats to our well-being. Eustress, on the other hand, is "good stress," causing happiness or pleasure. It is what drives us to achieve and to grow. Believe it or not, too much eustress in too short a period of time can be just as harmful as too much distress, because the body has trouble differentiating between the two and therefore reacts similarly to both. Consequently, becoming a parent for the first time presents a "double-whammy" of both distress and eustress, compounding potential stress-related problems.

The Primal Stress Response

Before addressing specific stress-management techniques for parents, another concept I'd like to develop is something called the "primal stress response." You may have heard of this as the "fight-or-flight response." We humans, when confronted with either real or imagined danger, exhibit a universal physiological response that we share with other mammals. This innate reaction prepares the body for vigorous muscular activity whenever a perilous situation is perceived. It has been theorized that our Stone Age forebears, having minimal natural defenses, relied upon the fight-or-flight syndrome for survival. When their safety was threatened, humans very quickly prepared either to fight the enemy or to flee from it, both options requiring vigorous muscular activity. If early man were immobilized by fear, he would be in imminent danger of extinction. Instead, fear and aggression, by preparing man for action, offered great value as a survival tactic in anticipatory response to a critical situation.

Today, however, our modern world presents fewer opportunities to cope with danger through vigorous muscular activity. In fact, society strongly dissuades us from physically fighting our adversaries or fleeing from our problems! Thus, when my boss yells at me for some real or imagined infraction, my innate reaction calls for either striking out at him or running for my life, while the response that is culturally appropriate demands that I engage in no action whatsoever. My body has just geared up for vigorous muscular activity, but my mind has yanked hard on the reins! The result is a lot of pent-up energy that, if allowed to build up in high amounts without relief, can be extremely harmful. It is little wonder that modern mankind, confronted with an ever-increasing number of stressors with no corresponding increase in the amount of muscular activity, is experiencing stress-related illnesses in unprecedented numbers.

Your Unique Response to Stress

Each of us reacts physically in a unique fashion to excessive stress in our lives. Our bodies have a way of telling us when we need to slow down. I subscribe to the "weak link" theory, whereby each individual has a weak link in his or her organ chain that manifests the effects of sustained, ongoing, unrelieved stress. Thus, one person might suffer a heart attack from too much stress, while another develops hypertension . . . or ulcers . . . or migraines . . . or backaches . . . or rheumatoid arthritis. While these are obvious stress-related illnesses, I'd like to discuss a number of more subtle, but nevertheless disruptive, common physical symptoms of stress.

Disturbed Sleep

One of the first indications that you are under too much stress will often be a form of sleep disorder or dysfunction. A sleep dysfunction is any sustained deviation from your normal sleep pattern, such as insomnia, excessive sleeping, fitful sleeping, or awakening early and being unable to go back to sleep.

Bruxus, or Teeth Grinding

Another common symptom of too much stress is a condition known as "bruxus," or teeth grinding. We humans act out negative emotions, such as anger, frustration, and hostility, by jutting our jaws and clenching our teeth. Unfortunately, many of us are unaware that we clench and grind our teeth in our sleep, resulting in worn teeth and chronic jaw pain. I have a good friend who, over the years, has ground his teeth down to smooth nubbins. Some of you, not realizing you are teeth grinders, may have awakened in the morning wondering why your jaw muscles were so sore. As a child, I had a recurring bad dream in which I would be descending some steep, narrow stairs into a dungeonlike place. The farther I descended, the greater my fear mounted. Invariably, toward the conclusion of my dream, my attention would be drawn to my jaws, which would begin to swell horribly in my dream. It wasn't until years later that I realized what I was actually experiencing during those dreams was bruxus, which was occurring in relation to stressful events during my waking hours.

Some people grind their teeth not only during sleep, but in their waking hours as well. Next time you're caught in traffic and are in a hurry to get somewhere, note what's happening to the muscles in your head. Very likely, your jaws are clenched tightly together, and your tongue is probably pressing hard against the roof of your mouth. Your tongue, for its size, is one of the strongest muscles in your whole body. Just relaxing your jaws and tongue can begin the relaxation process throughout your entire body. If you realize you are a teeth grinder, ask your dentist (who is probably already aware of your condition) to refer you to a clinic where you might be fitted with a device similar to a retainer, which will prevent you from grinding your teeth at night.

Chronic Muscle Tension

Whenever we are experiencing a "fight-or-flight" re-action, our muscles are in a state of tension. Prolonged muscle tension can result in tension headaches, chronic debilitating back pain, neck pain, and shoulder pain.

Increased Illnesses

During stress a number of hormones are released. One group is the endorphins, mysterious hormones that per-form a variety of functions. They are the body's natural painkillers, having the same chemical makeup as mor-phine. Endorphins also act as a trigger mechanism for the immune system. Because the body's capacity to manufacture endorphins is finite, however, too much stress can exhaust its ability to release endorphins. Con-sequently, your immune system functions less efficiently than it was intended, increasing your susceptibility to disease.

These are just a few examples of the physical man-ifestations of excessive stress. As mentioned earlier, heart attacks, ulcers, migraine headaches, eating dis-orders, some autoimmune diseases, and many psycho-logical disturbances can be considered stress-related diseases. While you may try to ignore the physical symp-toms of chronic stress, the stark reality is that you've got nowhere else to live once your body wears out!

In addition to physical symptoms, stress can make a parent irritable, impatient, and less tolerant of normal childhood behaviors, like whining and sibling rivalry. Stress contributes to feelings of resentment and depres-sion and may rob a parent of many of the joys of child-rearing.

Contemporary Sources of Stress

Stressors can be thought of as the external demands of life, as well as our internal struggles and mental attitudes in response to those demands. Countless sources of stress can be identified in contemporary life. If we examine some common life stressors, it soon becomes obvious that parents are particularly vulnerable to the effects of stress.

Worry

Real or imagined fears and anxieties cause virtually everyone to worry periodically. Routine concerns can range from relatively trivial matters, such as whether we'll be late to work, to oppressive fears, as of nuclear war or AIDS. In addition to the pervasive fears most people experience, what parent doesn't worry daily about their child's health, safety, development, academic performance, emotional adjustment, personal happiness, and future well-being? Parental worries never end—they just keep changing form. We wonder whether our baby will develop normally, react adversely to an immunization, become ill, or be injured. We worry about trusting our toddler to the care of others. Will he be kidnapped, injured, or abused? We worry whether our son will make friends at school or make the team. And will our daughter be invited to the prom, experiment with drugs, be involved in a car accident, or become pregnant?

Many people experience exaggerated, recurrent, and unreasonable fears, such as claustrophobia, fear of heights, or fear of flying. In addition to such common phobias, parents can develop intense fears involving their children, such as fear of a birth defect, crib death, kidnapping, or serious illness.

Family

The various interactions arising within a family are prime sources of stress. While all couples living together must deal with routine conflict resolution, problems of aging parents, and demands from other relatives, parents have multiple additional family stresses. The physical demands of infant care, routine toddler behavior, daily discipline, sibling rivalry, and adolescent acting-out add to family stress for parents.

Society

Our interactions with other people and our need for community acceptance and involvement often create stress. These social stressors can be greatly increased for parents, for example, if a parent worries about how his child's behavior in a restaurant affects others. Also, the relative isolation that can result from the increased demands of parenthood can be a significant source of stress for some parents, who lose social networks formerly important to them.

Change

Both numerous and rapid life changes as well as the absence of change can produce stress. While all adults move, change jobs, or change relationships periodically, parents, especially, must deal with continual life changes and transitions, beginning with conception. Major changes occur each time a child is integrated into the family, and marked parental ambivalence can accompany even minor childhood transitions such as weaning or starting kindergarten, let alone turning the car keys over to a teenager or sending a child to college. Conversely, the labor intensive, day-to-day care of infants and toddlers can make many at-home mothers of preschoolers feel their life is too stagnant and unchanging.

Workplace

Pressures and anxieties experienced at the workplace are often amplified for parents. For example, a mother's workplace may be her home, where she works a sixteen-hour shift and is "on call" the other eight hours. For parents employed outside the home, added to the routine workplace stressors are daily hassles involving their children. What to do if Stevie wakes up sick on a workday, the frustration of missing part of Julie's performance in the school play because of a work-related crisis, and afternoon telephone interruptions from a latch-key child are just a few examples of the daily conflicts facing working parents—even as they must deal with the ordinary stresses that arise in the workplace.

Decisions

The myriad decisions that face each of us every day can be highly stress-producing. Life has become so complicated and full of choices that even mundane decisions about what to eat or wear can be emotionally draining. Simply selecting a rental video to watch on your VCR can consume twenty minutes of indecision. We are bombarded by options every time we drive up to a fast-food restaurant, turn on the TV, walk into a bookstore, or open our clothes closet. For parents, additional stress is created by such heavyweight parental decisions as whether to have your son circumcised, whether to breast- or bottlefeed, whether and when to return to work, which daycare arrangement to choose, which pediatrician to select, whether to hold your son back in school, when to let your daughter start dating.

Physical Stress

Stress can stem from the physical demands placed on our bodies, such as pregnancy, lactation, sleep deprivation, inadequate nutrition, lack of exercise, or drug or alcohol abuse. Mothers of young children, especially, may be victims of chronic fatigue. Any abrupt change in physical activity also can be a significant stressor, including the sudden inactivity accompanying prolonged bedrest during pregnancy. Similarly, "the empty nest syndrome" can be a source of physical stress for parents at the other end of the childrearing spectrum.

Illness

Acute or recurrent medical problems can cause pain or stress, including migraine headaches, asthma, allergies, high blood pressure, arthritis, diarrhea, heartburn, backaches, and countless others. Parents of preschool and school-aged children may be exposed to various infectious diseases acquired by their children at school or daycare, such as strep throat, pink eye, colds, and stomach flus. Throughout my twenties, during which time my kids attended daycare, I was plagued by recurrent illnesses, including repeated bouts of strep throat.

Environment

Irritating aspects of our environment, such as cigarette smoke, exhaust fumes, excessive noise, broken elevators, or bad weather often contribute to stress in our lives. Again, parenthood notoriously involves excessive environmental stressors, such as prolonged crying, frequent whining, sibling bickering, messy diapers, spit up, dirty bottles, and cluttered rooms, just to name a few.

Specific Techniques for Managing Stress

Now that I've made my case for the parents of our society being particularly vulnerable to stress, what can you do to diminish the impact of stress in your life? There are many strategies to control both the stress we experience and our response to it.

Enlist Support from Others

One of the main differences between parenting today and parenting forty years ago is that the family unit has evolved from largely extended family networks to more isolated nuclear families. Years ago, we were primarily an agrarian society. Chances were, a family lived on the same piece of land as did their parents and grandparents. When your baby had colic, you ran to your mom, saying, "I can't understand why Jamie keeps crying. I've fed him and changed him, but I can't console him." Typically Mom would say something like, "Maybe I can help. You look tired—why don't you bring Jamie over here and let me watch him while you get some rest?"

That former, comforting reality is a fantasy today. We live in a highly mobile society that is comprised mainly of small nuclear families. Often there isn't even a co-parent present to share the daily childrearing responsibilities. The supportive extended family is largely a thing of the past.

In the absence of that extended family network, we need to cultivate whatever support system we presently have available or can implement. This involves actively communicating with, asking for help from, and listening to our partners, siblings, friends, neighbors, colleagues, and church members. I will never forget our insightful minister and his wife, Ken and Nancy Heflin, who recognized our frazzled condition when Peter was only three weeks old. They insisted we leave him with them for an evening while we escaped to spend some time alone together. I can't tell you how refreshing and rejuvenating that evening was for us.

Co-parents need to spend time alone together on a regular basis, even if this occurs only after the children have been put down for the night. Share your feelings, concerns, and wishes for your children and one another. Single parents *also* need time away with a member of the opposite sex. Good parenting doesn't require that partners neglect one another for the sake of their children; ideally, a couple's personal relationship is an important source of support through the inevitable stresses of parenting. All too often, however, parenting is made even more difficult by the presence of significant stress in the marital relationship.

Set Realistic Expectations and Pace Yourself

One of the greatest sources of stress in our lives stems from unrealistic expectations placed upon ourselves, our children, and others. Stress has been astutely defined as the difference between our expectations and the reality we experience. The best way to lower our stress is to lower our expectations of the world, others, and ourselves.

Stop believing that you have to perform at 100 percent efficiency at all times and in all life's arenas. It's physically impossible to be 100 percent super parent, 100 percent super spouse, 100 percent super professional 100 percent of the time. While it may be possible for you to strive toward excellence in any one of these at a given moment, you cannot be excellent in all three at the same instant. The idea that you can be all things to all people at all times is an absolute myth. As long as you continue to buy into that myth, your reality will fall short of your expectations, and you will experience constant stress. Furthermore, you will unnecessarily feel guilty and inadequate much of the time. Doesn't sound like much fun, does it?

Rather than striving to do and to be everything for everyone at once, begin prioritizing your responsibilities and aim at winnowing the critical few from the trivial many. To do this, make a list of everything that needs to be done and the time frame in which the tasks must be completed. Then categorize each item into one of the following three designations:

- *A Items*: The "critical few" activities that absolutely *have* to be accomplished today and that will be likely to generate the greatest results.

- *B Items*: The various maintenance activities that need to be completed eventually, but which could be put off until later without significantly compromising your overall results.

- *C Items*: The "trivial many" that either have no deadlines attached to them or are relatively inconsequential in terms of results achieved compared to effort expended.

In examining how most of us allocate our time, it has been clearly demonstrated that we typically spend only a small percentage of time on the most critical activities that will ultimately yield the greatest results. Conversely, most people tend to spend excessive time on unimportant tasks that yield only minimal results. It's almost as if we deliberately immerse ourselves in our C items in order to avoid tackling what's really important.

After assigning every item on your "to do" list an appropriate priority letter, force yourself to attack each of the A activities. When those are completed, plunge into the B tasks. C items should only be started after all A and B activities have been accomplished. Naturally, your intent will be to complete every task on your list every day, but we all recognize that there will be days when unanticipated intrusions on your time keep you from finishing everything you set out to accomplish. By daily prioritizing your list, chances are you can be satisfied with having completed your critical A items, even if some B and C tasks remain undone.

Give yourself permission not to do everything perfectly. That's not to suggest that you should settle for mediocrity in all things. Rather, it is meant to emphasize that some things justify being done adequately. By allowing yourself to do many things "adequately" and only a few things "superbly," you will free up precious time to devote to those priorities that are really critical in your life.

Maintain a Positive Attitude

The way we react to a particular event and the associated stress we experience are largely governed by our individual belief systems about that event. For example, I love to sail my sixteen-foot Hobie catamaran in winds so strong that one of the hulls lifts four to five feet out of the water. To me, "flying a hull" in high winds is tremendously exhilarating—it represents riding that thin edge between racing across the water or abruptly capsizing. Marianne, however, prefers more tranquil sailing; when one hull lifts out of the water, she immediately becomes uncomfortable and tenses every muscle in her body. In this instance, the same activating event or stimulus—flying a hull—can have dramatically different emotional consequences or responses in two different people—exhilaration or tension—based on their individual belief systems regarding the activating event. As Shakespeare said, "There is nothing either good or bad, but thinking makes it so."

Unfortunately, most of us embrace many irrational beliefs along with our rational ones. Irrational beliefs have no basis in fact. They often link *self* and *being* with *traits* and *performances*. They emphasize "oughts" and "shoulds," feeling guilty, laying blame, reliving past events, and building scenarios that are way out of proportion to the initiating event. It is most often our irrational thinking that gets us in trouble emotionally.

Stress management is mind management. It is the *pro*active control of the conscious mind over the *reac*tive subconscious. When we engage in worry about future events or feel guilty about past events, we do ourselves a great disservice. Learning the simple practice of positive self-talk can help quiet the mind and relieve the stressful effects of irrational belief systems.

With your eyes closed, try as hard as you can to think two entirely separate thoughts simultaneously.

Can't do it, can you?

You'll understand why if you remember a basic principle from high school physics: Two objects cannot occupy the same space at the same time. And since thoughts are comprised of electrical and chemical activity, thoughts are actually objects. You cannot, therefore, think two conscious thoughts at the same time. Once you understand that you cannot think more than one thought at a time, you will realize that when you are thinking positive thoughts, you cannot also be thinking negative thoughts. Similarly, when you are engaging in negative behaviors that do not work for you—such as guilt and worry—you are incapable of doing anything productive or proactive at that instant.

Examine Your Options

Until recently, I believed we had only two alternatives available when confronted by a stressor—we could either change the stressful event or we could learn to accept it. The philosophy of these dual options is summarized in the well-known *Serenity Prayer* from Alcoholics Anonymous:

> God, grant me the serenity to accept the things
>   I cannot change,
> The courage to change the things
>   I can change,
> And the wisdom to know the difference.

If you think about it, however, we really have a total of five alternatives for dealing with a stressful event. Some of these are more effective than others, but you'd be surprised how many people regularly choose the least appropriate coping styles. I believe that sequentially and realistically reviewing these options is the most effective way to approach a stressful situation in our lives.

Option 1—change it. This option is seldom easy because most changes involve giving up something valued in order to gain a new set of conditions. I know a woman who has battled an overweight problem for many years. Once she firmly resolved to lose weight and keep it off, she enrolled in a medically supervised very-low-calorie diet plan. She shed more than 100 pounds over the course of a year and has successfully kept the weight off by implementing permanent lifestyle changes. This woman's motivation to achieve her normal body weight exceeded her desire to perpetuate her former eating patterns. She found within herself the strength to do precisely what needed to be done to lose and keep off excess weight.

When something is causing you to experience excessive stress, do whatever is within your power to change the stressor. Talk to it . . . cajole it . . . move it . . . go under, over, around, or through it. Do whatever you are willing or capable of doing to change it to make it at least tolerable. If a stressor is not amenable to change, however, you will need to consider the next option.

Option 2—leave it. Several years ago, I left a corporation where I had been employed for over nineteen years. Companies change over time, just as people do. The last few years I worked there, a number of major changes in corporate philosophy and direction were implemented, some of which conflicted with my personal value system. I was powerless to change the new system, and I was unwilling to accept it. When I finally came to the realization that I no longer shared the company's vision, I chose to leave. Resigning from my position was one of the most difficult and painful decisions I have ever had to make. But it was the right decision for me.

After you have done all you are willing and able to

do to *change* a stressful situation—to no avail—consider whether you can or should leave it. Step back from the stressful situation and run a cost-benefit analysis to decide whether leaving is a realistic option for you. Examine the stressor in the context of the total environment in which it is occurring. If you have done everything you can to change the situation, without effect, in all likelihood the stressor is going to remain . . . whether *you* do or not. You are now confronted with a major decision: "All in all, with this stressor remaining, do I still find the rest of the environment rewarding enough that it overcomes the negatives created by this stressor?" If the answer is yes, then you will likely make a conscious choice *not* to leave the environment.

If, on the other hand, a stressor that cannot be changed makes the environment in which it is occurring intolerable for you, then you can elect to leave the environment altogether. If you choose this option, however, don't assume you've automatically eliminated the stressor permanently. You may find it recurring in your new situation. Before you leave, ask yourself, "Do I have a pattern in my life of having fled stressful situations in the past only to find the same stressors present in my new environment?" In other words, do you find yourself still living out the same patterns that have not worked for you in the past? For example, many people go from one bad marriage to another, or one abusive situation to another, or one intolerable work environment to another. No matter how often they flee an intolerable situation, these people discover the sad reality that "Wherever I go . . . there I am." If this is true for you, consider getting professional help to examine the sources of your ineffective patterns and to find ways to eliminate them.

Option 3—accept it. Occasionally, you may find yourself in a position where options 1 and 2 are not realistic choices. Parents of a child with muscular dystrophy, for example, can neither change the fact of their child's condition, nor can they leave it. Instead, they must find some way of accepting the permanence of their child's condition and of adapting to it. (See Chapter 10, "Accepting the Unexpected.") In your own case, if a stressor cannot be changed and you choose not to leave it, can you consider accepting it? There are a variety of ways to learn to accept something that we are unable to change and that we are unwilling to leave. One way is to begin changing the way you describe the event to yourself.

When you find yourself immersed in an internal dialogue over the unchangeable/unleaveable, begin to talk back to that internal voice, using phrases such as, "I refuse to let this bother me anymore!" or "I can handle this" or "This isn't the worst thing that could happen." Repeat these assertions over and over again to argue with the old set of beliefs trying to invade your thoughts.

You, alone, are in control of your thoughts. Your thoughts create your emotions. Your emotions have a direct impact on your behaviors. It all starts with thinking. Therefore, if we can find more effective ways to talk to ourselves about stressful events, we will find ourselves better able to accept those things over which we have no control. And, really, isn't most of our stress a direct result of feeling out of control? While we may not be able to gain complete control over the unchangeable/unleaveable event, we can certainly gain control over our own thoughts and feelings about it. Remember, you can only think one conscious thought at a time. So consciously replace negative thoughts with some phrase that works *for* you instead of *against* you.

Option 4—whine about it. Many people who can't change a stressor, won't leave it, and refuse to accept it seem quite content to just whine about it. I have searched for a kinder, gentler phrase to describe this option, and even went to my thesaurus, which offered "complain vigorously." Somehow, "complain vigorously" just doesn't have the same emotional oomph! and it doesn't generate the same mental images as "whine about it." Furthermore, "complain vigorously," if conducted in the appropriate setting, might actually have some impact, whereas "whining about it" is carried out with no expectation of changing the situation. It only serves to fuel your self-righteous feelings and to drive people away.

Option 5—wallow in it. Akin to whining, many people choose to deal with a stressor by wallowing in useless and immobilizing self-pity. These people have an external "locus of control" and a woe-is-me attitude. Factors outside themselves are always responsible for their problems, and they see no way to take control of their lives. Often these people don't even try to change, leave, or accept stressors. Instead, they seem to prefer to wallow in the comfortable constancy of their misery.

Among the five options just outlined, obviously only the first three are truly viable, proactive alternatives— fight it, flee from it, or flow with it. Although nothing useful is accomplished by "whining about it" or "wallowing in it," many people invariably adopt these latter two responses whenever they face any stressor, without even considering the first three options.

Put Things in Perspective

Next time you're feeling overwhelmed by "too much to do . . . too little time," try the following exercise to help put things in perspective. First, give yourself permission to stop what you're doing for the next few minutes. Take out two clean sheets of paper and a pen. At the top of the first sheet, write: *Things That Need to Be Done in the Next Twenty-Four Hours*. Now take a few minutes and write down your list of twenty-four-hour goals.

At the top of the second sheet, write the words: *Lifetime Goals*. This time imagine that you have lived to your full life expectancy of seventy-five or eighty years and you are now lying on your deathbed and reviewing what your life has been all about. Spend a moment or two writing down the sorts of things you would want to be able to say you had accomplished in your lifetime.

Now scan both lists. When viewed in the context of the things you want to accomplish in your lifetime, how much relevance do the individual tasks on your twenty-four-hour list really have? Typically, I find that most of the "to do" items I'm tempted to "stress out" over today are relatively inconsequential when placed in their proper lifetime perspective.

Another way to examine this process is to compare the *types* of activities on each of your two lists. Generically, look at the sorts of things you've listed on your twenty-four-hour list.

Very likely, they consist of things like:

- Pick up clothes at dry cleaner's

- Fill car with gas

- Make appointment for Suzie with Dr. Katz

- Call Fran about her part of the project

- Work on monthly report (due next week!)

- Send utility payment

- Buy birthday present for Ted

- Call washer repairman—try to get appointment for Monday afternoon

- Pick up prescription from drugstore

And now, examine the nature of the sorts of things you wrote on your lifetime goals sheet. If your list is similar to mine, it probably consists of such things as:

- My children and spouse have known that I love them

- I engaged in work I found fulfilling and meaningful

- My being here made a difference to others

- I experienced a great deal of love

- I led a happy life

- My shortcomings led to growth experiences

- I am at peace with my Maker and embracing what lies ahead

Tomorrow's goals are intrinsically different from lifetime goals. Lifetime goals are much more nebulous and difficult to define than daily goals; they're actually more like visions or missions than goals. While daily goals are usually independent events, with clear-cut beginnings and endings, lifetime goals are not so much destinations as they are journeys! You can draw a line through each daily goal as you complete it. But when you look back over your list of lifetime goals, how many would you be willing to draw a line through as though they were completed? Chances are you wouldn't be willing to cross *any* items off that page because none would ever be viewed by you as having been completely finished. Do you ever reach a point where you've loved your children *too* much? Are you ever *too* satisfied with the magnitude of the difference you have made in the world?

Lifetime goals are processes—they're methods of living life on a moment-by-moment basis. We need to find ways in which consciously to tie our day-to-day activities to our long-term goals, such that we see ourselves living out our visions. One way of doing that is to re-evaluate how you typically review your accomplishments at day's end. If you currently look at your "to do" list in terms of what *didn't* get accomplished, you are probably setting yourself up to feel not very good about the day as a whole. A preferable approach would be to ask yourself, "How did the things I *did* complete today contribute to my lifetime visions?" When examined this way, you will find yourself looking not just at what you accomplished, but at the manner in which you achieved it.

Instead of focusing upon the nuisance of having to fill your gas tank, pick up dry cleaning, and fight traffic on the way to the pediatrician, I'm asking you to find something of broader value in each of those experiences: "I got to spend time with Suzie in a way different than I otherwise would have spent it. She learned to help me pump gas; we talked about why we take my suits to the dry cleaner instead of throwing them into the washer with her playclothes; and while she sat on my lap waiting for the doctor, she began to learn how to tie her shoes. All in all, our time together was special . . . and wouldn't have occurred in quite the same way had I not had those particular tasks to accomplish!" Instead of browbeating yourself over what didn't get done, ask yourself, "Did I complete those tasks that were absolutely essential today?" If the answer is yes— and it usually is—find some way of rewarding yourself for, at the very least, surviving.

Learn to Relax

Tense minds and tense muscles go hand-in-hand. Have you ever tried to "just relax" when you were maximally stressed and worried? Mental relaxation often follows physical relaxation, but many people cannot simply sit and relax on cue without first learning an effective method of progressive relaxation.

Set aside fifteen to twenty minutes twice each day and devote them to becoming deeply relaxed from head to toe. Pre-recorded relaxation tapes, recorded "white" (or pink) noise, or calming music played quietly in the background can greatly aid the relaxation process. A number of environmental sound cassette tapes that are particularly suited to aiding the relaxation process have been produced. These can be found at most record stores.

You might find it particularly helpful to create your own relaxation tape. I've provided a text in the Appendix (pp. 315–17) that you can adapt to your own needs, if you're so inclined. Regardless of whether you use a tape of your own voice or a pre-recorded tape, the relaxation process is enhanced by using guided imagery cassette tapes. When they are used, there is less tendency for the mind to wander away from the task at hand and back to the everyday problems from which you are attempting to escape temporarily.

Find a quiet place, dim the lights, take the phone off the hook, loosen your clothing, get comfortable, and arrange not to be interrupted. It's best to learn progressive relaxation while lying down, if possible.

Two conditions are critical to the success of this process. First, you need to give yourself a series of directions that progressively relax various muscle groups in a specific order and manner. When doing this myself, I prefer to start with my toes and progressively move up my body to my head. I also find it helpful to imagine

281

my muscles becoming pleasantly heavy and flooding with warmth as I relax them individually.

Next, you need to create a vivid mental picture of yourself lying in a peaceful, sunlit outdoor setting where you are entirely alone. Keep yourself mentally in this setting throughout the duration of the exercise. Don't allow yourself to flit from one place to another. If your mind begins to wander, sharply say No! to each extraneous thought and force your mind back to the task at hand. This response will usually be effective in giving yourself permission to set aside the problems of the outside world for a few minutes. The reason this part of the exercise is so critical is that it provides you with a focus outside the immediate environment. If you're occupying your mind with peaceful, tranquil thoughts, it's physically impossible for unpleasant thoughts to be occurring simultaneously. Remember, you can't think more than one thought at a time!

Occasionally, people have told me that they experience a slight sense of discomfort—a feeling of being slightly out of control—when first trying this exercise. This is usually a temporary condition that results from having maintained your muscles in a fairly constant state of tension over a long period of time. If you keep yourself in a constant state of readiness or tension long enough, your muscles become conditioned to being always in a tense state. Then, when your muscles lose their tension during relaxation, a mild feeling of being out of control can result. If that is your experience, rest assured that it is a short-lived phenomenon and will soon disappear entirely as your muscles become re-accustomed to being truly relaxed.

Practice tuning into your body during your daily activities, and try to become more aware of when your jaw is clenched, your neck is tensed, or your forehead is furrowed. When you are performing a task, concentrate on relaxing muscle groups that aren't in use. Continued practice of these relaxation techniques will soon have you looking forward to these "islands of calm" during your daily schedule.

Cherish the Quiet Moments

Had I heard this advice when our children were very young, I might have laughed derisively, dismissing the merits of the idea as unrealistic. I can't overstate the importance of this simple stress management tool, however. Not only should we cherish the quiet moments, we need to actively schedule them.

I've read that Thomas Edison so immersed himself in his work that he typically got no more than four hours sleep each night. One of the reasons he functioned so effectively despite his seeming lack of sleep was that he took numerous fifteen-minute "catnaps" throughout the day. Each of us could benefit from similar daily respites during which we can nurture ourselves.

Dr. Spencer Johnson, in his book *One Minute for Myself*, makes a convincing case for asking yourself throughout the day, "Is there a way, right now, for me to take better care of myself?" His premise is that before we can take good care of anything or anyone, we must first take good care of ourselves. Taking better care of yourself right now might involve nothing more than taking a five-minute stroll outdoors, practicing progressive relaxation for a few minutes, stopping to paint your fingernails, taking a bubble bath, or pausing to read the newspaper. You'd be surprised how much better you can feel after spending only a few minutes pampering yourself. You can change your whole attitude in just one minute, and your attitude can change your outlook on your day. In the end, both you and everyone around you will benefit.

Sharpen Your Ax

The story is told of a conscientious, talented woodsman who was hired to chop down trees. He felled ten trees on his first day of work, and everyone marveled at his performance. As the week wore on, however, his efficiency declined without apparent explanation. On Friday, he worked feverishly to fell a single tree. The puzzled boss called the young man into his office to try to determine why productivity had declined so rapidly in such a motivated fellow. The employer soon determined that the young man had worked diligently all week, eventually refusing even to pause for routine breaks or lunch. The woodsman simply could not understand why he was presently unable to accomplish what he had on the first day. "Son," his astute employer began, "have you stopped to sharpen your ax?" "No, sir," the exhausted young man replied. "I didn't want to waste any time, so I've just kept working."

Many of us take the same misguided approach to our tasks, including parenting, refusing to pause to refuel or to renew ourselves. We "burn out" in our parenting, become filled with resentment and guilt, lose our enthusiasm and efficiency, and jeopardize our children's emotional welfare by our chosen martyrdom. Think about it. A race car running at peak performance can't possibly win at the Indy 500 if it never makes a pit stop. A battery will eventually burn out if not recharged. And the human body can't function indefinitely without pausing for sleep.

Give yourself permission to take periodic breaks from parenting, whether for an hour each day, an afternoon each week, or an occasional weekend away with your partner (see Chapter 2, "The Myth of the Superparent"). Preserve some of your pre-parenthood hobbies and interests and cultivate some new ones. Join a support group, an exercise class, or a bowling team. Go get a massage, a haircut, or a manicure.

Eat Nutritiously and Sensibly

In response to the fast-paced American lifestyle, many contemporary parents have little time to prepare nutritious meals and to dine together each evening. We tend to eat on the run, lured by the convenience of highly processed foods and fatty fast foods. One in five American women is obese, with associated increased health risks, and the probability that she doesn't feel at peak performance. Too many Americans still smoke, alcoholism is rampant, and drug abuse robs our nation of enormous monetary resources and human potential.

Increasing data have implicated the contributory role of dietary cholesterol and saturated fat in promoting cardiovascular disease. Few things can improve the health status of so many Americans as adopting the "prudent diet" recommended by the American Heart Association. Examine your eating habits and ask yourself whether you might look better, feel better, and live longer if you made some dietary lifestyle changes. If the answer is yes, the following guidelines can help you begin to implement some positive changes that will improve your immediate and long-term health and reduce your stress.

In general, it's best to eat a variety of foods in as natural a form as possible. Limit your dietary intake of total fat, cholesterol, and saturated fat. To do this, increase your consumption of fish and poultry, fresh fruits and vegetables, whole grains, and cereals. Eat less red meat, and trim the fat from meats and the skin from poultry. Use nonfat or low-fat dairy products. Broil, bake, or boil foods instead of frying them. Learn to read labels so you can note fat content and avoid saturated fats such as palm oil, coconut oil, and hydro-genated fats.

Avoid excessive intake of sugar, salt, processed foods, and caffeine. Eat adequate amounts of fiber and complex carbohydrates. If you don't smoke, don't start. If you do smoke, stop or attempt to cut down. Limit your alcohol consumption, and get help if you find yourself relying on drugs, legal or otherwise. Try to maintain your ideal weight, and consider taking a daily vitamin supplement, including B-complexes.

Exercise Regularly

Recalling how our body's fight-or-flight response to stress prepares us for vigorous muscular activity, it's easy to understand why so many stress management programs emphasize the importance of regular exercise. The recent enthusiasm for jogging, aerobic exercise, and health club memberships is motivated by the wide-spread desire to minimize the symptoms of stress, as well as to achieve improved physical appearance and cardiovascular conditioning. Ideally, you should aim for a minimum of thirty minutes of vigorous exercise at least three times each week, checking with your doctor first to be sure that you have no medical contraindi-cations to regular exercise.

You might elect to exercise in a structured environment like a health club or exercise class, or you may prefer simply to take a brisk walk or ride your bike each day. I try to ride my indoor exercise bike for thirty minutes each day while I read the newspaper. We also have a treadmill strategically placed in front of the TV to remind us to start walking when we turn the TV on.

Seek Professional Help

For some individuals, the effects of chronic stress are manifested as long-term psychological consequences such as depression, severe anxieties, or phobias. Professional psychotherapy may be necessary to help you change your lifestyle and relieve symptoms. If you are experiencing severe psychological symptoms, or if you ever feel like hurting yourself, I urge you to ask your physician to refer you to a licensed psychotherapist experienced in treating stress-related mental illness. You deserve to feel better and to experience life more abundantly. Countless people are helped by psychotherapy each year. For both your own and your child's sake, please take steps to see that you get the help you need.

Conclusion

During more than ten years of conducting stress-management workshops, one thing has become glaringly apparent to me: Stress is not a passing fad. If anything, the incidence of stress and stress-related illnesses promises to intrude even more heavily upon our lives with each passing day. Stress is a direct response to actual or anticipated change. In our contemporary society change has become the norm rather than the exception. The stresses associated merely with day-to-day living are compounded when the additional pressures parenting brings are factored in. Given the inevitability of stress in our lives, the key is finding ways to minimize its impact. Much of the daily stress we experience arises from the difference between our expectations and reality. Establishing realistic expectations, therefore, must be the first step in minimizing stress. Putting things in their proper perspective becomes the second step. And, third, determining which stressors can be changed, which should be left, and which must be accepted suggests the only viable proactive alternatives available to us. Since the impact of stress depends largely on our attitude, optimal stress management begins in the mind. Because some stress is both inevitable and necessary, our goal cannot be the avoidance of all stress. Rather, the emphasis must be upon minimizing unnecessary stress and learning to control and channel our responses to unavoidable stress in more creative and productive ways.

ADDITIONAL READING:

Borysenko, Joan. *Minding the Body, Mending the Mind.* New York: Bantam Books, 1988.

Charlesworth, Edward A., Ph.D., and Nathan, Ronald G., Ph.D. *Stress Management: A Comprehensive Guide to Wellness.* New York: Atheneum, 1984.

Friedman, Meyer, and Rosenman, Ray H. *Type A Behavior and Your Heart.* New York: Fawcett, 1974.

Glasser, William. *Take Effective Control of Your Life.* New York: Harper & Row, 1984.

Jacobson, Edmund. *You Must Relax.* New York: McGraw-Hill, 1978.

Johnson, Spencer. *One Minute for Myself.* New York: William Morrow, 1985.

Leider, Richard, and Shapiro, David. *Repacking Your Bags.* San Francisco, Berrett-Hoehler Publishers, 1995.

Selye, Hans. *Stress Without Distress.* New York: New American Library, 1974.

Veninga, Robert L., and Spradley, James P. *The Work/ Stress Connection.* Boston: Little, Brown, 1981.

10

ACCEPTING THE UNEXPECTED

One day, a member of my staff brought a greeting card into the office that gave us all a good laugh. On the cover was a drawing of a modest house, with the caption "All I want in life is someone to love . . . and a roof over my head." Inside the message continued, ". . . and I want to be happy all the time."

I think many of us have the unspoken expectation of being happy all the time. Unrealistic though it may be, the media would have us believe that certain products, like cosmetics and shampoos, when applied faithfully, can create the hairstyle and facial features of a model. We are convinced that celebrity workout tapes and stylish leotards can transform our cellulite into sculptured muscles, or that specific cleaning products used diligently can produce perfect homes. Similarly, many parents fantasize that the right childbirth preparation classes, specific nursery accessories, and the latest parenting books will guarantee them perfect children. The unspoken message is that if we do and buy the right things and simply try hard enough, our superbabies will grow into precocious children, compliant youth, and successful adults.

But in the real world, where the majority of us live, most children are average in ability and appearance, marriages often are troubled and many break up, some couples are infertile, and a few precious babies are born with birth defects. Learning disabilities, handicaps, and chronic debilitating diseases occur all too often. Even good children can get in trouble, and healthy children sometimes get hurt in accidents. In short, periodic disappointment and tragedy are an inevitable part of the celebration called life. Virtually everyone has to reconcile their expectations for life with their daily reality. For just about every life event, from Christmas to the prom, the old adage rings true—"Anticipation is greater than realization."

Because we as parents so often have greater expectations for our children than for ourselves, we have to learn to deal with the discrepancy between our expectations and the actual circumstances. Otherwise, instead of enduring happiness, life turns into a string of unfulfilled expectations. The only people who truly can be "happy all the time" are those few who have learned the priceless secret of being "happy in all circumstances." Happiness results only when we resolve to accept the things we cannot change, to choose a positive attitude, to find joy in daily living, and to reach out in love to others. Our ultimate happiness in parenthood is not found among specific memorable events, but rather it is experienced moment to moment in our sacred commitment to love our child unconditionally from zenith to nadir.

Becoming a Parent

We have some longtime friends, a couple older than ourselves, who married late and remained childless afterward. Larry originally met the man a number of years ago when they both owned and raced their Hobie catamarans. Now we still see them each summer at our favorite lakeside campsite. He is a lawyer and she is a schoolteacher, and both would make wonderful parents. Because of their age, however, even the possibility of adoption seemed remote. They always took a special interest in our children, and on many occasions I had thought that it was a shame that they had no children of their own.

One day a few years ago, Lisa called to tell me that she and Jim had just learned about an infant who was to be relinquished by his teenage mother. Several couples had written to the young girl and she had selected Lisa and Jim after reading all the letters. The baby had been born prematurely and was still hospitalized in another town. They asked if I would accompany them to see the baby and give my advice about the infant's health. He had experienced complications after birth, was on a ventilator for several weeks, and still required supplemental oxygen. In addition, routine testing had revealed that he had experienced some bleeding into his brain shortly after birth, as do many small premature infants. What did I think his chances were?

I have spent a lot of time in premature nurseries in my career, but I hadn't routinely cared for small preemies in several years. I contacted neonatology colleagues of mine and discussed the baby's long-term neurologic prognosis. The situation was extremely awkward for me. I desperately wanted my friends to have the long-awaited opportunity of becoming parents to this unknown baby who had entered their lives. On the other hand, I couldn't bear the thought of finding out a year from now that the baby they chose was severely developmentally delayed. While I felt I could get a good sense of whether the baby acted appropriately at this point, I doubted I could examine a two-month-old preemie and accurately predict the baby's future. I wanted to see my friends take a risk with this infant, but at the same time I felt responsible for how the child would turn out years later. That's what life is about, though, isn't it?—taking some personal risks, like choosing to parent a child who might be imperfect rather than continuing through life childless.

We set out that Saturday in a small, private plane that friends of theirs had volunteered. They arranged the flight on my behalf, to save me travel time. Unfortunately, I get airsick in small planes flying at low altitude, so the ride was nauseating. When we reached our destination, the winds were gusting so badly that we were unable to land after all, so we silently flew back to Denver without even seeing the baby. The disappointment was devastating for everyone.

We agreed we would start out again the next day, this time by automobile. Lisa and Jim felt bad that I would be giving up my whole weekend now, instead of taking care of the matter in half a day as originally planned. I reminded myself that nothing else in their lives might ever be as important as whether or not they adopted this baby.

During the drive, I tried to prepare my friends for how a preemie might look. I recall as a young intern being disturbed at how the newborn preemies under my care would change their appearance over time. Because the preemie head is so soft at birth, it can become elongated from lying on one side or the other all day. Eventually, however, the head rounds out. A preemie often has had an intravenous solution started in one of the scalp veins, and it is not uncommon for his hair to be shaved irregularly in search of a suitable blood vessel. They often look short and stubby; many suffer from an umbilical hernia.

After finishing my description of how a preemie might appear, we walked into the nursery and were confronted by the most beautiful baby you could imagine— lots of hair, perfect features, with only an oxygen tube taped under his nostrils to suggest he had been born early.

I busied myself with thoroughly reviewing Matthew's medical records to detect any clue suggesting he might have a hidden or potential medical problem. Had he had an eye examination to assure there was no sign of retrolental fibroplasia? Had his hearing been tested recently? When was the last ultrasound of his head? Are his ventricles normal size? What did his last chest X ray show? Has he been growing appropriately? Have the physical therapists seen him? Does he need any on-going therapy? Then, with a sinking feeling, I saw the dreaded diagnosis on the ultrasound report: "Periventricular leukomalacia." While it wasn't a guaranteed sentence, the appearance of periventricular leukomalacia after bleeding in the brain carried a poor neurologic prognosis. There was a very real chance that Matthew was brain-damaged.

Meanwhile, Lisa, Jim, and Lisa's sister were in the nursery taking turns holding Matthew and snapping Polaroids of the baby. They absolutely radiated happiness. Their initial awkward handling soon became more assured. "Look, he smiled. See his tiny fingers. Just feel that hair." Every feature of this miracle baby was perfect in their sight.

For a brief moment I thought, "How will I inform them that the baby might have neurologic problems?" I heard myself declare bluntly, "There is approximately a one-third chance Matthew has significant brain damage." How do you explain odds ratios in parenting? They responded, "Thank you so much for examining him and reassuring us about his health." Apparently they had selective hearing. There is no doubt this couple was going to keep this baby. I must admit, too, that when I held him I could not conceive that he was anything less than perfect.

Lisa and Jim left the hospital, giddy with excitement.

They would need a bassinet right away. What formula should they buy? They would have to get baby clothes. Their house was already on the market; they would need a larger one. How much time could Lisa get off for maternity leave? They would have to find a trusted babysitter before Lisa went back to work. They would need to have oxygen set up at home. In short, their lives would never be the same again.

We decided to stop at a salad bar before driving back to Denver. As we entered the eatery, we passed a young couple carrying their new baby, accompanied by smiling grandparents. "Oh, how cute!" admired Lisa. "How old is your baby?"

"Only two weeks," replied the proud new mom.

"Do you want to see our baby?" Lisa blurted out. Then she produced the photographs taken minutes earlier. "He was born prematurely and has been in the hospital for two months. His name is Matthew, and we're taking him home in a few days."

The other couple and the grandparents all admired Matthew, never realizing that Lisa hadn't given birth to him herself. I knew at that moment that Lisa and Jim had indeed made the emotional commitment to become Matthew's parents. They wouldn't reject this baby because of possible brain damage any more than other new parents would reject their child because of a heart defect.

On the way home, Lisa admitted that she was aware Matthew might have some "special needs." She believed that she and Jim would be ideal parents for such a child, since they were older, more mature, had some degree of financial security, and could provide the extra input that Matthew might need. She said she had given up hope of ever becoming a mother; if God had chosen to send this child into her life, how dare she worry about whether he would be perfect? She and Jim had decided to accept the baby on faith as a divine answer to prayers offered during all those painful years of childlessness.

Well, I must tell you how things turned out. Lisa and Jim and Matthew have become a beautiful family. Matthew was soon weaned from his oxygen and received several months of physical therapy and was followed carefully by various medical specialists. Despite the ominous "periventricular leukomalacia," he has thrived and developed, admittedly a little behind his peers. At two years of age, he walked and talked and laughed and played. He is a delightful, happy child who has brought countless joy to his parents and has been showered with love and attention in return. We saw him several summers ago at our regular campsite with shovel and bucket in hand. "How's Matthew?" I inquired. "He's perfection," Lisa quipped, "absolute perfection."

Matthew and his parents taught me a valuable lesson about taking risks and having faith. His birth mother, who recognized the special qualities of Lisa and Jim from the letter they had written and who loved her baby enough to let them raise her child, was mature beyond her teenage years. Mostly, I learned from their example what becoming a parent really is. It's making that wholehearted personal and public commitment to "our child," come what may.

The blockbuster movie *Parenthood* achieved its success partly because its message was so true to life. Parenthood is indeed more like a roller coaster than a merry-go-round. It is the very juxtaposition of the inevitable ups and downs in parenting that makes it so exhilarating. Parenting involves taking risks in life, being willing to survive and overcome disappointments in order to bask in and savor the cherished moments. The very instant you conceive or adopt a child, you board an emotional roller coaster for an unforgettable ride. Part of the time, your stomach may be in your throat and you may feel like covering your eyes with your hands in terror. At other moments, you will laugh uncontrollably and shriek with delight at the sheer enjoyment of it all. In the end, like most people who dismount from a thrilling roller coaster ride, you'll probably run to get in line again.

Reaction to Disappointment or Loss

All parents must periodically reconcile the discrepancy between their imaginary expectations and the reality of their circumstances. Each unfulfilled expectation represents a personal loss of varying magnitude to a given individual. Some disappointments, like the inability to breastfeed successfully, may represent only a mini-loss to one mother, while another woman might be emotionally devastated by her unmet expectation to nurse her baby. A birth defect or retardation may mean very different things to different parents. While a catastrophic loss may be equally devastating to different parents, they may handle the tragedy in highly diverse ways.

Although suffering is a universal experience, it is an intensely personal phenomenon. Personal suffering has been likened to a gas; whether a little or a lot, the gas fills all corners of a room. For many of us, even a little disappointment about our child can feel all-consuming at times. Comparing our plight to less fortunate others can help put our own problems in perspective, but people can't be expected to "buck up" just because someone else is worse off than they are. To an independent observer, a paraplegic may seem to be considerably better off than a quadraplegic, but that comparison doesn't minimize the permanent loss of function with which the paraplegic must cope.

Elisabeth Kübler-Ross, in her landmark book *On Death and Dying*, was the first to describe in detail the universal grief reaction people experience upon facing their own death or the death of a loved one. Similar stages of grief occur in response to any significant disappointment or major loss, such as a divorce, permanent paralysis, the birth of a premature infant, the diagnosis of a malignancy, the loss of a job, or the diagnosis of infant retardation. To some degree, these responses characterize our reactions to minor disappointments as well.

Shock and Denial

The usual immediate reaction is utter disbelief that such a devastating thing could have happened. Perhaps the initial shock and denial are psychological mechanisms the brain uses to soften temporarily the blow of the tragic news. "I can't believe it," "It just doesn't seem real," "I keep thinking I'll wake up, and it will all be a bad dream" are typical thoughts expressed by people who have just received very bad news.

As a pediatrician, I sometimes have had to deliver disappointing, and even tragic, news to parents. While assigned to the intensive care nursery during my residency training, I vividly recall one couple's amazing response to some shocking news. I had to tell them that their newborn son had Down syndrome, complicated by multiple medical problems, and that he wasn't expected to live. As we stood at the baby's bedside, the father announced that he, along with many friends of his religious faith, were praying diligently that God would perform a miracle by changing the number of chromosomes in every cell of the baby's body.

"Don't you believe in miracles?" he challenged. I felt helpless and didn't know how to respond. While I do believe that miracles sometimes happen, at that moment I seriously doubted the baby would be cured of Down syndrome, and I feared that praying for such a transformation was not helpful to the family.

"Yes, I believe in miracles," I acknowledged, "but sometimes the greatest miracle is our ability to ultimately accept that which we initially find utterly unacceptable." Eventually, after the shock subsided, acceptance was the miracle this family experienced.

Sadness, Guilt, and Anger

After the initial denial wanes, most people begin to experience fully the depth of their sadness and pain. They may be preoccupied and temporarily consumed by their loss, unable to think of much else. Excessive crying, loss of appetite, difficulty sleeping, disinterest in usual activities, inability to concentrate, and pervasive sadness are some of the early manifestations of intense grief. At this point, parents will doubt that life could ever return to normal again.

Eventually, angry feelings may surface or be turned inward in the form of self-blame. Expounding on the unfairness of life, one grieving mother wrote the following about her inability to produce sufficient breastmilk for her baby: "It's not fair that some people nurse with no sweat and their babies turn into blimps, while others of us nurse our nipples off and nothing happens. Nobody wanted to nurse a baby more than I did."

Parents may wonder whether their child's problem is genetic in origin, and if so, they want to know which one of them is to blame. Mothers may scrutinize every detail of their pregnancies, searching for some indiscretion they committed that would cause premature delivery or a birth defect. Women have confided in me that they wondered whether taking a medication, having sex, playing tennis, or skipping meals might have harmed their baby. Parents of children injured in an accident will re-enact the sequence of events leading to the mishap: If only we had taken another route; if only we hadn't turned our backs; if only we had checked the baby sooner.

A parent coping with a loss will often try to incriminate anyone, ranging from the physicians involved in their child's care to a babysitter, the paramedics, a drunk driver, or even God, for their misfortune. Unfortunately, many people get hung up in this stage of the grief process and carry long-term, self-destructive grudges or become immobilized in their own bitterness.

Those who succumb to prolonged anger soon discover that their rage only wounds themselves and the ones they love the most. In the end, they suffer greater pain and delay the healing process. One of life's most valuable lessons is the discovery that few burdens weigh heavier than a pack of grudges. Accusing and blaming serve to keep our focus on the unalterable past, thus blinding us to the possibilities that lie ahead. One father insightfully acknowledged that his profound anger over what had happened to his boy had prevented him from seeing the wonderful ways in which his "exceptional" son had enriched his life. Many stress-related illnesses can be traced to long-standing, unresolved anger about previous adverse life events. Perhaps worst of all, when we allow anger to fester in our lives, we provide an unhealthy, destructive model for our children, who will look to our example when they inevitably face adversity of their own.

Acceptance and Resolution

With time, psychologically healthy people effectively resolve their grief and manage to get on with meaningful lives. The originally unimaginable eventually becomes an accepted, unalterable part of everyday life. For most people, the old adage rings true: "Time heals all wounds." Resolution may occur ever so gradually, or acceptance may seem to arrive profoundly, at a specific moment in time.

Once, after I had been lecturing in another city, a woman approached me and shared her poignant story of acceptance and resolution. Marge's now six-year-old daughter had been born with one arm missing. Marge described her initial shock, followed by profound sadness. "First I cried for myself," she admitted, "for my own shattered dreams of raising a perfectly formed child. Later, I cried all over again, this time for Ashleigh," Marge continued, "for missed opportunities, hurt feelings, and self-pity. I remained depressed and overwhelmed by a sense of Ashleigh's incompleteness until she was a year of age. At that time, she was fitted with a prosthesis. As soon as she got her artificial arm, Ashleigh seemed whole in my eyes, and I began effectively to integrate the reality of her defect into our lives."

Another emotional crisis surfaced when Ashleigh was four. Marge had retained an exaggerated fear of Ashleigh's going to the beach wearing a swimsuit. Perhaps the beach scene represented for Marge a sort of personal "nakedness" where Ashleigh's physical flaw and prosthesis would be maximally exposed. Marge intended to hover protectively over Ashleigh, shielding her from any insensitive remark by a thoughtless bystander.

Instead, Ashleigh bounded ahead of Marge and was shortly surrounded by a throng of children her age.

From a distance, Marge stood teary-eyed, helpless to defend her child against potential verbal assault. "What happened to your arm?" an uninhibited young onlooker bluntly inquired. Ashleigh proffered her prosthesis and matter-of-factly explained how it worked, while Marge stood poised for the rescue. "Oh, wanta play?" the other child invited. And off romped the children together. "At that moment," Marge explained, "I knew both Ashleigh and I would be okay. I knew we both could handle this thing."

Coping with Unmet Expectations

Celebrate the Present

When forced to deal with adverse circumstances, it makes sense to concentrate on living fully in the present, instead of wasting precious emotional energy reliving the past or fantasizing about the future. Despite the sense of this advice, however, many people confronted with a crisis will attempt to retreat to the past or escape to the future, in their own minds. Two common ways people remain trapped in their past are through oppressive guilt and wallowing in their misfortune. Guilt is a useful emotion—for about five minutes following a remorseful event. Guilt serves to keep us from repeating an inappropriate action and reminds us of the need for restitution. Beyond that, excessive or prolonged guilt is nothing more than the past keeping us from living fully in the present. All the "what if's" and self-flagellation in the world will not change the present reality with which we must cope.

Sometimes we cling tenaciously to our guilt because we find it comforting to believe that we can control everything that happens to us. Blaming ourselves for things is one way of perpetuating the fantasy that we are totally responsible for everything in our lives. Although letting go of guilt frees us from the crushing grip of our remorse, it is a bittersweet freedom. By acknowledging that we are not responsible for everything, we are forced to admit that we also cannot control all the events in our life.

Another way we can obstruct our present effectiveness is by insisting on dragging our past around like a heavy anchor. Many people are immobilized, wallowing in their misfortunes, using the injustices of their past as an excuse for avoiding the present. While nothing about our past can be changed, we are free right now to change our attitudes and our actions—if we resolve to focus our talents and resources on the present.

People can also waste energy living in the future through worry and being convinced that life will begin "when" . . . when there's a cure for diabetes, when Greg's leukemia goes into remission, when Tamisha loses weight, when Curt can walk again, when Mitzi gets out of rehab, when I remarry, and so on. Some people act as if this particular life isn't really "it"—"it's" all going to start just as soon as their conditions for happiness are met. By the time such people realize that their imperfect experience was really "it," they may have missed out on a big chunk of their life.

Another common way people live in the future is through incessant worrying about what's behind every turn in the road ahead. Such people live with an uncomfortable sense of impending doom or dread expressed by the hopeless phrase "I just couldn't take it if . . ." They could be happy the way things are right now if they weren't so preoccupied with the possibility of losing one of their children, their health, their spouse, their job, or their possessions. In fact, constant worrying about every possible future scenario saps the joy of present moments. Worrying is another useless emotion; it does nothing proactive; it is simply the future keeping us from living fully in the present.

I just read an inspiring story in the newspaper about a couple whose three children all have an inherited, progressive, incurable disease, known as spinal muscular atrophy. For months after the diagnosis was confirmed in their first child, this couple was virtually immobilized by constant thoughts of their daughter's possible death. Once they came to realize that their hopeless attitude was actually robbing them of enjoying their child's life, they determined to stop feeling sorry for themselves and to start living joyously in the present. Although all three children now are confined to wheelchairs, this amazing family is so busy inhaling every moment of life right now that they don't dwell on the past or worry what the future may hold.

Seek Information and Support

The best specific advice for handling an unexpected parenting challenge is to become as informed as possible about the condition you face and to join a support group of other parents who are successfully coping with the same problem. Whether it's Sudden Infant Death Syndrome (SIDS), cleft palate, Attention-Deficit Hyperactivity Disorder (ADHD), cystic fibrosis, epilepsy, spina bifida, cancer, sickle cell disease, alcoholism, or autism you may easily feel isolated and overwhelmed when you first learn the diagnosis. Indeed, you may feel like the only parent who has ever had to deal with your particular problem under your particular circumstances. Discovering that many others have struggled with similar crises and have emerged intact can provide tremendous consolation and moral support. Hearing the personal stories of parents who confronted the same issue several years ago can offer invaluable perspective on your own situation. Eventually, you will probably find fulfillment yourself in serving as a resource and support person for others.

Because knowledge has a way of dissipating fear, find out as much as you can about your particular problem. Ask your child's specialist for any printed materials, audio- or videotapes on the subject. If there is a national association or foundation pertaining to your particular problem, contact it for additional educational resources. Write down your questions and insist on getting answers to all of them. Thus, if your child has diabetes, it would be advisable to have her followed at a children's diabetes center in addition to getting her regular pediatric care. You could subscribe to one or more diabetes magazines or newsletters, join a support group for parents of juvenile diabetics, send your child to diabetes camp, attend parent conferences on diabetes, and attend the annual diabetes Halloween party in your community. Once you become well-informed about the specific challenge facing your family, you will discover that you are less fearful and more proactive about your child's condition—and consequently, are a more effective parent.

Allow Adversity to Foster Personal Growth

Rather than being "broken" by tragedy, people often testify that, just as intense heat is used to turn iron into steel, withstanding extreme adversity can make people even stronger. When a negative experience is successfully resolved and integrated into our lives, we are able to use our emotional triumph over the event to empathize with and minister to others experiencing loss.

Adversity provides the opportunity to choose between bitterness and creativity.

I recall a resilient mother of a very premature infant, Jared, who had suffered severe brain damage. Katy's shock and denial lasted several years, during which she furiously complied with exhausting regimens of physical, occupational, and speech therapy, in a futile attempt to make her damaged child whole again. The ultimate reality of the extent of Jared's impairment was followed by chronic anger and outrage. Katy alternately blamed herself for delivering too early, the doctors for perceived lapses in care, anyone who ever displayed insensitivity to her child, her friends for neglecting her, and God for allowing such pain in her life.

By three years after Jared's birth, Katy had begun to resolve the experience and to fully integrate it into her life. She recalls a specific day when she realized she had come to terms with the permanence of Jared's condition and the fact that she could still love him as he was. Katy had agreed to babysit her friends' toddler, Aaron, while the couple vacationed for a weekend. The rambunctious Aaron was a flurry of activity, babbling, running, exploring, whining, while Jared was nearly incommunicative, locked in a palsied, immobile body.

A sudden realization struck Katy, as she wistfully watched the active toddler doing with ease the many things her own child would never master. "Instead of feeling jealous or resentful," she recounted, "I had a dominant sense of acceptance. For the first time since Jared was born, I could totally accept him just as he was, simply because he was mine and I had grown to love him. At that moment," she elaborated, "if I could choose either child for my own, I admitted that I would choose my Jared, despite all his limitations, over Aaron, who showed such ability and promise."

The story doesn't end here. As Jared grew older and bigger, his care became more difficult. Eventually, it

became evident that he would require full-time custodial care, thus raising the painful issue of residential
placement. After an exhaustive search, Katy could find
no suitable facility in her community where she felt
comfortable entrusting Jared's welfare to others. The
glaring need for a well-staffed, homelike residential environment for other severely retarded citizens soon
turned Katy's disappointment into creative energy. This
unassuming "mother with a mission" in a short time
raised hundreds of thousands of dollars and founded a
highly reputable facility to house and lovingly care for
severely retarded individuals in her community. Only
after the structure was erected did Katy learn that her
own son's application had been accepted. Katy was one
of the first parents who taught me that ordinary people
can be inspired and energized to do extraordinary things
in the course of enduring and accepting adversity.

What lost expectation about your child do you need
to acknowledge and accept? For example, thousands of
parents of gay youth and adults turn their backs on their
children by denying, ignoring, or condemning their
homosexuality. The parents' shock, discomfort, and obvious embarrassment about this disappointing aspect of
their child are often translated into outright repudiation
of the whole individual. Thus the condition of homosexuality becomes the basis for withdrawing the "unconditional love" that parents had pledged to their
child.

Have you ever thought about what conditions would
make you stop loving your child "unconditionally"? I
certainly wouldn't choose for my own child to be gay.
Neither would I want my child to be promiscuous. But
more important, I would not be willing to withdraw my
love on the condition of my child's sexuality, any more
than I would withdraw it on the basis of another personal attribute.

What, then, can you hope to learn from an unexpected parenting reality you face right now? For example one mother of a gay woman recently attended the wedding of her "straight" son. She observed that the entire extended family who were scattered over several states "dropped everything" to attend the young man's wedding. During the festivities, her lesbian daughter commented wistfully, "Not one of these relatives has even acknowledged my long-standing relationship with my partner, which means every bit as much to me as David's marriage means to him." Is it possible that learning about the obstacles facing certain individuals and viewing life from their perspective might make you more compassionate toward and more tolerant of all minority groups?

Another woman, whose first child was born with Down syndrome, explained to me that raising a child with retardation has taught her never to prejudge others, regardless of how different they may appear. She now recognizes that, prior to Denny's birth, she had been guilty of sometimes making value judgments about people, based on their ethnicity, income, education, or physical appearance. Today her greatest fear is that someone else will prejudge Denny, without getting to know the special individual he is. "I've learned to look beyond first impressions to discover the real person inside, because that's how I want other people to respond to Denny throughout his life," she said. "Denny has taught me to recognize the value of every person. Many people I know will never learn that lesson in their lifetime."

Choose Your Attitude When You Can't Choose Your Circumstances

Dr. Viktor Frankl is a Viennese psychiatrist who was a prisoner in Nazi death camps during World War II. Stripped of all possessions, nearly starved and frozen, brutally mistreated, and living under the daily threat of extermination, Dr. Frankl observed that the ultimate human freedom is the freedom to "choose one's attitude in a given set of circumstances." In his classic, best-selling book, *Man's Search for Meaning*, Frankl described the bestial conditions of his captivity and concluded that man is free to transcend his suffering and to find potential meaning under any conditions. He reiterated what the philosopher Nietzsche had deduced: "That which does not kill me, makes me stronger."

As a pediatrician privileged to hear parents' innermost feelings and raw vulnerabilities, I have witnessed countless personal heartaches and shattered expectations. Contrary to media images of cooing babies, endearing children, and promising youth, the reality is "Doo Doo Happens" in parenting. In fact, parenting is first and foremost risking—risking prematurity, birth defect, physical disability, medical illness, retardation, behavior problem, substance abuse, or school failure. Be it a congenital heart defect, or bed-wetting, virtually all parents can acknowledge something about their child's reality that fails to meet their expectations. We cannot choose whether we will face problems or which problems we will face, but we *can* choose how we will react to them. Thus, while troubles in life are inevitable, misery is definitely a choice. It's been wisely observed that "Some women have the best husbands, while others make the best of the husbands they have!" The same holds true for children, health, and jobs. The alternative to making the best of things is to miss out on a lot of satisfying living by wallowing in negative thoughts.

What, then, distinguishes the disillusioned parent who endlessly laments, "Spina bifida ruined my life," from the couple who starts the Sturge-Weber Foundation in the basement of their home to reach out to other parents and to learn more about the rare disorder that afflicts their daughter? For one thing, the latter couple accepts their child's condition and sees their child as a unique individual of infinite worth, despite the medical problems that accompany her diagnosis. They find hope in being optimally informed and in getting and giving support to other parents struggling to cope with the same syndrome. They don't look for someone to blame, nor have they put their life on hold until a cure is found. Instead, they live fully in the present and retain hope for the future. They work daily to convey to their daughter their unconditional love and to help her experience life to the fullest. And they recognize that the same grain of sand that serves as a constant irritation inside an oyster shell ultimately becomes the source of a beautiful pearl!

ADDITIONAL READING:

Bridges, William. *Transitions*. Reading, Massachusetts: Addison-Wesley Publishing, 1980.

Frankl, Viktor. *Man's Search for Meaning*. New York: Simon and Schuster, 1959.

Gaffney, Donna. *The Seasons of Grief*. New York: New American Library, 1988.

Kübler-Ross, Elisabeth. *On Death and Dying*. New York: Macmillan Publishing, 1969.

Kushner, H. S. *When Bad Things Happen to Good People*. New York: Schocken Books, 1981.

Peck, M. Scott. *Further Along the Road Less Traveled*. New York: Simon and Schuster, 1993.

A FINAL WORD

While many people dread public speaking, I actually enjoy addressing a crowd. Not only am I energized by the dynamic tension created between myself and my audience, but public speaking opportunities have taught me valuable lessons about communicating with others. Earlier in my career, whenever I had a speaking engagement I would automatically conduct a self-evaluation of my presentation to assess its effectiveness: Did my nervousness show? Was I articulate enough? Did I adhere to the time limits? Was I talking too fast? How did I think my talk went?

One evening, after addressing a crowd of parents, I silently scanned my mental checklist of my performance. It had been a long day, coming at the end of a busy week. My energy level was lower than normal, and I acknowledged to myself that tonight's presentation was not my most memorable. As soon as I descended the stage, however, a young woman in the front row approached me, beaming with obvious satisfaction.

"I want you to know how much your talk spoke personally to me tonight," she began. "I'm a single working parent, and I have been feeling so depleted and overwhelmed that I was seriously considering relinquishing custody of my two children to my ex-husband," she went on.

"What you said this evening about parents replenishing themselves was exactly what I needed to hear. While listening to you, I've decided to change my work schedule and to leave the children with a sitter once a week. I'm so glad I came tonight!"

Immediately a woman nearby interjected, "Thank you for making the comment about finding another home for a pet if no one is willing to care for it. I recently gave our dog away because no one in the family would take responsibility for Sheba, and I didn't have time to be her sole caretaker. The kids made me feel like an ogre for giving away the family pet, but your remarks have validated my decision and I refuse to feel guilty about it any longer."

A young couple gestured for my attention, and the wife began to explain, "We felt like you were speaking directly to us this evening when you talked about accepting things that can't be changed and living fully in the present."

"You see," the husband went on, "our two-year-old daughter was born blind. Initially we were so preoccupied with her disability that we overlooked her many strengths and doubted our own strength to handle the situation. Thankfully, with the support of our families and other parents of blind children, we were able to overcome our initial shock and subsequent depression. Now we have all the joys that other parents share, but the three of us work harder for every milestone, and we take nothing for granted!"

Then a man spoke up, grinning, "I was the youngest of seven boys, and I often wondered how my mother managed to preserve such a positive attitude most of the time. When you mentioned parents taking a few minutes for themselves, I suddenly recalled my mother saying to my father, 'Look, I can handle all this if I just know I can take a simple bath each evening, without the Boy Scouts around!' Your remarks tonight have opened my eyes to my own wife's need for a little time alone each day."

Talking in this way with members of my audience has helped me appreciate that the art of communication depends more on the listener's receptivity to a message than on the speaker's oratorical ability. The way an individual's heart is prepared to receive and respond to a particular message is, in fact, more important to communication than the eloquence of the words spoken or the mastery of their delivery.

Just as I have learned that each listener in an audience hears and takes away different key messages, I trust that this book has spoken to each reader in a uniquely personal way. My sincere hope is that each of you has found within these pages the specific insights you need to improve your parenting and enhance your family life.

I have shared in this book many lessons from the heart—parenting wisdom I have gleaned from professional training and clinical practice, coupled with personal insights I have gained from firsthand experiences. Whether seasoned or inexperienced, every parent who reads this material will inevitably recognize some mistakes they have made in rearing their child. But the first step toward better parenting is the honest acknowledgment of our shortcomings and a commitment to improving.

Once, after I had given a seminar on children's self-esteem, a reticent young woman hesitantly approached me at the break. "I am a single working mother raising my son alone," she offered. "I was in an abusive marriage which ended in a messy divorce, and my ex-husband provides no support," she explained. Then, lowering her voice and averting her eyes, she continued softly, "I'm ashamed to admit that I am guilty of every one of the examples you gave tonight about eroding a child's self-esteem.

"I've repeatedly told my son that he's just like his

dad; I've insisted he's 'bad' and threatened to send him to his father to raise. I constantly yell at him and punish him because I just don't know how to handle his behavior. I never realized until tonight how destructive my words and actions could be. Now I don't know what to do."

This young woman had never read a parenting book. She had minimal support and few role models. She simply didn't know a better way to be a mother. Yet she had many strengths on which to capitalize. She had recognized that a problem existed in her family; she had ventured out on a weeknight to listen to a parenting talk; and she had come forward to ask for specific help. That's a great start for doing better!

Because the talk was hosted at an elementary school, members of the administration quickly were able to connect this woman with a network of support, information, counseling, and other guidance. Her honesty and courage should remind us all that it's never too late to improve our parenting. Children's personalities and emotional outcome are not chiseled in stone or set in concrete by the age of three or five or even ten. Certainly, it's easier to shape young children positively than to reshape problem behaviors in older children; it's always easier to promote emotional wellness than subsequently to remold a child's psychological health. But it's never too late to recognize our deficits, to learn better parenting techniques, to enlist more support, to seek professional help, and to improve our relationship with our children.

Recently, I was in an airport in another city, waiting for the airline official to announce my row for boarding. I observed a lady in her seventies lovingly embrace a younger woman about my age who was preparing to board the plane. Both women fought back tears, and I overheard the elder one say to her daughter, "Thanks so much for coming; I just wish you didn't have to go.

Have a safe trip, honey. After all, you're still my little girl.''

The scene was so poignant that I got gooseflesh recalling my own tearful farewells with my parents several times each year. Parenting, indeed, is a lifelong commitment. We are never finished parenting our children, and we never stop learning ways to more effectively nurture, advise, support, encourage, and advocate for them.

Each of us juggles many competing interests and obligations in our life. Yet my heart tells me that nothing else which screams for our attention will ever rank as important as the one thing we daily are tempted to take for granted—our relationships with those people we love most, our families. Thus, I want to challenge parents to reorder the clamoring priorities of contemporary life in such a way as to keep our families first and foremost. A fulfilling balance of meaningful work and satisfying recreation seem naturally to follow once a rich and rewarding family life has been claimed first!

APPENDIX

A PROGRESSIVE
RELAXATION SCRIPT

The following is a script for a guided imagery that could be used to achieve relaxation. When reading into a cassette recorder, take special care to use a relaxed, comfortable tone of voice in a slow, measured way:

"Gently close your eyes and begin to focus on your breathing. Don't change your breathing just yet—simply become aware of your breathing right now. (Pause)

"And now, begin to focus upon taking deeper and deeper breaths of air into your lungs, completely filling them with each inhalation . . . completely emptying them each time you exhale.

"In your mind's eye, picture a place that's very peaceful . . . tranquil . . . a place that is outside . . . on a warm, pleasant summer day . . . with nobody else around. Lie down and totally immerse yourself in that place . . . create a 360-degree view. Feel the gentleness of the breeze, listen for the sounds of rustling leaves.

"As you lie there . . . breathing deeply and fully . . . relax your feet, your ankles. Let all the energy from your feet, your ankles drain into the ground below you . . . (Pause)

"Relax your lower legs . . . your upper legs . . .

As the sun gently warms your feet . . . your ankles
. . . your lower legs . . . your upper legs." (Pause)

"Relax your stomach . . . your lower back . . .
your upper back. . . . Breathing deeply . . . and
fully—no tension, no stress—a sense of peace
. . . of tranquility . . . as the sun warms your feet,
your ankles . . . lower legs . . . upper legs . . .
stomach . . . lower back . . . upper back. (Pause)

"Relax your shoulders—a lot of tension there—
let it go . . . let it go. Search your shoulders again
for any remaining tension and let that flow out of
you into the ground below.

"Relax your arms . . . your wrists . . . your
hands. Your arms become so heavy, you couldn't
lift them even if you wanted to.

"As the sun . . . warms your feet . . . your
ankles . . . lower legs . . . upper legs . . . stomach
. . . lower back . . . upper back . . . shoulders
. . . arms . . . wrists . . . your hands . . . breathing
deeply, fully—no tension—no stress . . . a sense
of peace . . . tranquility. (Pause)

"Relax your neck. Relax your neck even
more—a lot of tension *there*—let it go . . . let it
go. Let your jaw go slack—so that your upper and
lower teeth are not even touching. Let your
tongue fall to the floor of your mouth.

"Relax all those tiny muscles around your eyes.
Let your eyes roll ever so slightly upward . . .
comfortably. Smooth your forehead. Relax your
scalp.

"As the sun . . . warms your feet, your ankles
. . . lower legs . . . upper legs . . . stomach . . .
lower back . . . upper back . . . shoulders . . .
arms . . . wrists . . . hands . . . your neck . . . jaw
. . . tongue . . . eyes . . . forehead . . . your
scalp—breathing deeply, fully—no tension . . . no
stress—a sense of peace . . . of tranquility—your

entire body completely . . . totally . . . relaxed.

"Lie there for just a moment and soak up that feeling of total relaxation. (Long pause)

"In a moment, I'm going to have you come away from your place of relaxation, slowly open your eyes and sit up. But when you do, I want you to hold tightly to that feeling of total relaxation—bring it with you. (Pause)

"And now . . . when you're ready . . . open your eyes . . . and sit up."

INDEX

Abandonment. *See* Children, abandonment of

Abortion, as childbearing option, 22

Abuse
child. *See* Child abuse
alcohol, and stress, 267

Acceptance
of child's feelings by parents, 74–77
of failure, as value to pass along, 191–93
as option for dealing with stress, 275–76
social, as reason for discipline, 131–33
as solution for adversity, 300

Accusations

Acting out, adolescent, and stress in parents, 265

Actions
consequences of, accepting, as value to pass along, 183–85
of parents. *See* Parents, actions of

Activities
with child, as evidence of parental love, 86–90
special, after divorce, arrangements for, 249

Activity, physical, change in, and stress in mothers, 267

Accusations of children after divorce, handling, 239, 242–43

Adaptation, successful, of child to divorce, 252–53

Admitting wrong, as evidence of parental love, 90–91

Adolescent acting out, and stress in parents, 265

Adversity
attitude of parents in, 308–09
personal growth and, 304–07
for parents, 306
reaction of parents to, 296–301
solutions of parents for, 301–04

Affection, nonverbal as evidence of parental love, 77–78

Age
-appropriate expectations, maintaining, to prevent misbehavior, 140
of child, appropriate, for pet, 217

Aging of pet, as lesson for children, 213

Marital relationship (*cont.*)
see also Marriage
Marriage
counseling, as deterrent to
divorce, 224
partners, impact of divorce
on, 222
see also Marital relationship
Maternity leaves, extending, to
prevent unbonded chil-
dren, 163
Mazlish, Elaine, 102
Media
influence of, on childrearing,
25
see also Television
Medical problems
and stress, 267
see also Illness
Mess and clutter, and stress in
parents, 268
Middle child. *See* Children,
middle
Migraine headaches, and stress,
261, 263, 267
Mind, relaxing, and stress, 281–
83
Minority, ethnic, child of
fostering self-esteem in,
97–98
see also Children, vulnerable
Misbehavior
dealing with, strategies for,
146–59
parental ignorance and, 137
prevention of, strategies for,
138–46
punishments for, 147–61
reasons for, 133–37, 143
see also Behavior, problem
Mistakes, parental, and child's
self-esteem, 91–98
Moments, quiet, and stress
management, 283
Money
management, as value to
transmit, 188–91

mismanagement of, and family conflict, 189
worry about, as result of divorce, 233
Motherhood, surrogate, as option for childbearing, 21
Mothers
at-home, support for, to prevent unbonded children,
163
effect on, of working, 31
increased role of, after divorce, 227
sources of stress for, 267
working, effect on, of parenting, 23–24
see also Parenting; Parents
Muscle
groups, relaxing, and stress,
281–83
tension, chronic
and headaches, 263
and pain, 263
and stress, 263
Music, as outlet for anger over
divorce, 234

Natural consequences of misbehavior, as punishment,
148–50, 158–59, 183–85
Neck pain, chronic muscle tension and, 263
Neglect
and child's self-esteem, 72–75
child's, death of pet by, 214–
15
Neighbor, as source of help for
parents, 61, 98, 269
"No" saying, as strategy for
busy parents, 49–50
Nurturing behavior of children,
pets and, 212–13
Nutrition
adequate, and stress management, 285–86
inadequate, and stress, 267

Positive self-talk, and self-esteem, 80–81
Positive words, as evidence of parental love, 78–82
Poverty, effect of, on child-rearing, 24
Power, child's need for, and misbehavior, 135, 146
Praise
  as evidence of parental love, 78–82
  as reward for good behavior, 143–45
Pregnancy(ies)
  and stress in mothers, 267
  teenage, preventing, to prevent psychopathic behavior in children, 163
Preparation, as step in transmitting values, 173–75
Present, living in, as solution for adversity, 301–03
Pressures on at-home parents, 31–33
Presentation, as step in transmitting values, 173–78
Prevention
  of harm, as reason for discipline, 131
  of misbehavior, strategies for, 138–46
Primal stress response, 260–61
Priorities
  establishing
    as evidence of parental love, 89–90
    as strategy for busy parents, 41–45, 89–90
  urgent vs. important, 53
Privileges, loss of, as punishment for misbehavior, 157–59
Problem behavior. *See* Misbehavior
Problems, medical
  and stress, 267
  see also Illness

Progressive relaxation. *See* Relaxation
Promises, as incentive for good behavior, 144–45
Pseudomaturity, as trait of first-born child, 119
Psychological disturbances, and stress, 263
Psychopathic behavior. *See* Behavior
Psychotherapy
  and stress management, 287
  see also Counseling; Therapy
Punishments, for misbehavior, 147–61
Put-down
  by parent, and child's self-esteem, 93
  of self by parent, and child's self-esteem, 96

Quiet moments, and stress management, 283

Rahe, Richard, 258, 258*n*
Rebellion
  against control, 173–74
  against parents' values, 173–74
Reconciliation, false hope of, after divorce, 240
Reinforcement, positive, and preventing misbehavior, 143
Relationship, marital. *See* Marital relationship
Relatives
  as source of help for parents, 98
  see also Extended family
Relaxation
  progressive, 281–82, 283
    script for, 315–17
  sensations during, 282
  as technique for stress management, 281–83
  techniques for, 281–82

Sleeping difficulties (*cont.*)
  excessive, as sleep dysfunc-
    tion, 261
  fitful, as sleep dysfunction,
    261
Sociability, as trait of middle
    child, 120
Social acceptance, as reason for
    discipline, 131–33
Societal interaction, and stress,
    265
Society, strong, strong family
    and, 27
Sound, environmental, tapes,
    and relaxation, 281
Spanking
  as abusive practice, 159–61
  as punishment for misbehav-
    ior, 159–61
Special activities, arrangements,
    for, after divorce, 249
Spiritual faith, as value to pass
    along, 186–88
Sports, as outlet for anger over
    divorce, 234
Spouse
  house (term), 30
  relationship with. *See* Marital
    relationship
  as source of help for parent,
    56–57
Spy, using child as, after di-
    vorce, 243–44
Standard of living, decline in,
    after divorce, 227
Standard, lowering, as strategy
    for busy parents, 45–49
Statistics on divorce, 223
Stereotypes
  birth order, awareness of,
    118
  of firstborn child, avoiding,
    118
  fostering, by parents, and
    child's self-esteem, 96–
    97

of lastborn child, avoiding,
    121–23
of middle child, avoiding,
    121–22
sex role, self-esteem and, 193
of twins, avoiding, 124–25
Stress
  causes of, 260–61, 264–68
  forms of, 259
  manifestations of, 259, 261–
    68, 287–88
  parental
    causes of, 264–68, 270
    management techniques
      for, 268–87
    manifestations of, 264–65
    minimizing, to prevent mis-
      behavior in children,
      133, 143
  personal, causes of, 189
  -related illnesses, 261
    new parents and, 258
  response, primal, 260–61
  situations, options for dealing
    with, 273–77
  term defined, 259
Submissiveness in children, and
    parents' values, 173
Substitute caretakers and un-
    bonded children, 163
Superparent, myth of, 34–40
  television and, 35–36
  unrealistic expectations and,
    38–39
Support system, building
  as solution for adversity,
    303–304
  see also Help
Surrogate motherhood, as
    childbearing option, 21

Taboo, sexuality as, 195
Talking, as outlet for anger
    over divorce, 234
Tapes, environmental sound,
    and relaxation, 281